T0290079

'I have known John for over 30 years and his book is a must-read for every executive who wants to reach the top and make an impact. It helps you understand what and who the C-Suite is, and enables readers to level the playing field. John's unique understanding makes his book an excellent guide and enjoyable read.'
The Right Honourable Sir Hugh Robertson KCMG DL, Chairman of the British Olympic Association and Chairman of Camelot

'A timely and insightful guide to current thinking in governance and senior leadership, and what it takes to make it at the top of an organization.'
Alex Beard CBE, Chief Executive Officer, Royal Opera House

'Leadership at the executive level is demanding in a fast-changing world, and expectations are high. It has also never been more important that we encourage more diversity and people with all backgrounds and experiences to reach this level. This book, drawing on many sources, lays out the routes to the C-Suite, talks about the capabilities and skills needed, and should prove indispensable for those aspiring to get there.'
Peter Cheese, Chief Executive, CIPD, and author of The New World of Work

'So you aspire to the C- Suite? John Jeffcock's book – coolly analytical, attractively conversational, and authoritatively statistical – will challenge those of serious intent, stimulate those with high ambition and, perhaps most importantly, deter the naïve'.
Sir John Tusa, former Managing Director BBC World Service, and author of On Board *and* A World in Your Ear

'Understanding the dynamics of the C-Suite is essential for career progression, and achieving and retaining a leadership role. This insightful book is packed with advice and tips garnered from multiple expert sources. It will be a highly trustworthy companion on the journey into and through the C-Suite, as well as life afterwards, for anyone who wants to succeed in today's increasingly challenging world.'
Dame Janet Gaymer, Non-Executive Director, Business Banking Resolution Service

'There are echoes of some of my own experiences in C-suite roles, and on boards across sectors, throughout this insightful book. I recommend it for every stage of your life journey as you build towards, move into and seek to achieve in C-Suite and non-executive board roles. It includes a powerful source of advice, provided to provoke challenge and reflection as you progress. This rightly emphasizes the importance of actively building up a wide range of capabilities and experience in a diversity of contexts, with "integrity and courage", fuelled by "aligned passion".'

Dame Mary Marsh, Non-Executive Director, HSBC Bank plc

'John provides a fascinating compendium of advice for anyone aspiring to a successful executive career. His writing draws on a rich base of historical research and understanding – adapting and applying the lessons of the past to the challenges of the future. Much of his thinking resonates with my personal experience: the importance of expanding your own sense for how business works, of learning to add value right across your organization, and finally, of continuously challenging, updating and sustaining your competence.'

Michael Izza, Chief Executive, ICAEW

'This is an excellent book for current and aspiring C-suite individuals. Operating at C-suite level is not an easy task and can be a lonely experience, but *The Suite Spot* is full of shared experiences, knowledge and advice of how to navigate at the top. The combination of both the executive/personal and the governance aspects is valuable for any C-suite leader. I can highly recommend this book to anyone wanting to get their journey right.'

Charlotte Valeur, CEO Global Governance Group, and author of
Effective Directors: The Right Questions To Ask

'*The Suite Spot* is a delightful tour through governance and leadership models around the world, revealing not just what they teach you in business school, but the reality and peculiarities of what actually goes on in the foreign land called the C-Suite. This engaging and compelling account is a must-read for aspiring CXOs and a useful reminder that the most well-worn path to the top is not necessarily the only one.'

Sir James Wates CBE, Chairman, Wates Group and BRE
(Building Research Establishment) Trust

JOHN JEFFCOCK

THE
SUITE
SPOT

Reaching, Leading
and Delivering
the C-Suite

BLOOMSBURY BUSINESS
LONDON • OXFORD • NEW YORK • NEW DELHI • SYDNEY

BLOOMSBURY BUSINESS
Bloomsbury Publishing Plc
50 Bedford Square, London, WC1B 3DP, UK
29 Earlsfort Terrace, Dublin 2, Ireland

BLOOMSBURY, BLOOMSBURY BUSINESS and the Diana logo are trademarks
of Bloomsbury Publishing Plc

First published in Great Britain 2022

A catalogue record for this book is available from the British Library

Library of Congress Cataloging-in-Publication data has been applied for

ISBN: HB: 978-1-4729-8705-1; TPB: 978-1-4411-0023-8; eBook: 978-1-4729-8704-4

2 4 6 8 10 9 7 5 3 1

Typeset by Deanta Global Publishing Services, Chennai, India
Printed and bound in Great Britain by CPI Group (UK) Ltd, Croydon CR0 4YY

To find out more about our authors and books visit www.bloomsbury.com
and sign up for our newsletters

I would like to dedicate this book to my three daughters –

Josephine, Franziska and Philippa

– who have brought huge joy to my life and are the faces to whom I go when I cannot sleep on restless nights.

I would also like to thank my wife Katrin who, for over many weekends as I hid myself away to write this book, supported me and filled the gaps that this made in our family.

I think now comes the point when I am supposed to list and thank many famous business leaders. It is true that many of the ideas and approaches came from well-known CEOs and Directors but an equal number came from a wide range of people including strangers I have only met once and students who asked the right question. Many of these people will have never known the connection they triggered in my head. Thank you to them, the unsung heroes who are often far more important than they realize.

Importantly I need to thank the team at Winmark where I have the honour to serve as chief executive. A big shout out for all their work in running our C-Suite networks. Equally importantly are our C-Suite members and partners who have been my educators over the many years. A few of these I have named and are Alexia J. Maas, Amanda Burton, Andrew Allner, Andrew Cumming, Andrew Marks, Andy Halford, Bernic Waldron, Bryan Foss, Cameron Ireland, Caroline Brown, Celia Baxter, Cephas Williams, Charlotte Valeur, Chris Daly, Christopher Honeyman Brown, Dame Mary Marsh, Daniel Hulme, David Sole OBE, David Williams, Debbie Hewitt MBE, Dominick Sutton, Dr Elizabeth Hayward, Francois Coumau, Gavin Patterson, Hamish Taylor, Ian Dilks, Jane Tozer MBE OBE, John Dembitz, John Whittle, Justin King CBE, Ken McMeikan, Leon Kamhi, Mark Baxter, Michael Izza, Patrick Butcher, Patrick Dunne, Patrick McDonald, Peter Collyer, Pierre Danon, Richard Brooman, Rob Chestnut, Shereen Daniels, Sir Hugh Robertson KCMG PC DL, Sir James Wates CBE, Sir Peter Gershin and Wendy J Barnes.

Contents

Introduction

Patrick Butcher, Group Chief Financial Officer, Go-Ahead Group plc, started the meeting by introducing himself. He grew up in South Africa and he explained that 'I did not go to university, but got a job straight from school and did my degree through UNISA [the South African Open University] and then my wife and I came to the UK as immigrants, staying with relatives until we could afford to move out.' He asked people to think about that, then told another story: 'Both my parents went to Cambridge University, I was privately educated and my first job was arranged for me by my godfather, who was a partner at Deloitte.' Both stories are true but the way they are told give very different impressions of the same person. Twenty-five years earlier, I had just returned to the UK from Bosnia and Herzegovina, where I had been a United Nations operations officer and second in command of the Northern Cordon around Sarajevo. I was now doing an MBA in leafy Oxfordshire and we were being taught logic. The lecturer started by making a comparison between the economic sanctions against South Africa to shooting a zebra in the white stripe, as many were arguing at the time that the sanctions were having an equal or even more negative impact on the black community. She asked us students to put our hands up if we thought the comparison was a good one. Fortunately, I kept mine down but half the group raised theirs. She then rightly mocked us and questioned how we could possibly think it was a good idea to compare the economy of a nation state to the anatomy of a zebra.

In 2012, Nobel Prize Winner Daniel Kahneman published *Thinking, Fast and Slow*,[1] which still sits by my bed, mainly read. His book teaches us how the brain works and why we make choices. One story discussed in the book that is now well known is the experiment that Daniel and Amos Tversky conducted with students at the University of Oregon. Students were asked to guess the percentages of African Nations in the United Nations and then they span a wheel. But the wheel was rigged to stop at 10 or 65 and the average estimates of those who saw the 10 and 65 was 25 and 45 per cent respectively. Obviously, the wheel had nothing to do with the percentage of African Nations, which today is 54 – representing 28 per cent of UN membership.

Whether you are a business student, aspiring C-Suite executive, the executive leadership of an organization, or CEO of a Fortune 500 company, one of the largest companies in the US, you will come to this book with a head full of stories and good connections and that enables you to put this book and its words and meaning into context. This has great benefits as it means your brain can absorb the knowledge shared in an organized way and can file the content appropriately while you sleep, but it also creates 'unconscious bias' and brings in unconnected wheels.

This book starts by looking at governance and power and what today's C-Suite looks like in corporates and the digital giants. It looks at new skills and how to set your own direction before moving on to introduce the CXO methodology, Chief Expertise Officer, which is the golden thread running through the book. It addresses the knowledge requirements of a CXO, the difference between line and staff, and how to view your life and career, giving tips on how to level the playing field along the way. It takes on old theories and presents new models of thinking, such as tiara-shaped people and diamond-shaped departments. After a new approach to strategic networking, it focuses on key relationships before looking at how a world-class C-Suite operates. It has a whole chapter focused on the role of the CEO as leader of the C-Suite and the most powerful

[1] Kahneman, Daniel, *Thinking, Fast and Slow*. Penguin, 2012

person in the organization. Throughout these and other chapters, the book shares advice from some of the most successful CEOs and board directors of our time.

The last chapter of this book, C-Suite Musical Chairs, is about staying at the top and it highlights the importance of independent thought, the avoidance of bias. I would like you, the reader, to approach this book with an independent clear mind that is looking to grow 'the growth mindset'. I would also like to thank you for reading this book and all the far more able people than me who triggered the ideas, images and frameworks that have enable me to write it. Imagine it as a journey up a river, heading to the source, where you get to sit and listen while I as your tour guide get to steer and point out all the interesting caves and tributaries on the way, many of which you may never have noticed before. Hopefully, some of it you will find obvious – that it makes so much sense, it is obviously true.

The contents of this book may not be rigorously scientific but are based on evidence and research. This is not a single-idea book, indeed there are many tributaries, but every chapter presents new ways of looking at old and current issues, and the new ways are linked like a jigsaw. Sometimes you learn about different areas around different subway stations or bus stops, then one day, you walk a little further and suddenly you see how they connect and how the two maps join up in your mind. Writing this book forced me to walk a little further in many directions and in doing so, the linkages that I was not previously conscious of joined up in ways I had not always anticipated. My original hypothesis was in the right direction but the discipline of writing has made me a better tour guide.

When linkages do join up and the connections are made in my brain, I get a sort of euphoria and this has made the writing of this book an exciting project for me rather than a burden. That happy 'I get it now' feeling is hopefully something you will experience many times as you read through the chapters.

The purpose of *The Suite Spot* is to help more people from more diverse backgrounds to become C-Suite executives and

CEOs and ultimately to improve the resulting performance of the organizations they serve. The book does have an agenda, although not a political one, and that agenda is to help your understanding and careers. Every organization in the world, however small or large, benefits from having the right people doing their best in the leadership roles.

I

Today's C-Suite and How it is Evolving

'You need to know what you are breaking into'
John Jeffcock

The immortal line from Act Two of the musical *Hamilton* tells us that we need to be in 'the room where it happens'. In organizations the room where it happens, the room where the majority of key decisions are made, is the C-Suite and that is the focus of this book.

Things can go wrong and in this chapter we will look at governance, the separation of powers and who the stakeholders are, but first let me start with an example of when I personally got things wrong. It was my first board position, governor of one of the largest colleges in the UK, and I took it up as it was local to where I worked. I thought education was my thing, it would be a good thing to do and to be brutally honest, it probably appealed to my vanity. I remember the interview being slightly easier than I expected and I was quickly given a place on the Board, which should have been a warning signal to me.

My expectation was that it would be one board meeting a month and the papers would be quite easy to get through. I was not aware that the organization was embarking on a £450 million redevelopment project and each board meeting had a pack of papers several inches thick. Also, I had no experience of substantial property development projects and it quickly appeared to me that nor did anyone else on the Board. As a result, a couple of directors and I requested and found a property expert who could join the Board and fill our technical gaps in this area. We really wanted someone who could judge whether the plans being put forward by the CEO and consultants were realistic and good for the organization. However, we were told by the CEO and Chair that there wasn't an available space on the Board. Three months later, a person of a similar background was recruited as a consultant reporting to the CEO. For us, this defeated the purpose of the appointment and made the CEO even more powerful. Another red flag went up in my head.

It was at this point that I and others realized we had a weak chair who went along with everything the CEO wanted. To make matters worse, we also had a secretary who was keen to remind the Board about the limits of their authority. The biggest limitation was actually the strength of the Chair. We also had a finance director who kept telling us how clever she was and how brilliant and accurate the numbers were. That should have been another red flag but sadly, I was not experienced and confident enough to act. Had we had a better understanding of governance then in hindsight, we would have made better choices.

About six months later, three of the directors were coming to the end of their time and were up for renewal – one had actually fallen asleep in a board meeting! This might sound comical, but when you are involved, it is a very different experience. Like many things in life, it happens gradually and the little things on their own you may let pass. To me, this was an obvious opportunity to upskill the Board and I assumed, incorrectly, that the Chair would take advantage of this. What actually happened was that the Chair, who had known all three directors for many years, simply said in a board meeting with all three present, 'I assume no one has an issue with the three directors continuing on the Board for another term?' It was like I'd been ambushed. I looked around the table and a couple of other people had the same look on their faces, 'What just happened?' Again, I let it go, but that was the last time, I had learnt my lesson.

The truth is that if you have not experienced a similar situation before, you may not know how best to react and even if your gut is telling you otherwise, you may not always have the courage to speak up. This is what had happened to me the first time around – I had a combination of lack of experience and courage that meant on the day, I remained silent and let down the organization and the hundreds of people it employed. These situations are often compounded by additional pressures like time, length of papers and not wanting to be the person who always asks the difficult questions, extending the meeting sometimes by hours. At this point I downloaded a paper from a top consultancy on the top ten things to get right between a CEO and chair, emailed it to the CEO and requested a meeting. It was quickly apparent in the meeting that the CEO did not recognize any of the issues that seemed so obvious to me. Alone, I was not going to be able to effect any change.

For me, the final straw was when the Chair brushed over the remuneration committee meeting outcomes, saying nothing was material and shall we move on to the next agenda point in an already cramped agenda. The Secretary aided the Chair by quickly stating the number and title of the next agenda item and the meeting moved on. Again, I looked around the table and a couple of the other directors looked back at me with the same questions in their eyes: 'Did something just happen?' Again, we let it slip. This makes us sound incompetent and indeed we were, but we had just spent too long on the agenda item before as we had asked so many questions, so we trusted the remuneration committee and let this one pass. The remuneration committee interestingly was mainly populated by the three directors who had just been renewed.

The following day, all havoc broke lose. The employee representative on the Board emailed me and others asking why the CEO had been given a pay rise greater than the pay of those being made redundant due to financial pressures. As you can imagine, it made several of us board members very angry. We lost complete trust in the Chair, who had on purposely hidden information from us as he knew we would not have allowed the CEO's pay rise while we were letting people go. We gathered our views and quickly held an informal meeting to discuss how to proceed. It was agreed that I would write an open letter to the Chair, asking him and the entire remuneration committee to resign. To reinforce the seriousness of the issue, I resigned as a Governor in the same letter.

Six months later, the regulator was called in, who then wrote a damming report about the CEO, Chair, CFO, Secretary and governance of the organization, which was now in financial difficulties. The CEO had already moved on by this time and six months later, sadly committed suicide. To this day, I wonder had I behaved differently or done something else, would history tell another story? The CEO was not a bad person, he just needed a strong chair to keep him real but alas neither he nor the Chair realized this. I personally gleaned from the experience that you have to understand how governance works and what power you really have. In boardrooms, you must keep it real and always be brave, let nothing pass on your watch. This is why we need to start this book on the rather dry issue of governance, because it is really important and you may not be entirely conscious of the importance and eventual impact of every decision you make or sometimes more importantly, do *not* make.

C-Suite Definition

To start, we need to define what the C-Suite is and is not. Not everyone with a title beginning in 'Chief' and ending in 'Officer' is a member of the C-Suite. Title inflation has created many CXO roles of which only a few will sit on the top table and be part of the Executive Committee or C-Suite Executive. Here, we start by touching on the governance structure of organizations and then go into more detail on different C-Suite roles and how the C-Suite is evolving. We look at the merging and separating of C-Suite roles and consider the diversity or lack of it in organizations.

BOARDS & GOVERNANCE

Most organizations in Asia, the US and Europe have a Board of Directors or Supervisory Board and below this is usually a C-Suite or Executive Team. Nearly every organization in the World has a leadership team with executive responsibility and in this book to avoid confusion we are going to call the leadership team, C-Suite or Executive Team the C-Suite Executive. The Board is focused on governance, is presided over by the Chair and represents the shareholders and sometimes other stakeholders. Organizations with significant shareholders, such as Private Equity or a family, may have representation on the Board. So, the Board acts as the conduit in which governance passes from the investors or owners through the Board into the C-Suite Executive and organization. The value created through equity value or dividend then passes from the organization through the C-Suite and Board to the investors. This is well summarized by the billionaire Warren Buffet, who in June 1996 as Chairman of Berkshire Hathaway, issued a booklet entitled 'An Owner's Manual' and within it, one of the opening comments is, 'We do not view the company itself as the ultimate owner of our business assets but instead view the company as a conduit through which our shareholders own the assets.'[2] The illustration below captures the traditional governance model and value flow:

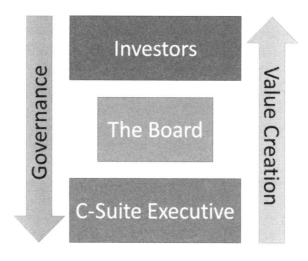

_____

[2] https://berkshirehathaway.com/ownman.pdf

In recent years, many people have been speaking about the shift of organizations from being a 'profit maximizer' to a 'value maximizer'. In other words, shifting from a single financial stakeholder viewpoint to a more balanced view from multiple stakeholders, including staff, society and the environment. This shift was given extra momentum in January 2020 at the World Economic Forum (WEF) at Davos, where natural capital, human capital and societal capital were all put on the agenda. At a session led by Bank of America and a number of fortune companies, they explained how they intended to adopt a framework to address this in 2020. Covid-19 impacted the initial activity but also made the framework even more important.

What happens in big companies tends to trickle down into smaller organizations and there is now a growing number of large organizations that are making the 'value maximizer' approach a reality. It appears that the investor market is polarizing, with some looking at value across all areas – such as BlackRock, Vanguard and State Street. The view is that although there are currently questions around shareholder returns, it is generally thought that an organization with a strong social purpose is likely to be more sustainable. The other investors, who were still the majority in 2020, were very much focused on earnings per share, but this approach makes it hard for the organizations invested in to progress strategically. Another underestimated force in this area is the big pension schemes, who have a longer-term agenda and can often be more interested in value.

People now talk about purpose rather than vision: why does the organization exist in the first place? Your purpose should be resilient and sustainable, include everyone in the organization and make the world a better place. Making money for its owners or employees is no longer a good enough answer. There has been considerable progress on Environmental, Social and Governance (ESG) and the inclusion of new and all stakeholders. Remember, without the 'G', the governance in ESG, then 'E', the Environment and 'S', the Social, go nowhere.

This market shift has meant that boards have increasingly represented all stakeholders and not just the shareholders. There is also significant pressure from consumers, with 81 per cent of global consumers[3] feeling strongly that companies should help improve the environment. In addition, and partly as a response to this customer pressure, governments have issued new governance codes and regulations that place a greater emphasis on stakeholders generally and are looking at the full range of stakeholders with a particular focus on customers, employees, the environment and society as a whole. So, the above model is rapidly evolving to include multiple stakeholders as illustrated by the more complex model below, which gives each stakeholder an equal weighting. Obviously, the reality is that the weightings are not equal, will be impacted by the strategic imperatives of the organization and how the C-Suite Executive are valued, measured and remunerated.

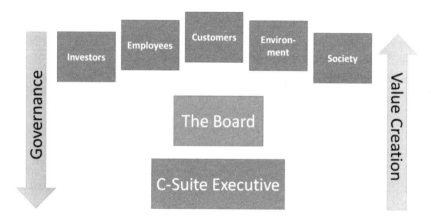

The employee as a stakeholder has been a prime focus and as a result, this has become an increasingly developed area, with regulation looking at remuneration including all aspects of pay, employees on boards, diversity and inclusion. Most significant change usually occurs when there is new stakeholder pressure, a new CEO or some form of crisis. For example, the food retailer Tesco, was criticized for delaying payments to suppliers and online

---

[3] https://www.weforum.org/agenda/2020/01/sustainability-green-companies-business-partnership/

fashion group Boohoo, for low pay and poor working conditions in its factories. Following negative attention in the media both Tesco and Boohoo significantly changed their KPIs (Key Performance Indicators). Tesco, who had developed a poor reputation with suppliers, focused on supply chain relations and Boohoo, focused on improving working conditions and production management. Now strong in ESG (Environmental, Social and Corporate Governance), Tesco is clear what they care about and they have done good work in this space.

Boards are asking the ESG and multiple stakeholder question of their C-Suite executives and their organizations are being asked to report on these areas to asset managers, pension funds and other owners. However, for the majority of the C-Suite, their remuneration is still almost entirely linked to financial performance. It is the remuneration committee that makes it real. There is a clear correlation between where investors and executive teams focus and this depends on where the light of attention shines. Although there is still some cynicism about the speed of this change, progress is being made and organizations like the International Integrated Reporting Council (IIRC) are looking at six different types of capital, which include social, natural, intellectual, manufactured and human. The conversations about these capitals and remuneration with the C-Suite tend to take place in stages, one at a time, as the organization learns how to measure and value them. In difficult times such as during the Covid-19 period, measures tend to retrench to financial as profitability becomes key to survival. It is sometimes said that ethics are a privilege of the wealthy and organizations like people retrench into survival mode in difficult times. Although for many organizations survival led to tough decisions during Covid-19, social media played an important role in holding businesses to account for the way they treated stakeholders, such as employees.

The C-Suite Executive is focused on execution, presided over by the CEO and represents all parts of the business so let's start by answering the question, 'What does a C-Suite executive actually do?' The good news is there is a clue in the title, Chief Expert Officer or CXO. Everyone in the C-Suite is a 'chief something officer', so the 'something' must be their area of specialism or expertise (X), whether tech, people, finance, HR, marketing, operations, legal and so on. There are around 45 C-Suite roles and typically, only five staff C-Suite executives in the executive team so they must be more generalist than their titles suggest and maybe a chief legal officer should instead be called the Chief Legal, Risk, Compliance, Data, Governance, Health & Safety, Company Secretary, Regulatory Affairs and Investor Relations Officer or CLRCDGHSCSRAIRO for short and the Chief Marketing Officer should be called a Chief Marketing, Communications, Public Relations, Brand, External Affairs, Employee Communications and Government Relations Officer (CMCPRBEAECGRO). In this book we will stick to the more common shortenings and look at the different elements of a CXO, not just the X.

The CXO Method – Definition

As stated, there is a clue in the title and the CXO role can be broken down into three constituent parts – C, X and O – and the CXO Method defines each of these constituents:

- **C – the Chief** – is the leader of the Department, strategic business unit or business stream. Business unit names may vary: at Toyota, a Japanese automotive manufacturer, they call them Global Business Units (GBU) and there will be a broad range of role titles but for the CXO Method, the 'C' is the leader of the Department. This individual will either be a member of the C-Suite or the next level down, reporting to a C-Suite member.
- **X – the Expert** – is typically the professional qualification and technical skills of an executive and more likely, the departments they oversee. Most would assume therefore that as someone's career develops, the areas of X, expert knowledge, need to broaden as they become more senior but this is not always the case. In larger departments of organizations, like Vodafone, a British

telecommunications company, there are often different career tracks. Amongst these there will be technical tracks and more general management tracks, just as there are in professional services. Someone taking the general track is more likely to become the Department leader but even in role, they will defer to the greater expertise of the expert careerist.

- **O – the Officer** – is about being a good company officer, putting the company first and adding value across the organization, not just in your area of responsibility. At McKinsey & Company, an American management consultancy, they talk about leaving your ego at the door and at Japanese multinational Canon, they always ask at the end of meetings, 'Have we made the best decision for the business?' The Officer role is key to careers. Thinking, operating and adding value outside your area is essential to business leadership and we will return to this later.

The C-Suite has had changing responsibilities over the last few years as they increasingly engage with a broader stakeholder group and focus on more holistic returns. They have an increasing number of objectives linked to environmental, social and stakeholder work and these are being discussed in appraisals but it is still relatively rare to find a link to their remuneration. This increased awareness, which also includes employee health and well-being, needs to be a collective responsibility with the Investors, Board and C-Suite all aligned and only when you have this alignment and run the whole organizations for all stakeholders do you have a chance of sustained success.

Company values can be a good way of achieving top-level alignment but it is how they are applied and translated into the real day-to-day business world in every decision that is key. One way of achieving this level of alignment is to present the investors, Board, C-Suite Executive and potentially employees with a list of different scenarios and questions, such as 'Do we think it's okay to increase production, profitability and resulting employment in an area that needs employment, if we know it will damage a local ecosystem?' The choice of questions is very important as they should highlight areas of existing alignment and potential non-alignment. The questions should also address areas that the organization will most likely face in normal and difficult trading conditions. In many areas the answers will be aligned and the process likely to confirm existing decision-making approaches. It is in the areas of difference where the debate should be had and these debates should result in a majority agreed position that guides future decision making. Once these areas are agreed, decision-making processes should become faster, potentially enabling the organization to react faster and improve its market share or position. Then as societies and ethics evolve, these positions will need to be revisited and reviewed to ensure majority alignment is still in place and relevant to its time.

The separation of powers between the Board and the C-Suite is considered important as it creates clearer lines of responsibility, achieves a better balance of power and ensures that the CEO and C-Suite are held to account. It is a similar approach to Government, where the governance is achieved through the political 'Cabinet' and the Civil Service are responsible for policy execution. To achieve this accountability, the Chair and CEO need to be different people and this separation is enforced by law in the UK, Germany and The Netherlands, whereas in the US and Switzerland, the Chair and CEO can be the same person, giving them significant influence. One of the advantages of not being chair as a CEO is that it takes a considerable amount of governance work off your plate and thereby frees up CEO time to focus on the business.

The US, UK, Switzerland and other countries follow a One-Tiered Board structure, again elected by the shareholders. The Board in this case performs the functions of the Board and supervises the executive committee. The Board functions can be vested in other committees. At Google Inc., what was once known as 'The OC' (Operating Committee) went by the more telling name of 'L Team' (Larry's Team). Larry Page was previously CEO of Alphabet, Google's holding company (Sundar Pichai has been in the role since December 2019), and was also an Alphabet board member, employee and controlling shareholder. Similarly, at Amazon, Jeff Bezos was listed as the President, Chief Executive Officer and Chairman of the Board. The success of Google and Amazon clearly illustrates that this approach to governance also works and it can be argued that the separation of powers means that the Board is too distant from the business.

The illustration below summarizes different approaches to governance of corporates from America, Europe and Asia. All the models have supervisory boards but how they are constituted varies, with shareholders having a say in all but employees having a larger say in Germany and banks a larger say in Japan. All the models also have some form of Executive Team, Committee or C-Suite, the difference being whether or not they have a legal status and in Japan, the President has a more specific role as the conduit between the Board and the Executive model. India has more options and can follow both the Anglo-American and the German models and may develop hybrids of both.

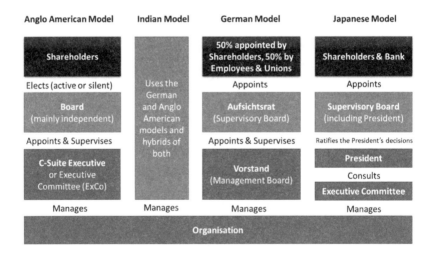

In the US, the Chair may also be called the President and the Chief Financial Officer may well be called 'Executive Vice President and Chief Financial Officer'. Typically, C-Suite executives are senior to Vice-Presidents but like Apple, they may be called Senior

Vice-President (SVP) and then the area they cover. Business unit leads or subsidiary leads are called Executive Vice-Presidents (EVP). If the business unit is significant or has even greater autonomy, the lead may be called CEO and then the area they cover. A good example of this is Walmart, where you have a President and CEO, Walmart U.S. and a President and CEO, Walmart International. Many organizations suffer from what the Chief Human Resources Officer (CHRO) calls 'title inflation' and as a result, it can be difficult to sometimes judge where someone stands in the hierarchy.

C-Suite executive teams are usually smaller than the Board although this again varies and there are around 45 C-level roles used regularly. The most common examples are the Chief Operating Officer (COO), Chief Finance Officer (CFO), Chief Information Officer (CIO), Chief Marketing Officer (CMO), Chief Human Resources Officer (CHRO), Chief Legal Officer (CLO). The initials are more commonly used than the full titles but this creates some confusion as is the CDO the Chief Digital Officer or the Chief Data Officer and is the CPO the Chief People Officer or Chief Procurement Officer?

SEATS OF POWER = CEO & CHAIR (OR PRESIDENT)

The two key seats of power in an organization are the CEO and Chair and if you combine the role into one person, like Amazon, it creates a very powerful leader. Most people would have guessed that the CEO was the most powerful person in an organization but the power of the Chair is often underestimated. Executives forget that the Chair has the authority to hire and fire the CEO and to adjust their remuneration through the remuneration committee. The Chair and Board can often act as a wise check on the CEO, which is why many say that having a CEO and Chair too close can present an additional unnecessary risk to the organization as that Chair check on the CEO is not fully in place.

Chair CEO Influence: I was not truly conscious of the influence of the Chair until I was lucky enough to sit in a non-executive director meeting at which around 20 non-executive directors (NEDs) were present. They were discussing how to manage CEOs and when we went around the table introducing ourselves, I asked the simple question, 'Have you ever fired a CEO before?', expecting the majority of NEDs to say no. To my surprise, everyone at the table had fired at least one CEO and one experienced chair had fired over ten. Since then, I have never questioned the authority of boards and the influence of board members.

Chair NED Influence: Chairs of material organizations tend to spend two to three days a week working with the companies they chair, whereas NEDs will spend two to three days a month on the organizations they serve. Therefore, chairs have both the Direct Positional Power of the role and a multiple of Indirect Personal Power through Information, Referred and Expert Power, as illustrated by the model below:

Bestowed by the Organization	
Direct Positional Power	**Indirect Personal Power**
Legitimate Power	Referred Power
Reward Power	Information Power
Coercive Power	Expert Power

At this point it is useful to talk about the power and different types of power an organization bestows on key members of staff and particularly the C-Suite. It is important to always remember that it is not the individual that is powerful but the role they perform. This is well illustrated by the Simon Sinek story of a former US Undersecretary of Defense speaking at a conference two years in a row. As Sinek tells it, 'They flew me here Business Class, they had a car waiting for me that took me to my hotel. Someone had already checked me in and they escorted me up to my room. The next morning, I came downstairs and there was someone waiting for me in the lobby and they drove me to the same venue. They took me through the back entrance and took me into the green room and handed me a cup of coffee in a beautiful ceramic cup'. He says, 'I'm no longer the Undersecretary, I flew here coach, I took a taxi from the airport and I checked myself in. When I came down the lobby this morning, I took another taxi to this venue, I came in the front door and found my way backstage. And when I asked someone, "Do you have any coffee?", he pointed to the coffee machine of the corner and I poured myself a cup of coffee into this here Styrofoam cup.'

He was the same person but now he was not in role and the power previously bestowed on him was now bestowed on another. The beautiful ceramic cup was for the role, not the person.

In 1959, the social psychologists John French and Bertram Raven[4] divided power into five distinct forms and six years later, added another to create the six forms of power illustrated in the above model. The six powers are broken down into two groups of direct positional power, which means as a direct result of the role bestowed on them by the organization, and indirect personal power, this is partly bestowed on them by the organization and partly earnt, although the earnt element may be more about perception than reality. Both direct positional power and indirect personal power have three different elements. Let us look at these and how they apply to the C-Suite.

Legitimate Power – This comes from the belief that a person has the formal right to make demands and to expect compliance and obedience from others. For example, a CFO may ask or demand a member of his or her team to create a cashflow forecast for the next quarter and is likely to set that task with a deadline, which is the expectation of obedience. The words may sound extreme but if you reflect on management systems which is not in the scope of this book, the systems like SMART (Specific/Measurable/Achievable/Realistic or Relevant/Time-bound (or timely)) objectives and the Balanced Score Cards are

[4] https://en.wikipedia.org/wiki/French_and_Raven per cent27s_bases_of_power

all based on a demand, a set target or objective and someone having to deliver to that demand, which means they will need to be compliant to it. So, every member of the C-Suite has legitimate power over everyone who reports directly to them and therefore collectively, they have legitimate power over everyone in the organization.

Coercive Power – If a member of an organization chooses not to carry out the task given to them within the set time frame, they may well be punished through a verbal reprimand or some form of performance management. Known as 'coercive power', it is a negative as opposed to reward power, which is often a positive. Coercive power comes from the belief that a person can punish them for noncompliance. Historically, in around 1800, people spoke of the 'carrot and the stick' when motivating one donkey to race against another, the stick being the coercive power and the carrot being the reward power, which we will look at in a moment. In most cultures across the globe there is a similar saying for reward and punishment – for example, in the German language they talk about the 'sugar bread and whip'. The stick or whip is the coercive power in action. For children, this might be no TV for a week or being grounded and for executives, it can equally take many forms such as the reduction or delay of a benefit, reduced money, a longer time to promotion or exclusion from a group or activity.

Reward Power – Reward and coercive power are one of the most effective types of power as they can tap into deep personal motivators like ambition and fear. Reward power can include financial benefits like commission, bonuses, profit shares and equity, and also benefits like recognition, Employee of the Month, promotions and other benefits. The appraisal systems carried out by most C-Suite executives – by them and to them – are all examples of reward power structures in action.

In 2009, McKinsey[5] research showed that non-cash motivators such as praise from immediate managers, leadership attention, including a letter from the CEO or one-on-one conversations, and a chance to lead projects or task forces were equal if not better motivators to financial incentives. The big question for C-Suite executives is about getting the balance between carrot (reward) and stick (coercive) right and being creative in what each could look like to achieve optimal performance. A weighting too far in either direction can lead to negative outcomes and corrosive cultures. The lead C-Suite Executive focused on this balance is the Chief Human Resources Officer. As a result, the CHRO has a huge influence over the deployment of reward power in an organization, always remembering that excessive or unfair deployments of reward power can be examples of real and perceived discrimination and corporate bullying.

In addition to the direct positional power members of the C-Suite have bestowed upon them, they also have indirect personal power and these take the form of referent, information and expert power. The first of these – referent power – also comes from their role in the organization, the Chief at the front of their job title whereas the information and expert power is more likely to come about as a result of the area of expertise they have come from. The Chief in their role title will account for four of the powers, the three direct positional powers and the indirect reference power, whereas the information and expert power comes from the X in their role. Let's now look at each of the three indirect powers:

> **Referent Power** – Referent power in the C-Suite comes from the height or seniority of their position and is the result of a person's perceived seniority. Although an individual may not directly report to them and they have no legitimate, reward or coercive power over them, a member of staff may perceive

[5] https://www.mckinsey.com/business-functions/organization/our-insights/motivating-people-getting-beyond-money

them as a peer to their boss and as a result, treat and respond to them accordingly. Star performers who are known or recognized and those who are particularly respected may also have referent power. A simple litmus test for referent power is whether you tell others about a person you met. When I teach power on management courses I give the example of a meal and ask those present a couple of questions. I ask them if they sat next to an Olympic athlete at a dinner, would they tell their friends about it the following day? Then I expand the examples to include Nobel Prize winners, movie stars, CEOs, politicians, even members of the nobility. If they say yes to any, those people have referent power over them. In business, this is far subtler and people drop into conversations things like, 'Well, when I spoke with Jane last week, she said …'. That immediately tells us that Jane has referent power to the person talking and probably to the group, or why else mention the name? The use of the name is designed to give weight to the position or argument.

Expert Power – Based on a person's superior skill and knowledge, Expert Power is the X in a CXO. It can derive from qualifications, experience and personal learnings. Individuals build this over their careers and often start off by qualifying as a lawyer, accountant or marketer. This is the bedrock of their expert power, which many will build on through doing further business degrees, such as a Master's in Business Administration or for a lawyer, a Master's in Intellectual Property. Each qualification is important, but most professions demand further practical experience before they can legitimize their expert power. For example, lawyers become trainee lawyers and accountants, trainee auditors for several years before dropping the 'trainee' titles. Once qualified, their names are often published in journals as a recognition of their expert power.

Within the C-Suite, staff executives such as the Chief Legal Officer wield significant expert power through their legal and regulatory knowledge and line executives such as CEO of a manufacturing plant may wield significant power due to their operational knowledge. The saying 'Knowledge is power' is often attributed to Sir Francis Bacon, Attorney General and then Lord Chancellor of England in around 1600. However, 1,000 years earlier, Imam Ali was documented in the book, *Nahj Al-Balagha*,[6] as saying, 'Knowledge is power and it can command obedience.' So the recognition of this type of power is not new and C-Suite executives should spend their entire career building expert knowledge and power as their roles and opportunities evolve. However, it is important for them to recognize that the expert power they had in one role may become much less or more important in a different environment. Therefore, banking on one area of knowledge for a career may be a dangerous and limiting approach. In the next chapter, we will look at the importance of knowledge and how this needs to change as people transition through middle management into the C-Suite Executive.

Information Power – The most transitory of the six powers because if a person was to give it away, that person's unique source of power would collapse to zero. People gain information power through holding information or having access to information. Negotiators through the nature of their trade are experts at using and manipulating information power. As a result, it is sometimes the withholding of information that gives the individual power over the other, often without the other knowing about it.

Let me give you an extreme example. In 1994, while in my twenties, I was a UN operations officer and second in command of the Northern Cordon around Sarajevo, the now capital of Bosnia and Herzegovina in Europe. One of our top British spies had been caught by the Serbs and we were very keen to have her back. She would have been a material loss and was someone who significant specialist assets would have been deployed to recover. As you can imagine there was a pre-agreed story in case of capture

[6] https://en.wikipedia.org/wiki/Scientia_potentia_est

and this was known to just her and the hostage negotiation team and they all knew the story intimately because a mistake could lead to a loss of life.

The story was that she was the UN General's Personal Assistant and that the General adored her like his own daughter. This approach immediately devalued the worth of the captured spy to the Serbs and created an alternative value of her worth to the UN General in the eyes of the Serbs. The Serb General had his own daughters, quickly understood how the UN General must feel and considered what he would do to someone who kidnapped his daughter. This was the subtly planted negotiation stick. Would that potential backlash be worth it for a PA? The Serb General released the British spy almost as an understanding gift from one father to another and never knew what he had done.

It is a great story about the use of information and storytelling and did you notice that I introduced it by saying that I was a UN operations officer at the time? This helped legitimize me and therefore the associated story. It is something people always do, they legitimize information through referencing where it has come from and this is a good example of why access to information can be as important as the information itself. Without the source being robust, the story or information value rapidly deteriorates. If I were to tell you something about Donald Trump, 45th President of the United States, you probably would not believe me and most likely, you would be right not to as I had no special access to his former administration. But if I were Donald Trump's PA, Nicholas Luna, why would you not believe me? PAs are often unique people as although the activities of their role may hold little information power, their access to information can be extraordinarily powerful. In addition, they are gatekeepers to a powerful person's diary so also control access to legitimate power. That is why it will always be in your interest to get on with Personal or Executive Assistants. PAs and EAs talk and arrogant young executives may find they hit a glass ceiling put in place by the very people they were demeaning.

Joseph S. Nye Jr, former Assistant Secretary of Defense for International Security Affairs and Dean of Harvard's Kennedy School of Government, talks of 'Soft Power' being the ability to get what you want through attraction and 'Hard Power' being the use of coercion, including military threat or payment. He identifies in our networked world a general shift from hard to soft power and more importantly, the strategic combination of both being optimal, which he defines as 'Smart Power'. Similarly, to get to the top of an organization you need to have experienced soft power, staff and hard power, line, roles. Strategically combining the two is smart and gives the optimal chance of success.

A major barrier to the digitalization of the workplace is the impact it has on power. When you digitalize a department business process or automate a manufacturing line, you effectively take information and expert power off individuals and capture it in technology. This is great for the business for many reasons – for example, it improves efficiencies and reduces error rates and risk. One of the risks it reduces is the impact of a key expert leaving the organization and the resulting loss of expertise or knowledge, as their expertise and knowledge has already been effectively captured in the machine. So, the balance of power between individual and organization shifts towards the organization. This shift towards the organization can have very real consequences on things like status, pay and influence. Many lawyers, accountants, surveyors and consultants unite in their distrust of technology for exactly this reason – they fear it is the path to unemployment. But hopefully in time, even the technology laggards will see that it frees them up to do more interesting work. This neatly brings us on to the depth of knowledge question. Technology is not typically a threat to people with deep and complex understandings as these can be difficult to replicate in technology. People generally will try to maintain power through not sharing everything they know. Those who know a lot are therefore often able to share more as they still have reservoirs of knowledge to fall back on. Average consultants may be less forthcoming as their knowledge may be shallower and quickly shared, thereby wiping out their value to the customer and destroying their income stream.

As indicated, some roles within a business will be positions of influence and some will be positions of power. We will look at how that can impact your career later in this chapter. For now, as we have a clearer understanding of power and how it may or may not be used, it is important to understand who actually sits in the C-Suite.

THE C-SUITE & DIGITAL GIANTS

Who sits in the C-Suite Executive varies from organization to organization depending on the maturity of the organization, the sectors in which it operates and on the strategic situation or opportunity the organization faces. For this chapter, we have taken the FTSE 100 companies listed on the London Stock Exchange. They are a good sample because they are a group of relatively mature organizations: over two-thirds of their total revenue comes from international business and they also represent a wide variety of sectors. The FTSE 100 companies are a good representation of multinationals generally and therefore a good place to start when looking at the C-Suite Executive make-up. The total value of the FTSE 100 was at the time of writing about £1.8 trillion.[7] However, the market value of the three digital giants – Apple, Amazon and Alphabet, owners of Google – is significantly greater. Because the digital giants represent such a colossal market valuation running into trillions of US dollars and may represent at least part of the future of business it will be important to include them in our analysis. They also represent a sector, technology and digital, and as a result, are a good illustration of some of the sector differences that can occur.

For ease, we will start looking at the average constituents of the top 100 FTSE company C-Suite Executives as a representative of normal large organizations and we will then compare that to the top ten digital giants. To help paint the picture, the FTSE 100 includes organizations such as GlaxoSmithKline, Rolls-Royce, Royal Dutch Shell, HSBC, Unilever, Vodafone, AstraZeneca, Rio Tinto, BP, Diageo, RB Group, Tesco, RELX and Barclays. For the

[7] https://www.londonstockexchange.com/indices/ftse-100?lang=en

digital giants, we have looked at just the top ten, which includes Alphabet Inc., Microsoft, Adobe, IBM, Intel, Amazon, Facebook, Cisco, Oracle and Apple.

We start with the FTSE 100 and the average FTSE 100 C-Suite Executive team consists of nine people, including the CEO. The eight remaining executives tend to consist of five staff C-Suite Executives and three line C-Suite Executives, as illustrated below. There are approximately 45 C-Suite roles commonly referred to and the staff C-Suite Executives of FTSE 100 companies and their frequency tend to be:

- 100 per cent   Chief Financial Officer (CFO);
- 67 per cent   Chief Legal Officer (CLO, sometimes known as the General Counsel);
- 67 per cent   Chief HR Officers (CHRO);
- 36 per cent   Chief Technology, Information or Operations Officer (CTO/CIO or COO); collectively, they are present 72 per cent of the time;
- 29 per cent   Chief Communications Officer or 28 per cent Chief Marketing Officer (CCO or CMO); collectively, they are present 57 per cent of the time.

It is worth noting that there are more CCOs than CMOs in FTSE 100 companies and around a third of the CCOs are titled Corporate or External Affairs. Although no organization fits the model perfectly due to their own needs, in general the five staff C-Suite Executives are the CFO, CLO, CHRO, a CTO/CIO or COO and a CMO or CCO.

The three line C-Suite Executives often have the title of CEO, Managing Director, President or Vice President, with a product area or region after their title. Of the line C-Suite Executives or Business Unit Leaders, most (58 per cent) represent a global product area with the remaining 42 per cent representing geographical areas and organizations have a mix of both approaches. For example, at

Unilever, the British–Dutch consumer goods company, you have a President North America (Geography) and a President, Foods & Refreshments (Product). What is interesting is if you look at small and medium enterprises, the size of the C-Suite Executive drops from nine to six people and there tends to be twice as many line as staff C-Suite Executives. The illustration below is the normal organization chart for FTSE 100 C-Suite Executive teams.

FTSE 100 C-Suite Executive

The CEOs of the geographic areas and product streams are all running independent business units with their own profit and loss. Depending on the size of the business unit and structure of the organization, they may have a repetition of the corporate structure in their own C-Suite Executive, with their own finance, HR, legal, marketing and tech or operations people. Or these departments may be centralized and managed through a business partnering approach or most likely, there is a hybrid approach with a combination of local and centralized resources.

Outside the C-Suite roles in the above illustration, the next most frequent roles to be found in the C-Suite Executives of FTSE 100 are in order the Chief Strategy, Risk, Research & Development or Scientific, Supply or Procurement, Compliance, Revenue, Sales, Customer and Health & Safety. In fact, there are around 45 of them and odd ones popping up for short periods of time, such as the CBO (Chief Brexit Officer) and the CRWO (Chief Remote Working Officer), which occurred during the Covid-19 pandemic. So, the question is, who do these people report to? The answer is the staff C-Suite Executive, not the line C-Suite Executive. This is important and you can quickly work out that 45 divided by 5 equals 9, which means each staff C-Suite Executive will have on average eight other C-Level executives reporting into them.

So, when people say you have to be a generalist in the C-Suite Executive, they are right – the chance of getting on to the C-Suite Executive representing only one area is near on impossible, you have to be a generalist manager and good at it.

Now, let's compare this to the Digital Giants. Interestingly, the digital giants C-Suite Executive teams are almost exactly the same size at nine people but then it changes slightly. Digital giants tend to have two-line CEOs compared to FTSE 100 three-line CEOs and six staff C-Suite Executives compared to the FTSE 100 five staff C-Suite Executives. In addition, the digital giants tend not to have any regional or geographic CEOs at all, instead they are all product or technology focused line CEOs. For example, Amazon have a Vice President, Worldwide Prime & Marketing, VP, Head Scientist, Alexa, VP, Performance Advertising, VP, Amazon Web Services Compute Services, VP, Amazon Fashion and VP, Worldwide Corporate Development. This may be a result of sector nuances and the US approach to geography can often be US and ROW (Rest of World), therefore regional breaks are less relevant.

The staff C-Suite Executive roles in a digital giant are also different. Like FTSE 100 companies, they have a CFO in 100 per cent of cases but they also have a CLO in 100 per cent cases, so CLOs are perceived as being more important in digital giants than in FTSE 100 companies. Coming next is the CMO, ahead of the CHRO this time, and then you have a CTO and also a COO. Just outside the standard six people, you also often have a Chief Product & Design Officer.

Digital Giant C-Suite Executive

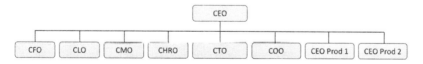

Of the top eight C-Suite roles, three remain the same (CEO, CFO, CLO) and in Digital Giants, marketing has a much higher priority, pushing down the importance of the other roles. The table below summarizes the change in priorities of different C-Suite roles:

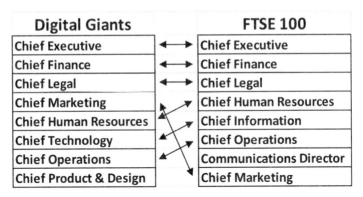

Digital Giants	FTSE 100
Chief Executive	Chief Executive
Chief Finance	Chief Finance
Chief Legal	Chief Legal
Chief Marketing	Chief Human Resources
Chief Human Resources	Chief Information
Chief Technology	Chief Operations
Chief Operations	Communications Director
Chief Product & Design	Chief Marketing

So, the difference between the digital giants and the FTSE 100 C-Suite Executive teams is not enormous but there are definitely some noticeable differences and this can impact your career. For example, good advice to European CMOs who want to be C-Suite Executives would be to join a tech company because they are more marketing-led and or travel to the US, where marketing is valued more.

TRENDS & DIVERSITY

Diversity takes many forms and one of the best models I found to summarize this is from the Thinking Ahead Institute, part of the Willis Towers Watson group. It surmises that there are four areas of diversity: surface self, personal self, doing self and thinking self. The area easiest to measure, report on and most often thought of is surface diversity, which includes gender, age and ethnicity.

The table below illustrates the gender splits in 2020 across C-Suite roles in the US, Europe and Asia. It illustrates that the US and EU C-Suites have a similar gender split, with approximately three quarters of the C-Suite being male and a quarter being female. Asia has almost exactly half the number of females at 13 per cent or one-eighth of the C-Suite. CHRO (Human Resources) is the only role in the US (62 per cent female) and EU (74 per cent female) that has more females than males. In Asia, CHRO also has the highest number of females in the CHRO role (35 per cent female) but it is half the amount at approximately a third of CHROs compared to two-thirds female in the US and EU.

C-Suite	USA		EU		Asia	
Role	M	F	M	F	M	F
CEO	94%	6%	95%	5%	98%	2%
CIO	80%	20%	95%	5%	99%	1%
COO	88%	12%	87%	13%	96%	4%
CLO	61%	39%	60%	40%	86%	14%
CFO	87%	13%	85%	15%	95%	5%
CHRO	38%	62%	26%	74%	65%	35%
CMO	69%	31%	61%	39%	69%	31%
Ave	**74%**	**26%**	**73%**	**27%**	**87%**	**13%**

This data is easier to see and understand if we graph just the female percentages, as illustrated by the graphic below. What you can immediately see is that the gender split in roles appears quite consistent across the global regions. CHRO (Human Resources) has overwhelmingly the largest number of females, followed by CLO (Legal) and CMO (Marketing). Asia has a similar percentage of females in the CMO role to the US and EU but falls significantly behind in the roles of CHRO and CLO. Female representation across all the geographical regions is materially lower in the CFO (Finance), COO (Operations) and CIO (Tech) roles, with CEO showing the worst representation. There are a couple of anomalies that include the US having proportionally more female CIOs (20 per cent female) than the EU (5 per cent) and Asia (1 per cent).

So, as a woman, the worst C-Suite role to have in terms of career prospects is a CIO in Asia (1 per cent female) and the best is a CHRO in the EU (74 per cent female).

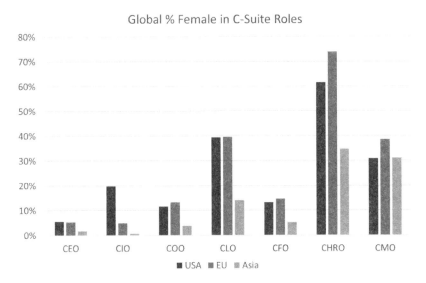

So, as a woman, the worst C-Suite role to have in terms of career prospects is a CIO in Asia (1 per cent female) and the best is a CHRO in the EU (74 per cent female).

The US, EU and Asia all still have a long way to go to achieve gender equality and as advanced societies, we have a choice of aiming towards equality of outcome or equality of choice. Equality of outcome would lead to a 50:50 split in men across all roles and you would therefore have an equal number of women in, say, Human Resources and Information Technology. This would take significant social engineering, probably stringent quotas and is a political decision beyond the scope of this book.

In Digital Giants, Marketing and HR are both dominated by women and as a result, Digital Giants tend to have two women on the Executive Team rather than the one on FTSE 100 executives. Digital Giants also tend to have more female chief financial and chief legal officers. Tech and Operations are dominated by men in both FTSE 100 and Digital Giants.

In Chapter 3, Career Planning & Strategies, we look at the age profile of the C-Suite as it relates to career planning, so let us now look at ethnicity. In the FTSE 100, ethnic diversity lags significantly behind gender diversity and although difficult to measure without self-declaration, a visual review indicates that around 5 per cent of C-Suite Executives are Asian and 1 per cent are of African descent. This means that only 1 in 20 FTSE 100 executives come from a diverse ethnic background. Although there appears to be much effort at present to address this, there is clearly a long way to go. However, the Digital Giants give us more hope and tell a very different story, with every C-Suite having ethnic representation and in some organizations like Adobe, white people are in the minority. It does appear that CEOs from non-white backgrounds tend to have more diverse C-Suites. In both the FTSE and Digital Giants, people of an Asian heritage are materially more present than those of an African heritage. As you might expect, there is no ethnic correlation with certain C-Suite roles as there are for women in either the FTSE 100 or the Digital Giants.

The C-Suite Generalist

We know from the FTSE 100 analysis that the average staff C-Suite Executive has eight C-Level roles reporting into them and in D alone, these can include roles like chief data, digital, diversity, development and design officers. Wikipedia goes further and lists over 70 C-Suite roles but for the purposes of this book, we are sticking with approximately 45 material ones. The naming of roles varies considerably – for example, in the FTSE 100 of the 29 Chief communication officers, ten are titled corporate or external affairs and their additional roles include corporate relations (three), investor relations (two), regulatory affairs (two), sustainability (two), government and brand. Two of the chief communication officers (CCO) have a marketing responsibility and three of the chief marketing officers (CMOs) have a communications responsibility. Three of the CMOs have sales in their role and five are chief commercial officers so could also be listed as chief revenue officers.

To take into account the breadth of roles each person covers, people often end up with dual named roles, some of which have a natural resonance but others are more unusual. At Unilever, for example, they have a chief digital & marketing officer, which sounds like a natural fit. At Dyson, the CHRO (Chief Human Resources Officer) was also made the CISO (Chief Information Security Officer) as they considered cyber security to be a human, not a tech issue. At PA Consulting Group, the HR function reported into the CMO (Chief Marketing Officer) as they focused on the employee brand. At Interserve, they gave the CHRO IT responsibility, so she became the CHRO and CIO and the reason they did this is because most tech initiatives tend to fall over when people get involved, especially when behavioural changes are needed, so pulling HR and tech together made sense for them.

At TalkTalk, they have a chief people and procurement officer and at first this may appear like an unusual mix. However, as Daniel Kasmir, Chief People and Procurement Officer at TalkTalk explains, 'The combination of People and Procurement is a strong combination. With so many organizations shifting fixed cost to variable costs (e.g. outsourcing), the joining up means that the supply and demand for people, whether employed directly or indirectly, sits under one function, which is then able to ensure cost optimization as opposed to backdoor organizational creep.' This is a key point as many organizations operate in functional or business unit silos, rather than looking at a core process or task issues. At TalkTalk, the issue of resourcing is more important than the department structure, likewise at Dyson, information security is more important than the department structure and at Interserve, technology implementation is more important than the department structure. If C-Suite executives are focused on their departments and have limited knowledge elsewhere they may without consciously realizing be presiding over a less-than-optimal business. C-Suite executives need to understand how the core processes run in the business and the key tasks within them. So what do boards and CEOs think of these dual- or multi-responsibility roles?

I remember once meeting the CEO of a large British construction company which had sales of in excess of £1 billion. We had a 20-minute coffee planned in a rather luxury mid-city café. I asked him what his major challenges were and it all poured out and our short meeting extended into what felt like a two-hour cathartic download of the problems he had with his top team. His main angst was that none of them could cover for each other, that they were all too siloed in their knowledge and skills and when a hole occurred due to an illness or resignation, he always ended up filling the gap. I know and deeply empathized with him as it had been a problem I suffered from in the small business I ran. It appeared that both of our top teams had been too narrowly focused and neither of us had adequate succession in place. The meeting triggered me to investigate the area and what boards and executive teams were doing to encourage a deeper breadth of understanding and skill. As a result of this research, we discovered:

- Holes between silos;
- Holes in language and perception;
- Holes in knowledge of business areas;
- Holes in resource (sick, transition, etc.);
- Potential internal rivalry.

We also discovered that this was not an uncommon issue, that it had been around for a while and there were several approaches already being practiced by some of the more innovative organizations. These approaches were all focused on creating greater understanding by exposing CXOs to other parts of the business and the top four approaches we found were:

- CXOs working in each other's functions;
- CXOs shadowing each other;
- CXOs being appointed as cover for each other;
- CXOs presenting each other's work to the Board or company.

Although in each organization there was some initial resistance to the above approaches the result was nearly always positive in that the individual CXO was often surprised by how much they learnt. Also, they very often had takeaways that they could action immediately to improve the activities of the organization.

When Mervyn Davies took over as CEO of Standard Chartered Bank in his first 100 days he travelled continuously, visiting 20 countries in three months. He ran focus groups with staff at all levels in places he had never been to before. He researched multiple stakeholders, including external people such as financiers, suppliers, consultants and customers. Davies wanted to understand how the organization was perceived, what it was good and bad at, and what challenges needed to be addressed and in which order. He and his top team then came together to review the findings and create a plan. After a few days there was a recognition of the challenges, a commitment to a stretch target and a sense of urgency to get things done.

The commitment to a stretch target was really important and Davies took three key actions. Standard Chartered launched a leadership course for senior managers, a 'Customer Week', where everyone had to spend a week listening to customers and a 'Song Contest', where every business unit had to submit a team to sing a song. The song contest was designed to pull together a disparate team, have some fun and also to give them a shared social experience. Here, I would like to focus on the customer week. I met one of their in-house lawyers who had personally experienced the customer week. At first, she was quite resistant to it and ended up spending a week in a car with a commission-incentivized sales person. She told me that she learnt more in that week about how the organization worked than she had ever learnt before. What she hadn't realized was that the sales person had already decided what he was going to spend his commission on, he had told his partner and they were looking forward to a mini break, but he hadn't actually made the sale yet. This put enormous pressure on him – he had to deliver the sale and it was something he may have unconsciously done to motivate himself. Either way, the team that got in the way of him closing and slowed down the process was the legal team and she was part of that team; she was part of the problem as far as he was concerned. Now the in-house lawyer understood the problem.

On returning to the legal team, she put in place a series of activities to help the sales person and the sales teams and as a result, the whole of Standard Chartered Bank ran a little bit better.

So, the moral of this story is working on other parts of the business works and can on occasion be life-changing. Admittedly, on rare occasions, the processes or practices identified can be an issue and although good to know about that new knowledge can result in short-term pain as behaviours, processes and sometimes people need to change.

THE NEW C-SUITE SKILLS

Four new and developing areas of expertise that the C-Suite will need to master are understanding society and communities, new medias and the art of soundbite communication, how stuff works (especially the new stuff) and leveraging variety and diversity.

Understanding Society and Communities

In 1920, there were an estimated 25 million horses[8] in the US, each eating acres of grass and creating tons of manure. Ten years later, cars per capita surpassed horses per capita for the first time and 30 years on, the horse population had dropped to 4.5 million[9]. In 2016, the US had 268.8 million registered vehicles or approximately 80 cars for every 100 people alive. The horse population has recovered recently, approximately two horses for every 100 people alive, but more as a leisure activity than for work. The engine that could achieve greater horsepower replaced the need for horses and has become more abundant.

Professor Hans Rosling was a leading Swedish Academic, whose TED Talks and posthumous book, *Factfulness: Ten Reasons We're Wrong About the World – And Why Things are Better than You Think*,[10] made him world-famous. He talks about the world having a Pin

[8] Equine Heritage Institute » Horse Facts
[9] https://sebestaconsulting.com/2019/09/peak-horses
[10] Rosling, Hans, *Factfulness: Ten Reasons We're Wrong About the World – And Why Things are Better than You Think*. Sceptre, 2018

Code and that Pin Code is 1114. There are approximately 7 billion people in the world today, 1 billion in the Americas, 1 billion in Europe, 1 billion in Africa and 4 billion in Asia. In 2100, Peak Human is expected to be at around 11 billion and the Pin Code becomes 1145, 1 billion in the Americas, 1 billion in Europe, 4 billion in Africa and 5 billion in Asia. The average person consumes approximately 1.5 to 2.5 kilos of food a day but sadly, our waste cannot all be reused as manure. The computer already has faster processing power than the brain in certain areas and technology has automated many human tasks, ranging from supermarket payment tills to event management.

The number of people in employment at the start in 2020 was nearing full employment in most Western nations[11] but many were warning of the automation of professional roles, which accounts for around half of all jobs in developed nations. This warning was coined by some as the 'hollowing out of the middle class'. The executive search industry has picked up on this and many agencies are increasingly repositioning themselves at the premium end of the marketplace or in the interim space. As one managing partner of a Brazilian search agency called BRAVA recently told me, 'The junior positions are going to go away.'

Raymond Kurzweil, Director of Engineering at Google, argues that computers would have human-level intelligence by 2030. An impact of Covid-19 was to accelerate the digitalization of businesses and it brought forward years of technology that in turn increases efficiencies and saves costs. Those costs being saved are people costs, they are jobs, and futurologists expect 30–50 per cent of jobs[12] to be automated and new jobs that don't exist today to be created. The big issue is how long is the gap between the lost roles and the ones being created, when does it start, how many jobs net are lost and how satisfying are the new ones: 'McKinsey predicts that 800 million people could be displaced in

---

[11] https://data.oecd.org/emp/employment-rate.htm
[12] https://www.huffingtonpost.co.uk/2014/01/17/rise-of-the-machines-economist_n_4616931.html

42 countries, or a third of the workforce, because of the Fourth Industrial Revolution.'[13]

Peak Employment & Peak Human
So, are we reaching Peak Employment potentially decades ahead of Peak Human? Different nation states will hit Peak Employment at different times, with developed nations leading the race and those following often leapfrogging technologies to keep pace. However, we can safely say that Peak Employment will occur in almost every nation state decades ahead of Peak Human. Some argue that Covid-19 brought forward technology by five to ten years, but a more accurate number according to McKinsey is closer to three years and as a result, we may have already seen Peak Employment. This will be the biggest challenge of our millennium that all societies will face, that is highly likely to be antagonized by mass immigration partly caused by factors such as climate change and the broadening wealth gap, in and between nations. It is important to note at this point that a large wealth gap in a nation state is bad news as it is often accompanied by a health and an education gap and reduced social mobility. The US has one of the highest wealth gaps in the world, the UK is not far behind and as a result, they both have much-reduced social mobility, which was the American Dream.

> The American Dream is a national ethos of the United States, the set of ideals (democracy, rights, liberty, opportunity and equality) in which freedom includes the opportunity for prosperity and success, as well as an upward social mobility for the family and children, achieved through hard work in a society with few barriers.[14]
>
> Wikipedia

So, if you are looking for the American Dream today, you may want to go to the state or country with the lowest wealth gap to see

[13] https://www.weforum.org/agenda/2019/09/fourth-industrial-revolution-jobs/
[14] https://en.wikipedia.org/wiki/American_Dream

the dream in action. In the US, the state with the lowest wealth gap is West Virginia, followed by Mississippi and the highest wealth gap is in Connecticut, followed by New York. If you are looking at countries, the lowest wealth gap can be found in Denmark, followed by Slovenia and the Czech Republic and the highest wealth gap can be found in Mexico, followed by Chile and then the US. So, if you are looking for the American Dream, go to Denmark.

Realists talk about the resulting knowledge and wealth gap increases, society becoming more fractured, increases in antisocial behaviour and civil unrest. Optimists talk of humans and machines working in harmony, three-day working weeks and Universal Basic Income (UBI) for all. When recessions hit, tax rises to the top of the political agenda. Likewise, if the employment gap between Peak Employment and Peak People is a society issue, rising to 25 per cent as it did in 1933 at the height of the Great Depression[15] or even further to 50 per cent, it will undoubtedly be a business issue, could lead to economic contraction and is likely to become one of the biggest challenges for businesses and their leadership teams. Robust and healthy social systems may become the most important competitive advantage of nation states and organizations.

The C-Suite will need to step up and become business and society leaders, engaging their community stakeholders in an intelligent and material way and ensuring that they are not excluded from the benefits resulting from the activities of the organization. This is not about brand or reputation management, but about looking after people, minimizing their pain, enhancing their lives and career opportunities and protecting the organization and society. Future leaders need to start today engaging with their local communities, developing those ties and the connectivity and learning and understanding of different micro communities. The public sector, too often mistakenly frowned upon by the private sector, may well become necessary or even essential sector experience for future business leaders. A major C-Suite skills and knowledge gap in 2030 and beyond will become 'community and civil service'.

[15] https://historyplex.com/unemployment-during-great-depression

Occasionally you may hear executive search companies recommend to people en route to the C-Suite to get more board experience. They recommend executives to become charity trustees and school governors and the third sector is often used as a board experience training ground for future business leaders. They are right to recommend the third sector but not just for the reasons they think. Through the third sector, executives can gain deep insights into different parts of society, understand better how their society works, what its concerns and motivations are and how they can better prepare for the future. The benefit is mutual, as for the third sector it is highly advantageous to have business leaders who recognize and understand the complexities of the environments in which they operate.

New Medias & The Art of Soundbite Communication
German inventor Johannes Gutenberg started the printing revolution in Europe in 1439 with the first movable type. Before newspapers existed, the first known newsletter printed in England was *Requests of the Devonshyre and Cornyshe Rebelles* in 1549, 150 years later the first daily English newspaper, *The Daily Courant*, was printed. Concurrently, in Germany in 1517, Martin Luther nailed a message to the Wittenberg Castle church door detailing what he thought was wrong about the Catholic Church. Few people had ever heard of him and the letter did not receive much attention at the time because the Church controlled communications. But the printing press was about to change that and between 1525 and 1545,[16] Luther published through different channels 5,651 documents and gave birth to the Protestant Christian faith. Today, there are over 800 million Protestants globally, making up 37 per cent of all Christians as opposed to Catholics, which now represent 50 per cent.

Imagine how history would be different if the Catholic Church had managed to keep the Protestants in their congregation. The Thirty Years' War would never have happened, there would be a

[16] https://medium.com/practice-of-history-2018/titlw-of-papweer-2adc4210dd24

different Monarch sitting on the English throne and many countries would not have the legacy of civil conflict caused by a religious divide that still haunts politics today. Two different examples of micro revolutions, only one successful but both recognizing the power of new media, print at the time, both using it to boost the voice of a political movement. Social media is the new print and can give voice to thousands whose voice has never been heard before, there will be many important voices and many misleading noises. Like print, some will be successful and others less so. Unlike print, there are new issues to manage such as fake news, viral disinformation and social media bots (robots or automated social media accounts) and like print, they can influence global politics. As mentioned, Sir Frances Bacon is often cited as the first person to use the expression 'Knowledge is Power'. More recently, this may have been usurped by the belief that 'perception is reality' and if the news is sometimes fake, that creates a significant problem for leaders.

The Apple iPhone was launched in 2007 and social media is still in its infancy, it will not take a hundred years to mature but still has some way to go. C-Suite executives need to be masters of this new media form, understanding how it works, how it can be used for good and bad, and most importantly, how to respond to reputational issues at both personal and corporate levels. They need to be social media philosophers able to use logic to counterargue, mitigate risk and direct perceptions, and able to do all this in a soundbite. They will also need to have the word discipline of poets and the communication skills of newspaper editors.

How Stuff Works, Especially the New Stuff
Barings Bank, the oldest British investment bank, was founded in 1717 in Exeter in the UK by a German called Johann Baring. Within 100 years, it had become a global powerhouse. In 1803, Barings financed the acquisition of Louisiana by the United States from France for $ US 15 million; it was the bank behind many famous brands like Guinness, Whitbread and Vickers and represented the Bank of the United States, Government of Upper Canada, Argentina, Russia, India, Italy, Japan, Turkey and the

State of Czechoslovakia. It funded railways in Canada and Bengal, a bridge for Constantinople and the London Underground, and had offices worldwide.

Barings plc sadly collapsed in 1995 as a result of unauthorized trading by Nick Leeson in Singapore and was sold to the Dutch bank ING for £1. Leeson was a derivatives trader who asked for control of both the front and back office in Singapore, a move that meant the bank lost its governance checks and no one registered the associated risks. Years later, the British Chancellor, Kenneth Clarke, presented the findings from a review that found 'serious problems of controls and management failings within the Barings group'.[17]

Today, financial products like derivatives are much better understood and governed within banks, but artificial intelligence, machine learning and cyber are not. Large numbers of executive teams and boards do not understand how it works and the risks are not under control. The Co-operative Bank, included as a case study later in Chapter 2, see pp. 91–94, is another example of governance failure due to lack of understanding.

How can you control or govern an instrument, service or product if you don't fundamentally understand how it works? The answer is you can't. People will counter-argue this by saying you can drive or govern a car without knowing how the engine works. They would be correct but they are not making and selling it. You can't make a car without understanding how it works, that would be madness. You need to deeply understand how the stuff you make and sell works. If your organization is on the front edge of science, engineering or all the techs, like fintech, biotech, proptech, insurtech, legaltech, femtech, edtech, medtech, regtech, foodtech, cleantech, etc., you need to understand what you do enough to be able to control and govern it. If you cannot do this, you are exposed to unlimited risk and will never be able to truly reap the benefits of what you do.

17   https://www.theguardian.com/business/from-the-archive-blog/2015/feb/24/nick-lees on-barings-bank-1995-20-archive

Line business leaders tend to have a better understanding of how stuff works than staff business leaders due to what they do and their closer involvement. Either way, it is essential you stay on top of what your business does, are permanently curious and if you have knowledge gaps, you fill them fast. When big software companies release patches to their software it takes the hackers approximately five days to reverse-engineer the patch to work out what the design, architecture or code fault was. Once they have done this, you are exposed, which is why techies always recommend that patches are implemented quickly. Likewise, if you do not understand how your stuff works, either it will come back to bite you, a competitor will use your ignorance to bite market share off you or a third party, like a hacker, might just punish you for fun. In each scenario, the organization you represent loses because you didn't know what it did or how it worked.

Leveraging Variety & Diversity

'The business case for diversity' stems from the progression of the models of diversity within the workplace since the 1960s. In the US, the original model comes from the equal opportunity employment objectives implemented in the Civil Rights Act of 1964. The idea was that an individual qualified for a specific job should have equal opportunity to obtain that job without being discriminated against. The compliance-based model, the enforced version, led to accusations of tokenism by the majority cultures and some who have benefited from it have said they would rather be promoted on merit but they still took the opportunity and show no regrets on that decision. Although much good has been achieved through the compliance-based approach, the process is open to criticism.

In 2003, Norway made it compulsory for all Boards to have at least 40 per cent female representation on the Board. Firms were given five years to comply and the figure is now around 42 per cent. Critics would say that a female succession pipeline of talent in corporates was not in place and this led to a prominent group of Norwegian women who had multiple board directorships to be given the nickname 'the golden skirts'. However, promoters would argue that it was a master stroke achieving gender equality while improving performance and governance all at the same time. In 2010, in the UK, Dame Helena Morrissey, Chief Executive Officer of Newton Investment Management, founded the 30% Club, which grew to have Chapters all over the world. By 2019, female representation on all FTSE 350 company boards in the UK was 32.5 per cent so the 30% Club had achieved its aim of over 30 per cent female representation. Therefore, it looks like the compliance-based model to diversity will most likely kick-start the process faster and deliver the desired result in half the time; five years in Norway as opposed to almost ten years in the UK. It also appears that corporates will tend to aim to beat the given quota and in both the above cases this is achieved by 2 per cent, which tells us that where the compliance or voluntary target is set is incredibly important. The compliance approach may lead to a lag in the skills and knowledge catching up, if the organizations do not have a good succession pipeline, so a compliance route can undermine the process if a less skilled person is promoted over a more highly skilled one but it may also help less confident people make the step. Likewise, if the voluntary approach is too slow, governments and regulators may threaten a compliance-based approach to drive more action.

There is evidence from the US, UK, Malaysia, Iraq, Spain and other countries that indicates that organizations that have women on boards tend to have higher organization performance, measured by return on assets. In 2010, McKinsey & Company published a report called 'Women Matter 2010',[18] which said that companies with gender-balanced executive boardrooms are 56 per cent more profitable than all-male boards. That may sound great, but if you are a woman or from a minority group, it still feels that access to the top executive team and board roles, that of CEO and Chair, is even harder to achieve. This intuitive feeling can be supported by actual data. In the US and Western Europe, most C-Suites now have at least one woman and or a minority representative and most

---

[18] women_matter_oct2010_english.ashx (mckinsey.com)

boards are now around a third female, with ethnic diversity lagging behind at around 5 per cent. This enables corporates to present a more diverse leadership but unfortunately when you look at the two power roles, of CEO and Chair, there is still remarkably little diversity. The data tells us that it is easier to move from being a C-Suite executive to becoming CEO than it is from a non-executive director to the role of Chair – statistically, the difference is material. This may be because boards still need to catch up and the diversity in the C-Suite has not yet had time to progress into the boardroom. It may also be because of the gender staff and line divide.

In 2020, McKinsey & Company explain that 90 per cent of CEOs in the S&P 500 companies are promoted or hired from line roles, yet only 20 per cent of women in senior VP positions hold line roles. Line roles are roles that have a direct impact on the objectives or deliverables of an organization, such as sales and production, while staff roles are those that support or advise the line roles, such as finance, legal and human resources. Another way to look at this is that line roles are positions of power and staff roles are positions of influence and to make it to CEO, it is important to have had the experience of positions of power. The CEO is clearly the top position of power and putting an individual in that role who has not held a position of power before obviously comes with some risk.

Line managers and leaders preside over business areas and core processes whereas staff managers and leaders preside over areas of knowledge and activity. Combining the two areas creates a matrix structure and to optimize a matrix structure, it is essential the different areas have a reasonable depth of understanding of the other areas. This once again brings us back to the need for staff managers to have line management experience. Staff functions like legal, tax, finance, compliance and governance have in the past been known as the 'control functions'. However, recent trends show these merging with government and public affairs and being repositioned as the 'transparency functions'.

This difference between line and staff roles should make organizations reflect on their succession pipelines across the business and particularly in line roles. Based on the current status and trends, McKinsey suggest that it will take more than 100 years to reach gender equality in the C-Suite.

What diversity includes and the motivation behind diversity become important because they represent different philosophical approaches and the depth of approach is critical to its sustainability. Government sector and social enterprise organizations unsurprisingly want to represent the populations they serve and therefore tend to focus on Surface and Personal Self, gender, ethnicity, age, health, family, caring, belief and sexual orientation. Governments also tend to adopt the compliance approach for their own organizations but allow more freedom to private enterprises. For example, corporates and private enterprises focus on competitive advantage and are therefore also interested in the Doing and Thinking Self, which would also include education, experience, level, reward, energy, how individuals source information, make decisions and approach challenges.

Kevin Sullivan, former VP of Apple Inc., said that 'diversity initiatives must be sold as business, not social work'. Black business leader Sir Kenneth Olisa, OBE, Lord-Lieutenant of Greater London, when he talks to a business audience says that diversity is not about social justice, it is about being competitive and out-performing the competition. If you are an Asian subsidiary of a US company and all your board and executive team are American or a European subsidiary of a Japanese company and all your board and executive team are Japanese, do you have diversity? Does a woman add diversity to a board because she is female or because she has had a different lived experience and thinks differently? If a white, Asian and black man all go to the same school, university and take the same professional qualification, do you have diversity? As Dr W. Thomas Boyce M.D. explains in his book, *The Orchid and the Dandelion: Why Sensitive People Struggle and How All Can Thrive*, a brother and sister can be brought up in the same family, go to the same school, study the same subject at university but have very different life experiences due to the order they were born in. Interestingly, secret intelligence services to profile prospective candidates often ask the child order question and other questions such as, until what age did you share a room?

As illustrated by the diagram below, organizations need to consider and act on diversity in their recruitment and selection processes. They need to focus on equal development opportunities of competencies and experiences in their staff and line management roles, making sure their internal selection and promotion processes are also free from bias and encourage less represented groups to step forward. Only this combined action will achieve the much-desired 'belonging' status. As the social commentator and influencer Verna Myers so beautifully put it, 'Diversity is being invited to the party, inclusion is being asked to dance and belonging is being able to choose the music'.

Therefore, the key to someone having a successful career at an organization, regardless of diversity, is their ability to develop the right competencies and to have had the right experience. These areas of knowledge are shared in the next chapter and for now, we will focus on the process of how to build your CV and career. Individuals who make it all the way to CEO do not do so by coincidence and instead, like all good businesses, they start with a purpose and then create a plan of how to achieve it. If you talk to board directors and ask them what advice they would give to their children, they would say within your current role always look for new experiences and challenges, do not just sit still. Volunteer and be at the front of the queue and make sure you stay current. Push yourself to make sure your skills do not go out of date and keep building your CV. By this, they mean internal CV and not for external purposes. To stay successful, you need to stay current, ensure that you are progressing and always be looking for new things.

SETTING YOUR DIRECTION

This is all good advice but it needs to sit within a framework that can guide your direction or you may end up with huge amounts of redundant knowledge. I remember once listening to a woman in her early thirties who had just moved to a new investment bank. At a networking drinks, she approached three more senior-looking women in banking and asked for their advice on what she should do. The advice was to identify the most senior woman in the organization she had just joined and to invite her out for a coffee. At that coffee to ask her how a woman can become successful in this organization and to ask her to share her career journey and how she overcame challenges on the way. Organizations are permanently evolving so the shared journey should be received as an example, not as the only way. You need to start by setting your own purpose and understanding the routes up, then you need a mentor probably two levels up from your current role and peers in other parts of the organizations that can act as ambassadors for you. Your plan can be divided into the three career Ps:

Purpose – People like organizations need a purpose, where do you want to get to? When Ian Callum was 14 years old, he knew what he wanted to do, design cars and more specifically design Jaguar cars. He loved them and was inspired by the XJ6. He wrote to Bill Heynes, Vice Chairman of Jaguar, asking for advice and enclosing some of his own car designs. Heynes' responded, advising Callum to study art and engineering drawing and Ian followed his advice. Ian later became Jaguar Director of Design, a role which he held for over 20 years.

Once you have a purpose, you can ask others how they made their journey, you can look at the different routes they have taken, the common ground and create a guiding framework to achieve your purpose. Always remember that although your purpose may remain constant, your framework is likely to need to be able to evolve as you learn more and as the situations unique to your life evolve. You have limited sensory power and focusing this on your purpose will alert your sensory antennae to spot the appropriate opportunities as they arise. Similarly, as a business leader, you should ask your high performers if they have a purpose or bigger ambition that they would like to fulfil and then once known, assist them on their journey.

From the role and gender data shared earlier in this chapter you can identify which roles are more prevalent in the C-Suite and which roles tend to have more diversity. This means you could choose a role that is more likely to be represented in the C-Suite and a path more familiar to people like you. This could be a sensible approach, as could choosing a route where you are the more diverse candidate. This latter, path-less-taken route may be a better approach but as a result is likely to demand greater personal resilience from you and that would be your personal choice to make. As a former infantry captain, I often agree to meet up with people who are leaving the services and debate what they should do next. I always give them the same advice: spend your life creating value and just do something. You won't know what you like and don't like until you have tasted it. Services people tend to be loyal by nature and therefore see their next career step as a lifelong decision whereas career changes are more common today than they have been for many generations.

Because you start as an in-house lawyer does not mean that the summit of your career, your purpose, has to be becoming a Fortune 100 chief legal officer, having spent a lifetime as an in-house lawyer. Jim Collins, one of the world's best-selling business authors, has a list of his top ten business leaders and surprisingly, a significant number of them trained as lawyers. He argues that business schools teach you about the best solution whereas law schools teach you how to ask the best question, and that the latter is more important. What is important about this small group is that none of them became Fortune 100 chief legal officers and although they all trained as lawyers, they all changed direction early in their careers. In some organizations it may be easier to change from one role to another – for example, to a line role from a staff role – at certain points in time or stages in your career. Human resources and senior leaders may well be good guides to help you recognize when these doors are more open. We will look at these career choices in Chapter 3 of this book, Career Planning & Strategies, see also pp. 151–165.

Promote Mentor – People often say you need to have a mentor or champion two levels above. One layer is too close and might be felt as threatening to the mentor and more than two may be too distant. This is the person who guides you to the next level and may even be an important internal advocate. They are a sort of 'well of inside knowledge' on your journey. On the other hand, we have all met people who are good at being promoted but less good at doing the job. These people usually get caught out later and then complain about unfair practices and glass ceilings to defend their reputations. Your 'promote mentors' role should be to help you move up in your career, partly because they help you become better at what you do. Developing personal competencies is a key aspect of your career that you should continually be building on. Some people have very successful careers following their 'Promote Mentor' as they make their own way up the corporate ladder. Others have different promote mentors throughout their careers that take them to the next phase of their careers. Super senior people are not good promote mentors as they are unlikely to advise you on the detail in your next step, but they can give you the framework to achieve your purpose.

People Peers – People peers are the people in your organization at a similar level who you know and they can be more valuable, the more distant they are from you. Take Clare, an executive in the Human Resources department, as an example. She is well known and good at what she does, she is well liked and often going out on socials with her peers in her HR department. Emma joined at the same time and is less social with the HR department but knows the production teams really well. On her induction, she met Rachel from production and they became good friends. As a result, she is invited to all the production socials and has a unique insight into what is going on in that business unit. So, who is more valuable to HR and the business, Clare or Emma? The advice is to work on your internal peer network and we will cover this in more detail in the next chapter.

Key Learnings from Chapter 1

Purpose & Stakeholders

- Corporates should focus more on purpose than vision and corral their organization and all its stakeholders around this and then manage all their stakeholders accordingly.
- Remuneration committees need to consider Environmental, Social and Corporate Governance (ESG) and the different types of capital when setting their policies and C-Suite Executive pay.
- There are around 45 C-Suite staff roles and boards and CEOs need to decide on which should be represented in the C-Suite Executive today and in the future.
- The Investors, Board and C-Suite must be aligned in their views and this can be achieved through organization values and highlighting and debating areas of difference.
- Stakeholders are important and experience with different stakeholder groups can help further a career.
- Regardless of the role, new managers and leaders should start their role by consulting all their stakeholders and understanding their point of view. They should then pull together their team and come up with a plan, backed by the collective impact of the team.

Power & Knowledge

- Executives and organizations alike should aim to ensure that they have a breadth of knowledge of how the organization works and this can be achieved at all levels through things like placements, shadowing and appointed cover.
- Organizations should capture knowledge and information in their systems and executives to maintain and develop their knowledge power, should build knowledge in areas that are more difficult to commoditize and capture in technology.
- Executives should look to develop areas of expertise in understanding society and communities; new medias and the art of soundbite communication; how stuff works, especially the new stuff and leveraging variety and diversity.
- Chief Human Resources Officers (CHROs) are key influencers in how power is used in an organization and individuals can build power through their position, expertise and knowledge, but staying relevant is key. Those who have access to power should be treated with the same courtesy as those that hold the power.
- It is the role not the person who is powerful, it is important to understand the sources of power and to have appropriate checks in place.

Career & Breadth

- Like organizations, people need a purpose and a plan on how to achieve it. The plan needs to be flexible enough to take into account the inevitable blows that may knock you off course for a while or reveal another route.
- Executives planning a smart career should strategically combine line and staff role experience, and line is essential to get the top power roles of CEO and chair.
- Executives should develop general management skills and experience to be considered for the C-Suite; they should

also look at which sectors value their areas of knowledge or expertise more highly and try to transition into those sectors.

- Executives aiming for the C-Suite need to reflect on who will be included when they are 'promotion ready' and should try and ensure that they are included in the top succession group.
- Look for a mentor or adviser that can guide you to the next stage of your career and develop peers and friendships in different parts of the organization – these can be important knowledge links.
- Make sure you are always challenged, be curious and push yourself. To stay successful, stay current, ensure that you are progressing and always look for new things.

The CXO Method & Glass Doors

'Preparing for promotion, breaking in and overcoming the untold hidden barriers.'

John Jeffcock

At school, we are taught maths but teachers seldom explain why or how it can be used later in life. If we are lucky, we get involved in team sports but how does this help our personal development? And those that star, unlike me, win awards for coming top of the class or first in the race. Similarly, at business school, you are taught cash flow management as part of the finance modules and Maslow's Hierarchy of Needs in the human resource modules and may even win a prize for doing particularly well. But very few schools teach you what a chief financial officer or a chief human resources officer actually does, yet we are expected to make career choices in our twenties and thirties that have lingering effects on the rest of our lives.

This chapter explains how careers develop and what C-Suite executives actually do and how their functions or departments are changing. Prime Minister Sir Winston Churchill once said, 'Dictators ride to and fro upon tigers from which they dare not dismount. And the tigers are getting hungry.' Department leaders are not riding tigers but they are captains of shrinking departments as the impact of technology sweeps across every business, eating up jobs. So, it is important when we look at C-Suite roles to also look at the changing responsibilities and departments they lead.

THE CXO METHOD – ROLE

First, we must remind ourselves of the Chief Expert Officer (CXO) Method, where the Chief is about leading a team, the X your area of expertise and the O about being a good company officer. Once you understand the elements of the role, it is possible to look at what each element does and there are general similarities that can be drawn across all CXOs, as illustrated below:

- **C – the Chief** – Chiefs tend to spend their time setting and implementing the department or business units change agenda, managing the department and business to ensure optimization. They are a business and change leader, a consultant and key business partner.
- **X – the Expert** – The Expert in the CXO Method tends to spend their time involved in business as usual (BAU) activities, responding to requests and innovating to find faster and better ways of serving the business.
- **O – the Officer** – Officers are more future focused, making connections within and outside the business, looking for opportunities to serve customers better, deliver greater value, working with all stakeholders and aiming to outperform the competition, thereby always striving to enhance the business model.

THE CXO METHOD – CAREERS

In almost every industry, whether you start as an apprentice or a recent graduate, you start by learning your expert skill. Albert Einstein started out as an assistant examiner at the Federal Office for Intellectual Property, Melinda Gates in marketing at Microsoft,

Steve Jobs as a technician at Atari, Christine Lagarde as a trainee lawyer at Baker & McKenzie, Barrack Obama as a financial researcher at Business International Corporation and the list goes on and on. So nearly everyone starts as an executive, learning their first area of expertise 'X'. Entrepreneurs can be an exception to this as many do not complete university, start working for a start-up or start a business immediately after graduating. Jeff Bezos of Amazon, Bill Gates of Microsoft, Larry Page of Google, Elon Musk of Tesla and Mark Zuckerberg of Facebook are all good examples of this.

But for most of us, as we do well and get more senior we start to run a team, we become a manager and then sometimes a director or vice president. Historically, over time the number of people we are responsible for grows until we are running the department or business unit. I say 'historically' as technology is changing this and responsibility is increasingly better measured through other means, such as customers, geography and finance. So, our time shifts from being expertise focused to management and expertise focused, then on to more management focused. So, we become a 'C'.

Moving from an X to a C within the same team, where we were once co-worker and are now manager can be challenging. Our relationships need to change and previous personal relationships need to adjust to take into account our new responsibilities. HR can provide support and a good way to avoid perceived favouritism is to start by conducting a team review or audit. Asking your team about their ambitions and worries, how they think you could help them, what you expect from them and how what they do fits into the bigger picture. This clearly positions you as more senior with the individual and thereby establishes you as the team leader but do make sure you spend equal time with each, as differences could rightly or wrongly be perceived as bias.

As the triangle of people narrows, your view of the organization becomes more panoramic and your influence grows, you can increasingly achieve more and are able to add more value across the organization. This value add can take many forms, from strategic direction to risk mitigation to stakeholder management to market opportunities. Now you have become an 'O' and as you can see in the illustration below, your career goes **X -> C -> O**:

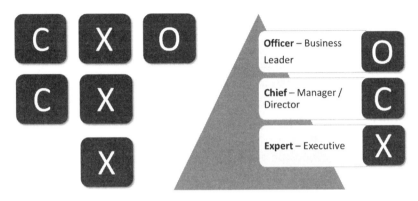

To become an 'O', you need to be involved in the broader business. Do not wait to get involved until you have been promoted as this will leave you with a bigger gap to fill when the time comes. You need to make sure that you are promotion-ready as early as possible and one way of doing this is to show the people who will enable your promotion that you are almost already doing the job. This gives confidence to those in charge, reduces risk and makes the promotion easier for others to understand. For example, committees that pull together different communities within the business can give you useful internal connectivity and influence as well as demonstrating to others your interests and ability to add value in multiple areas. Acting on this connectivity and seeing the opportunity when the time arises is what makes the difference – do not wait to be asked to step forward.

Smart Thinking

During the Covid-19 crisis a father-of-three was stranded at a holiday resort in southern Europe. At the bar one evening, he met a Chinese man and they got talking mainly about being stranded but during the conversation, he discovered that the man had a manufacturing plant in China. The next day, he asked if he made medical equipment and the Chinese man replied by saying only 'protective clothing'. The father-of-three had remembered that he had attended a course ten years before with an American who was now a senior government official in a southern US State. Over the next three months, he sold that state $40 million worth of medical clothing on his mobile phone from a hotel bedroom. You have to see the opportunity, make the connection and trigger the solution.

So, let's apply this example to how we all turn data into action, as illustrated by the model below. In the model, the brain processes the data and turns it into information. This is then analysed and banked as knowledge, the brain connects this knowledge, often when we sleep, with other knowledge and judges its validity and value in the current situation. Then, based on the value and opportunity this knowledge presents, you take action. Sleep is an important part of the connecting process and many people have their best ideas as they are falling asleep or when they wake in the morning. Which is why entrepreneurs, scientists and authors all have a notepad or recorder by their beds.

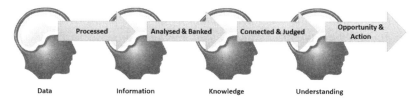

In this example, we jump over the data phase as this had already been given to the entrepreneur by the Chinese man. The entrepreneur then analyses what he has heard and probably visualizes the manufacturing capability in his head. He sleeps on it and makes two connections with already banked knowledge that resides in his memory, one connection from a course he went on years before and one connection with knowledge gained more recently through the media. If he had not already banked this knowledge, he might never have made the connections and would be considerably poorer for it today. The connections are made almost simultaneously, one to the macro environment and need for certain types of medical equipment and another to a person who might have that specific need, who he already knows. He has now made a judgement of a potential need-and-supply opportunity and the action he takes is to verify these. He needs to validate the need with his old American acquaintance and validate the capabilities of his new Chinese acquaintance. Once done and both being positive, he seizes the business opportunity.

What this example illustrates is the need to have different banks of knowledge and what can be missed through siloed or narrow thinking, something we will discuss later in this book. At business schools they sometimes call these banks of unutilized knowledge 'redundant knowledge' and the idea is that you collect these deposits of knowledge over your lifetime, through reading books, conversations, personal interests and other activities, and then at different points in your life and career a connection may suddenly trigger a knowledge bank to open its doors to a new approach or opportunity. The key is to always remain curious like Bill Gates, who reads about 50 books a year,[19] about one a week, which gives him a huge deposit of redundant knowledge that he can access at any point. So, what knowledge banks do C-Suite executives need to be able to access and hold to be successful?

CXO KNOWLEDGE = NOUGHTS & CROSSES

The CXO Method shows as an executive you develop expertise (X), how as a chief (C) you learn how to manage and then how you develop further to become a business leader and good company Officer (O). Let's call the Xs crosses and the Os noughts. One of the differences between different levels of management is knowledge and a British C-Suite knowledge and connections company called Winmark Limited investigated this to quantify

[19] https://www.inc.com/marcel-schwantes/bill-gates-reads-50-books-per-year-but-only-these-6-leadership-books-made-his-list-of-recommendations.html

the knowledge difference. Board members were asked to rank the knowledge expectations across 18 areas for middle managers and then for C-Suite executives. The 18 areas covered include most areas of business activity but there are clearly some areas missing and different organizations and sectors will have different lists. So, the list of 18 is a generic list that should apply to most organizations and is useful to demonstrate differences in roles and expectations. The list includes:

1. Clients & Accounts;
2. Cyber, Risk & Ethics;
3. Digital & Data;
4. Diversity, Inclusion & Culture;
5. Environment, Climate & Society;
6. Finance & Tax;
7. Governance, Structure and Processes;
8. Innovation & Product Development;
9. Legal, Regulations & Compliance;
10. Marketing & Sales;
11. Operations, Processes & Sustainability;
12. People, Talent & Performance;
13. Production & Manufacturing;
14. Stakeholders (including investors);
15. Supply & Procurement;
16. Tech, Architecture & Systems;
17. The Business Model;
18. Vision, Purpose & Values.

The knowledge was measured using a 0 to 100 percentage framework, where 0 means no knowledge at all and 100 means complete knowledge. The results showed that the average knowledge requirements for a middle manager is 62 per cent across the 18 key areas, so more than average, which would have been 50 per cent.

The average knowledge requirements for a C-Suite executive, however, is 73 per cent across all 18 areas. So, for middle managers to successfully enter and operate in the C-Suite, they need to increase their knowledge by 19 per cent across all areas to achieve a higher average score of 12 per cent in each area. Twelve per cent in each area is almost equivalent to a middle manager learning four new areas from scratch so the knowledge gap is material and many would argue that the workload and therefore time commitment are equally increased.

To ensure knowledge diversity within the C-Suite executive team, you would not want this uplift in knowledge to be spread evenly across the C-Suite. This is usually resolved by the functional knowledge of C-Suite leaders, such as the CFO, CLO, CHRO, COO, CIO and CMO. In addition, boards and CEOs when promoting individuals into the C-Suite look to fill the team's knowledge gaps, so it is important you have the right knowledge when the gap arises or you will not be considered.

This knowledge change is best illustrated by the 'Noughts & Crosses' model below, which is based on the Winmark board research. As you will see from the illustration, the crosses start off in the lead but in the end, the noughts have the highest score. So, in C-Suite noughts and crosses, those that back crosses, expertise, start off leading the race but in the end, the noughts, the value creating officer role, is the winning area of importance:

	Executive			Manager			C-Suite	
100			100			100		O
80			80			80	C	X
60			60	C	X	60		
40	X		40		O	40		
20			20			20		
0	C	O	0			0		
	Executive			Manager			C-Suite	

The three big jumps that the above 'Noughts & Crosses' model illustrates is the jump in expertise (E) that a graduate makes when they start their new role and become an executive. Larger organizations tend to have graduate induction programmes, where the graduate spends time with different areas of the business. Once complete, they are allocated to an area partly based on aptitude and their preferences and based on what the organization needs so they actually start being trained a little in O areas but are then often siloed into an X area to deliver.

The next big jump is when someone moves from executive to manager, their chief (C) score makes a big jump and interestingly, their (X) score continues to grow at the same time but not by nearly as much. This tells us that when someone becomes a business area leader, they do not drop their technical background or area of expertise and instead continue to develop their knowledge of it. So, what gives? What they drop is the practice of that functional skill – they become the manager of the activity rather than the doer or deliverer.

In sales, you often hear of the top sales performer campaigning for and then being promoted to the sales manager. This sounds sensible but the negative impact can be material because the roles are fundamentally different. In this example the doer becomes the manager and stops selling, the thing they were best at and probably liked most, and the personal achievement motivator that made them a good sales person does not necessarily make them a good team leader, which is about team, not personal achievement. So, the organization ends up losing the sales revenue the sales person generated and potentially having an egocentric sales manager and subsequent team performance and retention issues. Similarly, not all footballers (X) make good football coaches (C).

Finally, when they move from manager to C-Suite executive, the officer (O) related knowledge makes a significant jump and leads the field, while the C and X still advance by a comparatively small amount. Whether the C or X is higher for middle managers depends on the needs of the business and the preferences of the individual. Some managers need to do the expert work and others just like doing it and find it hard to step away. Even CFOs like diving back into their spreadsheets occasionally, there can be something comforting in them. Only recently, I spoke with a CFO of a trade association, who explained how proud they were of the numbers they had produced.

If you take the same 18 areas of management and look at what are the most important ones for middle management and for C-Suite executives, you come up with different lists. Three of the six remain the same and they are: 1) The Business Model; 2) Vision, Purpose & Values and 3) People, Talent and Performance. Although the knowledge expectation for each of these areas is higher and the order changes, they do still remain in the top six. This means that for an ambitious middle manager, it would make sense to focus most attention on the three that remain rather than the other three. But there are caveats to this: Digital and Cyber are still underrepresented skills at the most senior management levels and therefore if a CEO is looking to fill a knowledge gap, you may have a better chance if you have unique expertise in these areas. Also, clients and accounts are king, because cash is king and customers are where cash comes from, without which you have no business, so representing these key stakeholders and key income streams can also be immensely valuable.

Middle Managers Top Six Knowledge Requirements	C-Suite Executives Top Six Knowledge Requirements
1. Vision, Purpose & Values	1. The Business Model
2. People, Talent & Performance	2. Vision, Purpose & Values
3. The Business Model	3. Stakeholders (including investors)
4. Clients & Accounts	4. People, Talent & Performance
5. Cyber, Risk & Ethics	5. Governance, Structure & Processes
6. Digital & Data	6. Diversity, Inclusion & Culture

The big movers. Stakeholders moves from being the least important, eighteenth, for middle managers to being the third most important area of knowledge for C-Suite executives. Governance also jumps from being the seventeenth most important area of knowledge for middle managers to being the fifth for C-Suite executives. This very clearly shows that getting stakeholder and governance experience early on might be critical to whether you get into the C-Suite or not.

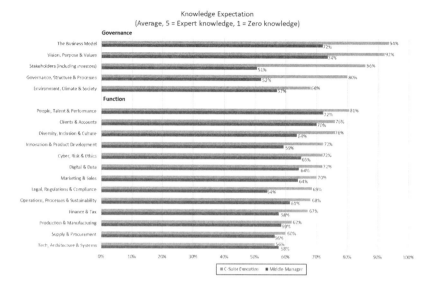

Knowledge Expectation
(Average, 5 = Expert knowledge, 1 = Zero knowledge)

Governance Experience

One of the ways you can gain stakeholder and governance experience is to do external work such as becoming a school governor or a trustee of a charity. You can also attend Annual General Meetings, organize to meet investors, sit on employee committees and attend courses and have relevant mentors. I remember vividly listening to a top executive search consultant talk to a very senior group of chief legal officers. The session was titled 'How can a Chief Legal Officer become a Non-Executive Director?' She started the talk by saying that she had gone through the CVs of every person in the room and how impressed she was by some of them. She then said that she would not consider a single person in the room for a non-executive director role and the mood in the room changed significantly. You could see people thinking, 'How dare she', 'What does she know anyway?' and 'I knew she wouldn't be a good speaker.' She then explained why. She started by saying that they look for a minimum of ten years' board experience; she wanted people who had lived through good and bad times in a boardroom environment and could bring that wisdom and experience to other organizations. She recommended to start getting board roles as early as possible and advised those present to start with not-for-profits and to take up roles like school governor, charity trustee and in local community groups.

But still there is a catch and it is the same for boards as it is for the C-Suite. For a chair and CEO to ensure knowledge diversity within the Board and C-Suite Executive teams respectively, they would not want this uplift in knowledge to be spread evenly across the Board or C-Suite. You need diversity in many areas including knowledge or you will always get the same answers. Morgan Stanley is reputed to have said, 'If you have two people on a board that always agree, you have one too many.' As mentioned, this knowledge diversity is usually resolved by the functional or business unit knowledge of C-Suite leaders. When promoting individuals into the C-Suite, CEOs look to improve decision making through filling knowledge gaps and skills in their teams so you may have spent considerable time building knowledge in a certain area already present in the C-Suite executive team and if you don't have the knowledge that is needed, you will not be considered.

Knowledge alone will not get you into the C-Suite, things like leadership style, personal attributes and internal connectivity would also be very important and are covered later in this book. Attributes you should start thinking about and developing now are:

- **Great Judgement, Integrity & Self Belief**: Includes asking the right questions and being trusted with information;
- **Strong Interpersonal & Conflict Management Skills**: Includes being a senior corporate negotiator;
- **Great Antennae**: To know where to look and to identify risks before they become issues and opportunities to exploit.

This list of three attributes were first told to me by Patrick Dunne, author of the 2019 book, *Boards: A Practical Perspective*.[20] Patrick

---

[20] https://www.governance.co.uk/product/boards/?preview=true&v=79cba1185463

has trained and placed hundreds of board directors into private equity backed businesses and is someone I have always admired as he teaches conflict management to the boards of some of the largest organizations in the world and also goes into prisons and teaches prisoners how to manage conflict.

A C-Suite Case Study: Chief Legal Officer

Before going on to look at the shape of C-Suite roles and their departments, it is useful to review an illustrative case study. For this example, we have taken the legal department and the role of chief legal officer. This example is important as it brings into the CXO Method the issue of organization maturity. Over time, businesses and departments become more mature as processes, behaviours and ways of working develop and embed themselves. In 2015, I remember being in a CEO meeting with General Electric (GE) and eight other CEOs. GE were sharing their experiences of lean and agile working practices. One of the CEOs in the room asked a question about an issue he was having in embedding the process. GE's response was we dealt with that in 1980 and then explained what they had done, so in this example, GE were managerially 35 years ahead of the other company.

The chart below illustrates how a legal department can evolve in terms of maturity and when taking up a new role, it is always important to understand how mature the organization and your area of the business is as it will have a significant impact on what you do during your first 100 days.

Commercial Counsel (CC) (X) →	General Counsel (GC) (C) →	Chief Legal Officer (CLO) (O)
The reactive old world 'no' department	The proactive current status quo for the majority of departments	A world-class department

Using the above coding CC for Commercial Counsel, GC for General Counsel and CLO for Chief Legal Officer, we look at five key areas of business activity and how they might differ at different levels of maturity.

Strategic Direction & Operating Model

- **CC (X)**: No clear vision of the future or operating model and very limited proactive intervention;
- **GC (C)**: Established purpose but not yet clarity around a three-year vision and model. Immediate priorities being addressed but these do not sit in a broader strategic framework. Risks and mitigation actions identified and being worked through;
- **CLO (O)**: Established purpose, clear three-year plan and supporting operating model. A plan of how to achieve the three-year vision being implemented with clear roles and responsibilities. Business as usual risks addressed and systematic reviews of 'black swan' risks also taking place.

Reporting, Stakeholders & Customers

- **CC (X)**: Metrics are limited to external spend and comparative costs. A reactive function to Stakeholders & Customers with potential spots of high-risk exposure. Limited influence at board level and seen as a cost base.
- **GC (C)**: Metrics are limited to inward-looking function metrics, such as hours spent on different tasks, and they have difficulties justifying value. The GC does trigger inventions and is respected by the business and key stakeholders and customers. Good business account management and partnering is in place.

- **CLO (O)**: Full metrics are in place that add value to other functions – for example, sales contract turnaround times. A business enabler function that is held up as a good internal benchmark. Stakeholder management and business engagement plans are all in place and experienced business partners understand and add material value to the business units they are serving.

Business Processes & Technology
- **CC (X)**: Very limited, as everything is bespoke, but sum Microsoft Excel reporting sheets;
- **GC (C)**: Core processes understood and mapped. Processes unbundled and a uniform set of flowcharts and templates exist. Demand understood supported through a work triage approach. Limited improvements made to date due to constraints;
- **CLO (O)**: Core processes evolved based on three-year operating model and fully embedded in working practices. High-value and irregular work triaged and predicted based on company and market knowledge. Automated self-service for volume/routine work with inbuilt reporting.

Partnerships & Strategic Procurement
- **CC (X)**: Limited central control, a high level of hidden costs, with business units buying direct without consultation utilizing their own local budgets.
- **GC (C)**: Strategy and framework in place and being rolled out across the entire business. Conscious of business spend but still have limited influence over it. The GC is the legal lead for alliances, partnerships and mergers and acquisitions (M&A).
- **CLO (O)**: Identifies, supports and leads on major deals, ranging from M&A to product alliances to sales

distribution. Business is adherent to a clear strategic procurement framework that includes diversity, the environment and the organization's values and standards. The framework also caters for and exploits alternative providers and new technologies.

PEOPLE & CHANGE

- **CC (X)**: Poor retention or left with the 'b' team;
- **GC (C)**: Team in transformation in terms of skills and commerciality. Competency framework partially built and skeleton transition plan in place;
- **CLO (O)**: Best team in place and performing well. Clear roles, responsibilities, recognition, careers and staff feeling challenged and in control. Alumni go on to be GCs in other great organizations.

Most leaders of in-house legal departments will strive to run world-class legal departments as a chief legal officer. However, the majority are in reality still at general counsel level and on the journey to world class. The issue is often what you inherited from your predecessor; when you move into the leadership role you could inherent a department anywhere on the maturity curve and the more immature the department, the greater the transformation needed. When the new chief legal officer joined Fujitsu Europe, he did not wait to be told by his fellow business leaders what they thought should be done, instead he went direct to his internal clients, gained feedback, produced a new model for the department and told the C-Suite what he would be doing and the benefits of it. He drove through a substantial change programme and was immediately perceived by the leadership as an 'O' and sits in the C-Suite executive team. So, what does the Chief Legal Officer of Fujitsu and a twenty-first century chief legal officer look like in terms of competencies? The competency table below is aligned to the above department table and summarizes some of the key competencies:

Positioning	Role Positioning	Core Skills/Competencies	Core Tasks
Corporate Leadership	Business leader & legal counsel (thinks like a CEO)	Diversity of thinking (in boardroom) and constructive challenge. Networking with directors (across global footprint). Good legal advice and judgement. Influencing skills.	Independent thought. Company director & secretariat (own country and International subsidiary boards). Staying on top of key legal knowledge at corporate, sector, product (innovation & liability) and supply chain levels.
Strategic Direction & Operating Model	Strategy consultant	Business design and modelling. Legal strategy. Financial analysis. Commercial acumen.	Environmental/horizon scanning. Legal compliance (international). Corporate alignment. Find and deliver optimal economic model. Optimize linkages with procurement, IP, HR, Finance, etc.
Reporting, Stakeholders & Customers	Trusted business advisor and partner	Business outcome focused. Governance authority. Managing conflict expert. Data analytics, privacy and security. Filtering, identifying and communicating salient issues.	Governance review. Policy creation and execution. Budget and financial management. Legal head in times of crisis. Educating the business.

Positioning	Role Positioning	Core Skills/Competencies	Core Tasks
Business Processes & Technology	Chief operating officer (legal function)	Understand and comfortable with agreed risks. Process mapping and design thinking. Contracts management. Agile project leadership.	Monitoring and enforcing contracts. Unbundling and building new and better processes. Fastest way to lose credibility is to not know or understand the numbers. Optimal resource utilization, including outside the function (i.e. tech within procurement).
Partnerships & Strategic Procurement	Chief partnerships & procurement officer	Leading on key negotiations. Business representation. Project director.	Lead negotiator on M&A, key distribution agreements, product and service alliances, supply chain, etc. Managing increasing contract aggression.
People & Change	Inspiring active leader	Capability framework and development plans. Social skill (resulting from Emotional Quotient).	Educating team in how the business makes money, creates value and competes within the sector dynamics.

T-Shaped Managers

Some people reading this may translate the C and X into the vertical element of the T-Shaped Manager and the 'O' into the horizontal top of the T. The T-Shaped Manager is quoted often by business leaders and in business books and one might argue that it is a widely accepted management concept but that does not make it entirely correct. In the 1980s, the term 'T-shaped man' was used internally by McKinsey & Company for the recruitment and development of men and women but the most popular reference is David Guest from 1991. The metaphor then gained real popularity after the CEO of IDEO Design Consultancy endorsed the approach for recruitment.[21]

In March 2001 issue of the *Harvard Business Review* (*HBR*), Morten T. Hansen and Bolko von Oetinger wrote an article titled 'T-Shaped Managers: Knowledge Management's Next Generation' and they defined the T-shaped Manager as follows: 'We call the approach T-shaped management. It relies on a new kind of executive, one who breaks out of the traditional corporate hierarchy to share knowledge freely across the organization (the horizontal part of the 'T') while remaining fiercely committed to individual business unit performance (the vertical part).' And Wikipedia defines T-shaped skills as: 'The vertical bar on the letter T represents the depth of related skills and expertise in a single field, whereas the horizontal bar is the ability to collaborate across disciplines with experts in other areas and to apply knowledge in areas of expertise other than one's own.'

In the *HBR* article, BP (British Petroleum) are given as a case study and they explain how business unit managers are judged on their ability to meet targets and also rewarded and promoted on how effectively they share knowledge with others outside their units. They explain how lone stars can remain and perform at BP but are not promoted.

Business schools and books also talk about X- and I-shaped people. X-shaped people are good at working in multiple areas,

[21] https://corporatefinanceinstitute.com/resources/careers/soft-skills/t-shaped-skills/

typically have good interpersonal skills and are good at convening groups. The many arms of the X illustrate their connectivity. I-shaped people, however, can fit in the T-shaped people, in that they represent the vertical bar of the T. The I-shaped person is an expert in one given area and not connected outside their area of business. So, could you translate I, T and X to the C X O approach as the chart below suggests?

I an expert with limited connectivity -> **X** – the Expert

T-shaped manager   -> **C** – the Chief

X multi worker and communicator   -> **O** – the Officer

Sadly, reality is as ever slightly more complicated and as Albert Einstein said, 'Everything should be made as simple as possible but not simpler.' I fear the T-shaped Manager is easy to explain but is an oversimplification of reality. It implies that cross organization and internal communication is the domain of senior management, which obviously should not be the case.

THE TIARA-SHAPED C-SUITE

Modern knowledge and communication systems such as Microsoft Teams for organizations with different teams, Slack for a chat-powered workplace, Google Chat for G-Suite users and Yammer for enterprise social networking all allow communication across the organization at all levels. So, the communication element of the T, the horizontal bar, should in today's world be at the bottom, not the top. Students at business school and executives in large organizations are all encouraged and given facilities to network and connect much earlier. In fact, as soon as they join, it is probably one of the first things they are taught how to use in their organization. Those who do not make these connections are considered not to be team players and their careers can be very quickly stifled. The T-shaped manager was created in the 1980s at a time of siloed functions and more formal working relationships and no longer reflects a reality people want or have. It is time to flip the 'T' into an upside-down 'L'.

We also know from earlier knowledge research that a single area of knowledge, the vertical bar, is not sufficient or even close to sufficient in nearly all roles. It is not a true reflection of most people's reality at work. The reality is you need lots of vertical bars that represent different knowledge banks or areas to different depths. We also know that as you move from an executive to a middle manager and a middle manager to a C-Suite executive those areas of knowledge get deeper or now, as we have flipped the 'T', we should say higher. It is interesting that in academia we talk about higher education and yet at work we talk about someone's depth of knowledge. We talk about people being at the top of their game or representing the height of professionalism. Is it 'down to you' or 'up to you', does one imply blame for failure and the other fame in success?

As this book is all about helping people become more successful, let us stay on the positive side and push knowledge up, not down. With this in mind, if you combine the upside-down 'T', the 'L', with the expected 18 areas of researched knowledge covered earlier, you can see that your T-shaped executive turns into a brilliant Tiara, as illustrated below.

There is a striking difference between the executive role and the middle manager role in terms of height and breadth of knowledge. For some middle managers this may come as a relief as it is not unusual for an executive to assume and say that they could do everything their manager can do. If you are still using the T-shaped model, this view could be justified but in the Tiara-shaped approach, the difference cannot be ignored. The T-shaped executive has only one vertical line of knowledge whereas the middle manager has 18. The jump from executive to middle management does not happen overnight, you cannot go from having one area of knowledge to 18 and people who are promoted before that time will suffer from only having a fraction of the knowledge areas in place. Similarly, executives who have developed knowledge across the 18 areas will be much easier to promote and the risk of their promotion is much mitigated.

The lines in the Tiara illustrations are representative and for illustration purposes and do not represent the exact height of each area of knowledge. A precise image of the C-Suite knowledge heights can be found below:

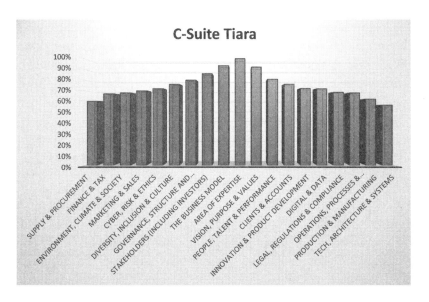

Chief HR officers talk about competency frameworks and develop their staff in line with these frameworks, which detail the knowledge, skills and experience that individuals need to have to do certain roles. Typically, each competency area has multiple competencies that form them and HR plots different competency requirements for different roles. The competency levels build up and are often ranked to dictate the performance and seniority of the individual being assessed. If you plotted these competences and the different levels in an infographic similar to the one above, you would get a very similar-looking image. As an individual becomes more senior, the competency levels continue to rise in a similar pattern to the C-Suite executive role.

The C-Suite executive role resembles more closely the middle manager role than the executive role and both have Tiara-looking roles, with the C-Suite executive role being taller. The above illustration does not show you which each individual line represents so you cannot see the movement of importance, but you can clearly see that the level of knowledge increases significantly. Again, middle managers may assume that they know everything that a C-Suite executive does and like the executive in the above example, they would be suffering from unconscious incompetence. What is noticeable about the C-Suite Tiara is that the gap between that principal area of competence or knowledge, for example marketing, and the next area is considerably smaller than the gap for middle managers. This further illustrates that C-Suite executives are by nature generalists and far more generalist than middle managers. This need for generalists is a good argument for job rotations, internal secondments and business school programmes.

CONSCIOUSNESS, COMPETENCE & GENDER

As touched on earlier, the height and number of the vertical knowledge lines are witnessed by more junior colleagues but they are not conscious of the height and breadth of the knowledge required. In psychology, they talk about the four stages of competence or the conscious competence learning model. For example, when a baby is born, it does not know it cannot walk, so it is unconsciously incompetent. Then the baby realizes that it cannot walk, so it becomes consciously incompetent and then as it starts to learn to walk, it becomes consciously competent. Finally, as the walking becomes natural, the baby becomes unconsciously competent. Similarly, in careers when people apply or start new roles, they may be unconsciously or consciously incompetent and then after they have gained enough experience, they become unconsciously or consciously competent. The interesting question is, at what point should you apply for the new role or promote the individual?

A Hewlett Packard internal report found that men apply for a job or promotion when they meet only 60 per cent of the qualifications, but women apply only if they meet 100 per cent of them.[22] This is important because if we assume that both sexes learn at the same speed then a man is often applying for the next role 40 per cent earlier than the woman. Multiply this across the span of someone's career and the difference could be exponential but this is not the case because if the man is successful once they are in the role, they need to become consciously competent before they can apply for the next role. A woman once explained to me that the difference between being a man and a woman in a corporate is that the man is standing on the career escalator and the woman's escalator is not working so they have to walk upstairs.

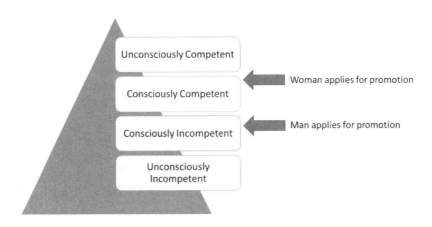

---

[22] https://hbr.org/2014/08/why-women-dont-apply-for-jobs-unless-theyre-100-qualified

Is this because men are more confident than women, less intelligent or just greater risk takers or some combination of other factors that are not quite clear? Males being greater risk takers is potentially a factor and this starts from a very young age. There was an interesting series of experiments trying to establish whether the gender difference was based on nature or nurture. One experiment involved mothers lifting one end of a plank covered in carpet to a height they were comfortable with for their one-year-old baby to crawl down. The mothers were asked to adjust the height of one end of the plank to the maximum height they were comfortable with for their child to crawl down from. What was fascinating was that the mothers lifted the plank substantially higher for male babies than female babies so nature certainly plays a role and upbringing and society may offer males more opportunities to take risk.

The scientific research on gender and risk is mainly based on the Domain-Specific Risk-Taking (DOSPERT) Scale, which measures five content domains: financial decisions, health and safety, recreational, ethical and social decisions. There are plenty of research articles that have been published highlighting the difference between male and female risk taking and some go as far as to say that in times of stress, male risk taking increases and female risk taking decreases. Both in the UK and US, the ratio of male to female prisoners is around 18 to 1[23]: does this demonstrate this or that women are better at not being caught? In the US, there is a clear difference between early male and female death rates, as illustrated in the table below, but recent research by Dr Thekla Morgenroth and Professor Michelle Ryan from the University of Exeter and Professor Cordelia Fine and Anna Genat from the University of Melbourne has shown that the DOSPERT Scale may measure male risk types and that females take risks in other ways. Either way, there is clearly a gender difference and therefore the need to have a more gender

[23] UK https://www.gov.uk/government/statistics/women-and-the-criminal-justice-system-2019/women-and-the-criminal-justice-system-2019; USA https://www.bop.gov/about/statistics/statistics_inmate_gender.jsp

balanced C-Suite becomes imperative to ensure a more balanced risk profile:

Death Rates US[24]	Female	Male	Difference
Suicide	1,225	5,027	310%
Road Traffic Accidents	1,972	4,817	144%
Homicide	671	4,233	531%
Poisonings	1,438	3,592	150%
Other Injuries	194	748	286%
Drowning	67	402	500%
Falls	27	185	585%
Drug Use	65	84	29%
	5,659	19,088	237%

In 2003, psychologists David Dunning of Cornell University and Joyce Ehrlinger of Washington State University conducted an experiment to look at confidence and more specifically, the difference between men and women.[25] The study used a science test and asked the candidates first how good they thought they were (Am I good at science?) and then after the test asked them how well they thought they had performed (Did I get this question right?). As the table below illustrates, it was found that women underestimate their abilities and performance and the reality of the performance in this experiment is close.

	Am I good at science?	Did I get this question right?	Actual score
Women	6.5	5.8	7.5
Men	7.6	7.1	7.9

Afterwards, having no knowledge of how they performed, men and women were asked if they wanted to take part in a science

[24] US Death Rates as reported in 2018 by https://www.worldlifeexpectancy.com/usa-cause-of-death-by-age-and-gender
[25] https://www.theatlantic.com/magazine/archive/2014/05/the-confidence-gap/359815/

competition that had prizes. Seventy-one per cent of men applied and only 49 per cent of women; proportionally, this is similar to the HP job application statistics. Is this a confidence issue when applying for a role and can it be translated into the 'imposter syndrome'? In 1978, Dr Pauline R. Clance and Dr Suzanne A. Imes published 'The Impostor Phenomenon in High Achieving Women: Dynamics and Therapeutic Intervention Syndrome'.[26] And so the imposter syndrome was born and research showed how professional women, despite external evidence to the contrary, can doubt their accomplishments, believe that they do not deserve their position and have a persistent internalized fear of being exposed as a 'fraud'. Subsequent research says that men and women equally suffer from the 'imposter syndrome' but the depth and knowledge of the syndrome for men is less researched.

A good friend of mine who worked for a top institute had always thought that he was too nice to get into the C-Suite and he never even considered a CEO role. But he was good at what he did, hired a coach to personally help him and was soon promoted into the C-Suite. When the CEO role came up, he bravely stepped forward again. He understood all the challenges well, knew the lay of the land, now wanted the job and knew what he would do in the first 100 days. He got the top job, he felt, because he was authentic with himself, was focused on value-based decision making, had a vision of the future and wanted the organization to be successful. He may have looked steely on the outside but for the first three years on the inside he felt like a hunchback, beaten and tired. At around the three-year point as CEO, he started to enjoy the role, the success of the institute and the increased profitability gave him inner confidence. He looked back on what he and others before him had done and realized that he had been comparatively successful.

In Chapter 4, we look at the CEO Life Cycle and it is not surprising that this inner confidence comes at the three-year point, known as the Recovery Phase in the CEO Life Cycle. On reflection, he thought he may in the past have been too subservient and advised me to know where my energy comes from: 'You must

---

[26] https://en.wikipedia.org/wiki/Impostor_syndrome

know where energy comes from, energy has a big impact on you and people working with you.' He explained how you can source energy from physical, emotional, spiritual and mental sources so energy can come from enjoying the company of friends to staying fit to going to church, and the majority of CEOs I know have had some form of physical regime. Whatever the combination of factors that drives this difference of when men and women apply for roles, it means that women are more likely than men to have a full Tiara of knowledge and are therefore almost certainly better decision makers as they make decisions from a more informed position. So, if you have a man and woman applying for the same role, all other factors being equal, logic would suggest you should always employ the woman as she is more likely to be competent even if she does not know it or thinks she is. If we expand this further into all forms of diversity, you might argue that a diverse candidate in a selection process is likely to be more competent than a less diverse candidate. The case put forward for diversity is often centred around different thinking approaches due to cultural background, social differences and lived experience, but this research shows another reason – more diverse candidates may be more competent or have a fuller Tiara. Great organizations who want to stay successful need to actively encourage women and people from more diverse backgrounds to apply for more roles.

A modern example of this was at an Artificial Intelligence (AI) consultancy called Satalia. CEO Daniel Hulme explains that they have an internal voting system of how much each person should be paid in the organization. The individual puts forward a number and it is voted on by everyone. A competent woman in the organization put forward her number and the votes from her peers rejected it, saying she should be asking for more. She increased the number and again her peers rejected it, once again saying it should be more. After two rounds, she came to a significantly higher number that they agreed on.

This gender difference and glass ceilings are explored more later in this chapter but first, it is important to share a case study of what can go wrong if those in charge are not competent.

The Co-operative: A Case Study

The Co-operative's birth can be traced to 1844, when the 28 'Rochdale Pioneers' set up the Rochdale Society of Equitable Pioneers. The 'pioneers' were artisans, many of them weavers. Having endured workplace abuse and seen their earnings halve within ten years, they formed their 'Society' as a self-help organization.

A Failure of Governance

In 2013, the Co-operative had 8 million individual members and was linked to 170 affiliated groups. The members elected (through a one-member, one-vote system) a pyramid of ever more powerful committees. The pinnacle of this structure was a 20-strong board elected by 600 people. The Co-operative's governance system, as explained below, was the root cause of the troubles it faced.

- **An unmanageable board led by a bully.** The Board was too big; it was populated by tradesmen rather than professional business people (moreover, 5 of its 15 lay members were also members of the National Executive of the Labour Party); it had poor selection processes; many members had no banking experience and a lack of transparency meant that it was not possible to hold board members to account. The chairman was revealed to be a bully, who had intimidated other board members, ensuring their contribution to discussions and decisions was limited.

- **An over-promoted executive.** A tradition of internal promotions meant that the executive was insular and homogeneous. Its members typically had 'territory agendas'; many had their own pet projects and a significant proportion were promoted beyond their competencies. Those who led the Co-operative Bank would never have been employed at a comparable level outside the organization. Even though salary levels were average by industry standards, their limited Tiaras of knowledge meant that their remuneration was excessive.

- **A disparate structure.** The Co-operative had evolved into an incoherent collection of businesses. Its grocery chain and farm businesses were not supporting one another (unlike rival Morrisons, which used its agribusiness to supply its shops). Only 5 per cent of the Co-operative's farming production ended up in Co-op groceries. The Co-operative also had a funeral business, a pharmacy chain, the Co-operative Bank, a travel agency, an electrical business, motor dealers and an insurance arm. These activities have now been rationalized, with some sold – for example, the pharmacy business was sold in July 2014[27] for £620 million to meet the collapsed bank's capital needs.

- **A lack of financial transparency.** In early 2013, the Board learnt that there was a £300 million hole in the bank's balance sheet. By March, this had grown to £600 million and by June, the deficit had reached £1.5 billion; subsequently, an additional £400 million was required. Although economists would have decided not to save the bank, the Board decided to fill the hole in its finances, owing to the Co-operative's altruistic principles. It was felt that as the bank had failed on the Board's watch, the Board was morally bound to resolve the issue.

- **Irresponsible mergers & acquisitions.** The Board showed exceptionally limited directorial skills, especially in the area of M&A. In 2013/14, Sir Christopher Kelly reported that the 2009 acquisition of the Britannia Building Society, which had been intended to upscale the Co-operative Bank's business, had been a mistake. The bank inherited the Britannia's corporate loan book, of which £802 million in loans (mostly, commercial real estate) had to be written off. In Sir Christopher's opinion, 'due diligence' by the bank's Board had been 'cursory' and its assessment of potential losses 'woefully inadequate'. He concluded the Board paid

[27] https://www.bbc.co.uk/news/business-28361977

little attention to a series of warnings 'clearly and consistently identified by the regulator over a long period of time'.

- **Damaging processes.** The apparatus for collecting and distributing profit to 'good causes' – to take just one example – was so complex and ill-managed that the cost of the administration process exceeded the sum distributed. This wasteful process led to destructive internal faction-fighting between the groups that were earning the money and the groups that spent it.

How did the Reform Team Fix the Problem?

The key to the change was to get the governance structure right. Barriers to achieving governance reform were twofold.

- **Denial.** The 20 board members and the 600 electors behind them denied that there was any problem and resisted the reform and their own displacement.
- **Leaks.** When attempts were made to sell off parts of the Co-operative to meet its debts, members of the Board began leaking information. Private investigators halted the leaks through an investigation that led to the removal of two board members and the issuing of warnings to two others.

Because of the bank scandal, the Co-operative's membership had fallen to 5 million by mid-2014. The reform team appealed to ordinary members to endorse their proposed reforms over the heads of the old guard. They did so by insisting that their programme would deliver on the Co-operative's founding goals in the following three ways:

- Articulating the purpose of the Co-operative (an objective that had been lost).
- Identifying what was in the interests of the Co-operative's individual members and business sectors.
- Pursuing those interests by recycling the Co-operative's profits to its members and businesses, rather than to third parties.

At the May 2014 AGM (which was open to the public), a majority voted to change the Co-operative's rules and structures so that the existing Board, the incompetent homogenous group, could be removed and the new governance structure put in place. By September 2014, two-thirds of the Co-operative had endorsed the proposed reforms, enabling it to move from a £2.5 billion loss in 2013 to a £216 million profit in 2015.

The above case study illustrates the need to have at least consciously competent people in the C-Suite. The alternative being a recipe for disaster. Now we must look at the shape of the departments the C-Suite oversees.

DIAMOND DEPARTMENTS

The impact of technology is sweeping across every part of every business and in most organizations those that have ignored this change have or will soon be quickly moved on. There are different levels of technology intervention from automating a process to the proactive use of knowledge and we will look at this later in this book. For now, we will look at how it is transforming the shape of departments and this time we will use the finance department as an example.

I remember being at a CFO dinner which we organized. There were around 14 CFOs in the room and they all came from well-known real estate companies. We had a broad discussion that went from the increasing flexibility of leases to the digitalization of their departments. Towards the end of the dinner, a CFO asked the group by what percentage do you think finance functions will be able to reduce their costs through technology? The group agreed that it would be around 5 to 10 per cent but when I left the room, a CFO whispered in my ear, 'It is going to be more like 20 per cent.' This caught my interest and the following day, I met another real estate CFO and asked the same question. He was merging two finance functions and expected to reduce the total cost of the combined function by 40 per cent. Then within the month, I met a FTSE 100 CFO, who had a five-year plan in place to reduce his department from over 1,000 people to just over 100.

The digitalization of a department can take several years and the CXO leader needs to first understand what (s)he wants the department to look like in five years' time. Once this is done, the current business-as-usual model needs to be reviewed and current processes mapped and improved, where appropriate. It is only at this point that the CXO lead can start engaging with internal and external technology solutions as it is essential they know what they are automating. 'Automation applied to an inefficient operation will magnify the inefficiency,' according to Microsoft co-founder Bill Gates, probably the most famous entrepreneur of the microcomputer revolution.

One obvious impact of automation is the reallocation, reskilling or loss of people and this tends to happen to the more junior people who are involved in more monotonous type work, which is by its very nature more easy to automate:

> Growing automation adoption adds to the challenges that women face in the workplace. MGI research found that the share of women whose jobs are replaced by machines and will likely need to make job transitions due to automation is roughly the same as for men: up to one in four over the next decade may have to shift to a different occupation. Between 40 million and 160 million women globally may need to transition between occupations by 2030, often into higher-skill roles.[28]

The higher the work complexity or knowledge required, the more expensive it is to automate in terms of both time and money. Although it should be said at this point that Artificial Intelligence is catching up fast. Automation has many benefits around risk and speed that I will not go into now but it also has two lesser-known impacts. It shines the light of transparency on what work is being done and not everyone is always happy with that. Those

[28] https://www.mckinsey.com/featured-insights/diversity-and-inclusion/ten-things-to-know-about-gender-equality

who have enjoyed a certain level of work–life balance may find their lives rudely interrupted by automation and as a result, may be inclined to slow its implementation path. That same light of transparency when applied across the organization often finds pockets of previously unknown and off-policy work and as a result can actually increase workload before decreasing it. It can therefore be advisable not to overstate the financial benefits of the new technology implementation in its business case. The return on investment does not start when the new technology is turned on, it starts when the behaviours of those around it change.

Like the T-shaped model, we need to look at the shape of departments in more detail. Departments move from being triangular-shaped to more diamond shapes as the more repetitive tasks and roles are automated.

Yesterday's Function Tomorrow's Function

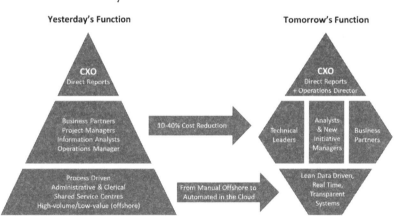

Source: John Jeffcock, 2020

So, we move from T-shaped executives running triangular-shaped departments and business units to Tiara-shaped executives running diamond-shaped departments and business units. The bottom of the triangle high-volume and process-driven work had already been outsourced or offshored by some organizations. However, as the above diagram illustrates, the bottom of the diamond is not being offshored any more but rather being onshored digitally and automated into the cloud. This change is starting to have a devastating impact on the outsourcing industries and the countries where outsourcing is an important economic sector. As part of the transition many roles need to change so restructures are inevitable in the majority of cases. The good news is that the new roles will be more interesting, more value adding and as a result, more personally fulfilling. The bad news is very bad indeed as the roles going are skilful ones and their loss has been referred to by *The Financial Times* as the hollowing out of the middle class. Therefore, the systematic digitalization of the workplace, although essential to remain competitive, is a major catalyst in the widening wealth gap in many Western economies and the inevitable repercussions of which may haunt our children for many decades.

Department Types & Maturity

Whether you are looking to join the C-Suite executive or are already part of it, it is essential to understand how the organization and the different departments and business units are structured. Many factors impact the structure of an organization, ranging from how it grew to the sector norms in which it operates. As part of the role of the leadership team is to ensure that the organization is run as efficiently as possible, it will be important to ensure that the supporting structures are aligned to the purpose and strategy of the organization. Structure is important and is one of the key elements of McKinsey's famous 7S Framework.[29] Developed by Robert H. Waterman, Jr and Tom Peters, the 7S Framework looked at seven elements of an organization that need to be aligned to ensure it is successful. In the centre you have the shared goals and values, surrounded by hard and soft elements. The hard elements include Strategy, Structure and Systems and the Soft Elements include Skills, Staff and Style – style is really Culture. These elements are briefly described below and the idea of the business model is that they all connect with each other. The hard variable of Structure, for example, has an impact on strategy, processes, culture, etc.

[29] https://en.wikipedia.org/wiki/McKinsey_7S_Framework

Hard Elements
- Strategy – Purpose of the business and the way the organization seeks to enhance its competitive advantage;
- Structure – Division of activities; integration and co-ordination mechanisms;
- Systems – Formal procedures for measurement, reward and resource allocation.

Soft Elements
- Skills – The organization's core competencies and distinctive capabilities;
- Staff – The organization's human resources, demographic, educational and attitudinal characteristics;
- Style – Typical behaviour patterns of key groups, such as managers and other professionals.

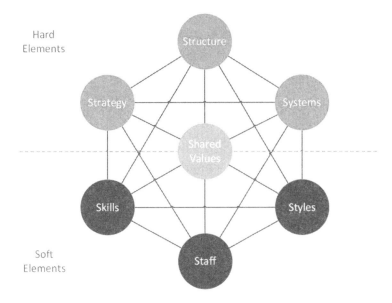

Whether you are reading this book on the New York City Subway, Shanghai Metro or London Underground, you can probably quickly see the links and apply it to your own organization. Often when taught in businesses, employees will say things like 'They say we should be more tech and modern (Strategy) but my PC takes 20 minutes to turn on in the morning (Systems)' or 'We are told we should have a collegiate culture (Style) but we have an "eat what you kill" commission structure (Systems).' It can be useful to run a team exercise with a view to identifying the top three areas of 'rub' or friction. From a management perspective it is the areas of 'rub' that walk through the door and complain at you. Rub are the areas of non-alignment and can become areas of disenfranchisement as they may appear hypocritical to an employee. Generally speaking, it is easier to see, measure and manage the hard variables than the soft variables and if that is the case maybe the labelling is the wrong way round.

Let's now look at the different structures a department may have and why the maturity of that part of the business is important. To jump into practice rather than theory, let's use the HR department this time as the example. There are different types of HR departments and different types of HR directors or people who can be naturally more suited to certain types – some chief HR officers, for example, may be more practiced in certain approaches and as a result may only apply for roles where their preferred structure is in place. This can be a sensible specialist approach but as illustrated in other sections of this book, its narrowness may also be career limiting and suggest a lack of flexibility.

There are two main functional approaches, the larger, centralized approach and the smaller, decentralized approach, and the impact these can have on the CHRO role is described below:

- **Large, Centralized** – You can have large, centralized functions similar to what the big oil companies, like Shell, BP, Sinopec, Chevron and Total have. HR directors in this environment would spend a lot of time in meetings, would be politically very savvy and spend considerable time running the function.
- **Small, Decentralized** – You have decentralized small head office functions with dotted lines across the business units and often across the world – like Bunzl plc, a British distribution and outsourcing company. CHROs in this environment are much more hands-on, have deeper

involvement with the business and need to be exceptional at influencing business leaders and prioritizing workstreams.

Once you have assessed whether it is the right sort of structure for you, you need to look at your sector, environmental and maturity fit. It is also important to consider your sector fit – for example, you may enjoy working for a high-knowledge company like a law firm, with creative personalities in a media organization or blue-collar workers in an Amazon warehouse. You may also be moving into a company operating in a tough external environment, like during the Covid-19 outbreak, or a sector in general decline, such as the high street retail was in 2020.

When people talk about 'Function Maturity', they are really referring to the systems, culture (Style) and skills elements of McKinsey 7Ss. It is important to understand through an interview process, whether externally coming in or internally taking responsibility for part of the business, how mature the business unit or department you are managing will be. Some CHROs, for example, like to set up HR functions and all the respective processes, whereas others prefer to run already existing well-established departments. The matrix below compares department structure type against department maturity and provides brief descriptions about how each option would impact the role of the CHRO:

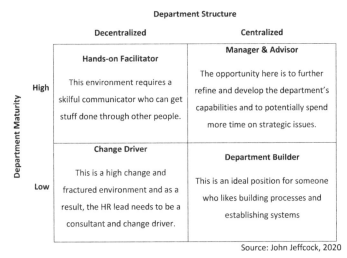

Source: John Jeffcock, 2020

Corporate structures can be difficult to change and may be changed for reasons that are not at first obvious. I remember counselling an Oil & Gas chief legal officer who was coming to the end of a global restructure of his legal department. The operating businesses were all organized by business process and his function had historically been organized by geography. He was realigning his department to reflect the business processes rather than geography and at the same time he wanted equivalent job titles across the global department. The biggest barrier to this change was asking his US reports to follow the same job title system as their European counterparts. After much persuasion and many heated discussions, he eventually gave up and kept the US job titles the same, saying it was not worth the fight.

Similarly, I remember once talking to a senior executive of HP (Hewlett Packard) about the 2002 acquisition of Compaq. HP at the time was run by Carly Fiorina, the first woman to lead a Top-20 company as ranked by *Fortune* magazine. Carly was keen to shift HP from being a product-focused organization to being a more customer- and sector-focused organization but after a couple of years in the role not much had happened and then she bought the personal computer manufacturer, Compaq. Why? It seemed to disagree with her publicly shared strategy and she was widely criticized in the media for her actions. So, I asked my HP friend, why did she do it? He said, 'Take a look at the Board,' and I said, 'What do you mean?' HP had for many years been organized into four product areas, known internally as the four Roman columns, and these product areas were huge – some at the time were bigger than other Fortune 100 companies. This meant that the CEOs of these columns ran big businesses and were powerful people. They were not going to give up their seats of power to support Carly's customer- and sector-focused strategy without a fight. So, what does she do? She smashes another big company into HP – that was Compaq – that enables her to restructure and most importantly, change the leadership team.

Compaq CEO Michael Capellas became the HP President and the combined HP Compact C-Suite became predominantly

Compaq people – well, at least that was the internal perception. The truth is probably only known to Carly but it clearly illustrates that power and structure are intimately related and the biggest barriers to change are often motivated by status. Some of the most delicate and important conversations that HR and CEOs are involved in are attempts to sideline powerful people who may not recognize that they are part of the problem.

C-Suite 5 Influencers

Similar to Porter's 5 Forces Framework that analyses the competition of a business, the diamond-shaped department has five key influencers. The first influencer is internal and is the home team itself: what are the capabilities and ambitions of the department or business unit team and what should the C-Suite executive be doing to develop and look after them? Then come the other two internal influencers, the Board and C-Suite Executive itself and the other departments and business units you co-exist with. Again, what do they want from you and how can you best serve and lead them? Externally, there are also two influencer groups and these can be prioritized by their relevance and importance based on a risk benefits analysis. The two external influencers are those that supply directly to you and those that influence your environment. Those that supply directly to you are your suppliers and outsourced services – these may include technology suppliers, external experts like a consultancy, lawyers and accountants, and outsourced offerings that may be on- or offshore. The other and final influencers can be grouped into shareholders and sector influencers. These will include the environment, society and media, and also your relevant regulators, politicians, pressure groups, trade and professional associations and any other external body or grouping that has sway in your area of business. Shareholders, particularly when a family, when the holder is significant or when there is an active investor, might be thought of as the Board's main influencers.

Shareholder engagement needs to be underpinned by open dialogue and communication. By giving shareholders clear visibility of the business, the Board gets an accurate picture of shareholder sentiment in return. They also minimize the risk of miscommunication, which can lead to time-consuming and unprofitable disputes relating to both governance and strategy. Briefings should be regular but proportionate and timely, reflecting results, trading updates and major developments. A relationship formed early on, long before any crisis situation develops, can lay the foundation for mutual trust and support in the event of a business crisis. Engagement is key and the worst approach when engaging with sceptical shareholders, or even activists, is to ignore their concerns – this will isolate them further and fuel their agendas.

The five influencer groups are summarized in the model below:

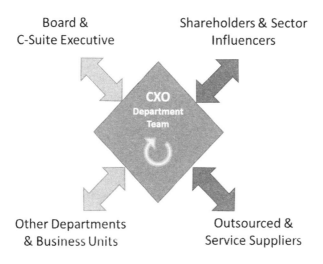

When reviewing your approach to these five influencers it is important to keep focused on the organization's purpose and resulting strategic objectives and rally all influencers where possible around this. You should work out who the key stakeholders are in each of the five influencer areas. Ask what they want from you and how they will measure it, trigger the relationship and create a plan to work with them. Ensure you partner well with each of the key stakeholders, creating multiple positive touch points. Where possible, get involved early on in discussions and bring with you a broad knowledge of the business, remembering the 'O' part of your role. Try and always be a force for good, champion diversity, allow risk taking, create a safe environment and be an honest friend, wise counsel and trusted confidant and adviser to all influencers.

THE IMPORTANCE OF LINE

When I first drafted this chapter and this section on diversity, I walked away from it feeling that something was missing or I hadn't quite nailed it. All psychology issues like impostor syndrome, propensity to take risk, level of conscious competence all seem important but when I met business leaders and spoke with them that was not what came across. Sure, a percentage of business leaders might be tyrants, but although high-profile they represent a very small percentage of business leaders. Then one day I was speaking with a woman who was running an organization focused on trying to get more women into the C-Suite and she said that the issue was 10 per cent impostor syndrome and 90 per cent internal politics, but when I questioned her internal politics, on what she actually meant, her answers were wobbly at best. Then that night, at about 5 a.m., it came to me and I think she was about right: the glass ceiling within the C-Suite is 10 per cent psychology and 90 per cent something else, and she was calling that something else politics.

Bear with me for a moment, I would like to give you a military example and then bring it back to business and explain why the same thing is going on. In the British Army, you have three teeth arms, combat units that engage in close combat, and they are the infantry, armoured and aviation units. Behind these teeth arms, you have all the support cores and these include catering, medical, transport, etc. The support cores are really important, ensuring the teeth arms are effective, but you would never appoint a general to lead a battle from a support core as they have virtually no frontline business experience. Similarly, the operating business units of the organization exist in a hostile environment with fierce competition and you would want your CEO to have a comprehensive understanding of that environment and this is why line experience is so important. The 90 per cent is line experience.

In Bosnia, we had soldiers digging trenches in a blisteringly cold winter to protect the northern cordon of Sarajevo and the powers that be thought it would be a good idea to have an intelligence officer attached to us. The regiment I was in, the Coldstream Guards, recruited predominately from the North-east of England and therefore was full of people who looked a bit like Vikings and now attached to this team came a rather short female intelligence officer. She was looked at sceptically to begin with, but she helped dig the trenches, never complained and within a few weeks, she was part of the team. Had she been appointed a platoon commander, would the soldiers have minded? No, they wouldn't because as far as they were concerned, she had become one of them. To prove this, they presented her with a blue red blue watch strap, the colours of the Guards Division.

I remember the general counsel of a real estate company complaining to me about their leadership team. Comments had been made to them like 'You're not really one of us' and they had been offended by this. We had both made assumptions about what 'one of us' meant; we thought it was referring to gender, but in this case, it was referring to them never having run a real estate practice. In Chapter 1 we talked about the difference between positions of influence and positions of power and the resulting difference between staff and line roles (*see also* p. 54), but there is more to it than this. Line roles are judged almost entirely on financial performance and value creation, the results are more transparent to see and the competitive environment is external and relentless. You will find a similar level of camaraderie in manufacturing plants, because the work is tough and less so in the offices that sit above them.

Similarly, nurses and doctors have a closer bond than those who administrate the hospitals. People who operate in these environments, just like the teeth arms in the military, have a high level of respect for each other and a level of camaraderie not found in the same way in the cores. So, there is a glass ceiling within the

C-Suite between the teeth arm business units and the supporting services like finance and human resources. That is why 90 per cent of CEOs in S&P 500 are recruited from line roles. The CEO who has typically been promoted from a business unit has a closer bond and affinity with the business unit CEOs than with the C-Suite departments – they are probably more like them and are even likely to have common banter.

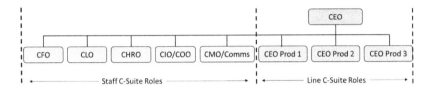

To achieve diversity, we have to diversify the line and line experience is key not just for experience but probably more importantly because it makes you 'one of them'. The problem is we draw the top team organization chart wrong; the truth is that the business is the three product CEOs reporting to the CEO, the C-Suite departments exist to help those businesses. So, the organization chart for the C-Suite should actually look like the model below, with the three business unit CEOs reporting direct to the CEO. Essential services, the staff roles, are typically collectively financially equivalent to one of those business units.

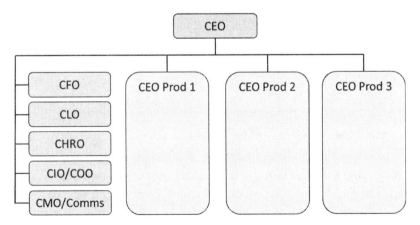

Each product area CEO almost certainly employs around the same number of people as the collective staff count of all the support functions. Owing to sheer size, they probably had to fight through more layers of management and compete against more people to become CEO. So, in summary, line leadership is different from staff in several ways:

- **Environment** – Line operates in a fiercer competitive and more dynamic environment, and as a result, line managers need to be more creative and decisive. All entrepreneurs are line managers.
- **Performance** – Line measures are more financial and transparent to all, which makes line managers more personally exposed. Weaker line managers are weeded out quickly and stars are spotted faster.
- **Culture** – Line roles are likely to have a closer bond, camaraderie and respect for their peer group and as result, look out for each other more.
- **Size Matters** – Getting to the top of a bigger business unit is harder as the internal competition is more numerous and therefore those that are successful are likely to be highly skilful.
- **Promotion Gap** – Similarly, a move from a divisional CEO to group CEO is likely to be an increase in multiple of responsibility, people and financial, of under-five, whereas from a support department lead to CEO is likely to be a multiple of over ten.

The importance of line management experience cannot be underestimated for those who want to be CEO.

Glass Houses, Diversity & Appraisals

What is the glass ceiling, who does it apply to and where in an organization does the glass ceiling appear? The glass ceiling is a metaphor used to represent an invisible barrier that is not seen and yet is unbreachable. Typically, it rests at the top of an organization and prevents access to the most senior roles, these roles being the most prestigious and highest-paid in an organization. It was originally coined by feminists and then extended to include ethnic and other minorities, such as the LGBTQ groups. Sometimes it goes by different names – for example, East Asians in America sometimes refer to the 'bamboo ceiling'. Whatever the reason, it is an unseen barrier at the top of an organization that clearly exists as a result of discriminating factors. Whether these factors are conscious or unconscious is slightly irrelevant, they create the unseen barrier. In the overwhelming majority of cases discrimination will be the driver behind this glass ceiling, however, white men have also complained about hitting a glass ceiling, as have senior executives wanting to break into the C-Suite, so there is more to it than we first think.

The career ceilings can be categorized into three broad groups, which are explained below although the glass ceiling specifically refers to discrimination:

- **Society Imposed** – These include factors such as social mobility, stereotypes, power players and class, which we will look at in the next chapter. There is also a senior business etiquette and understanding that has its roots deep in society.
- **Organization Imposed** – This includes discrimination, all forms of bias (including affinity), conscious and unconscious (the glass ceiling), lack of innovation in or ability to attract and welcome variety, selection criteria based on organization need and the CEO and C-Suite team's personal fit and preferences.
- **Self-imposed** – This is when someone may not want the role, may not feel psychologically safe or have a fear of rejection. They may not have the necessary knowledge or experience (no 'O'), may have no profile, reputation or stakeholder experience or no direct line power experience.

Several years ago, we had the CEO of a large telecommunications company talking to our chief marketing officer network. He was a white male and he gave an excellent presentation, answered questions thoughtfully and genuinely triggered a few light-bulb moments in the heads of everyone attending. Everything had gone really well, but then as he was about to leave the final question caught him off guard. He was asked, 'How can a chief marketing officer become a chief executive?' and he laughed. It took a few seconds before he had realized what he had done. His previously grateful audience now had a look of offended aggression on their faces. The facilitator intervened gracefully and asked why he had laughed. He apologized and then explained that 'The truth is none of you understand a balance sheet and how can you possibly think you can be a CEO if you don't understand a balance sheet? You are not even considered for the list.' This is an example of a real or perceived knowledge gap that could occur in many places but here, the perception was that marketing people do not have a good enough understanding of finance to become a CEO.

More recently, I was speaking with Gavin Patterson, CEO of BT plc and now President & Chief Revenue Officer of Salesforce. Patterson had started his career in marketing at Procter & Gamble (P&G). He explained to me how grateful he was to P&G because they gave you financial profit and loss responsibility, as a country brand owner, at a comparatively young age. He then rolled off a list of other CEOs who had all been his contemporaries at P&G and were all now running large organizations. The problem today, he said, is to get the same level of financial responsibility that he had in his twenties – you probably have to be a national marketing director and that means in your mid-thirties. This BT telecommunications CEO example tells us that marketing people can go all the way to CEO but only if they have the appropriate general management experience and knowledge. So, has the development of future business leaders actually slipped back?

In 2020, *The Irish Times*[30] reported that Deloitte, Adobe and Accenture have either dropped performance appraisals altogether

[30] https://www.irishtimes.com/business/work/why-performance-appraisal-systems-are-doomed-to-fail-1.3747881

or radically simplified their appraisal systems. Those that do appraisals tend to have annual appraisals and six-month catch-ups. On top of this, most line managers have monthly catch-ups and you would hope they would raise any feedback issues immediately or at these meetings rather than wait for a formal appraisal. There are inherent conflicts in appraisals, which include their purpose – for example, are they for establishing future development needs, giving feedback on or ranking for administrative purposes like setting the individual's pay? Although many appraisal systems are now highly refined, all too often the appraisers are not trained and the scoring of people can be inconsistent across an organization, making comparisons potentially futile. Individuals also nearly always rank themselves higher than their peers and managers rank them, which can lead to demoralizing conversations.

Hamish Taylor, former CEO of Eurostar Group, explained that the problem with appraisals is that they tend to focus on what people are not good at and instead we should treat them as we do brands, find out what they are good at and focus on that rather than their weaknesses. Perhaps not surprisingly, Hamish came from a marketing background, having also started at P&G as a brand manager.

The big shock comes when someone scores better than a peer in their appraisals and then it is their peer that gets promoted into the C-Suite or executive committee. Is this discrimination or is something else going on? The problem with appraisals is that by their very nature they appraise the historical performance of the individual. They typically appraise the technical skill of how someone performed their role and how well they fit with their team or culture. In other words, they appraise the C and the X, but not the O and what we now know is that it is the O that gets you into the room where it happens.

Recently, I was interviewing the Chair of a $3 billion private real estate and construction company. He took the view that CEOs probably have a shelf life of around eight years, after which they tend to lose energy and their ideas start to wither so, five to ten years is probably about right for tenure. They were looking for a new CEO who had a more strategic than operational focus and as a result, needed someone with a broader knowledge of the company and how it operated at the most senior level. They were keen to have an internal recruit and after a rigorous process, eventually the CFO got the top job. When I asked why, there were three main reasons given:

1. Emotional intelligence was important and chemistry with the Board and family stakeholders was key;
2. They wanted someone that the executive team would look up to, would gain good advice and guidance from and someone from whom the executive team would continue to learn;
3. And they wanted someone who was technically good, a competent operator who had a good grasp of the finances.

In other words, they wanted an O first as the stakeholders were key, then a good top team leader, a C, and finally, someone who was a technically competent X. CFOs develop through their roles a keen understanding of governance, the business model and stakeholders through investor presentations. These are the three key areas of C-Suite knowledge, often making them the best-positioned staff officer to become CEO. This fit with the CXO model is useful and what was interesting was what happened to the two unsuccessful candidates. One candidate could not reconcile the fact they were not appointed, maybe they hit their glass ceiling or used the glass ceiling metaphor to explain their lack of success? Either way, they soon left the organization. The other was a serious contender that did not have enough board and broader business experience or enough O to get the CEO role. They were keen to keep this individual and to ensure a healthy succession pipeline and as a result, appointed them to the Board to help fill the experience gap and gain a broader business understanding. At the time you are reading this book that individual may well be the CEO in place today.

So, is the glass ceiling for some actually a lack of O and is O the something that they cannot see, the reason they look inside but are not invited into the room? Does this glass ceiling exist because no one told them about the O, because they were too studious in scoring well in the C and the X that they overlooked the O or because their friends, network and mentors let them down in explaining the reality of what organizations need? Can this glass ceiling be smashed by them developing their O, or more specifically, their knowledge and skill in the areas of:

1. Stakeholders (including investors);
2. Governance, Structure and Processes;
3. Diversity, Inclusion & Culture.

Whatever group or society you associate yourself with, it is essential to ensure you have enough O to be in the selection pool to get into the C-Suite, the room where it happens, and to then ultimately secure the top job of CEO.

Key Learnings from Chapter 2

CXO Method

- Chief is for Chief, running the team or unit, X is for Expertise, the area of expertise you developed, and O is for Officer, the role that adds value across the organization. You start as an X, grow to become a C and they may move on to become an O.
- When moving from an X to a C in the same area, it can be useful to conduct a talent audit to start with to reposition yourself as the leader.
- As you start your career, the X is the most important area but for entering the C-Suite, O is the key that will let you in. The uplift in knowledge from middle manager to C-Suite executive is substantial and sits at around 19 per cent across all areas.

- Try and gain financial and stakeholder experience early on in your career and remember, appraisals focus on the X and the C and it is the O that gets you into the C-Suite executive. When boards look for a new CEO, they look for O first, then C and then X.

C-Suite Knowledge

- To get into, and be successful in the C-Suite, you need a comprehensive understanding of The Business Model; Vision, Purpose & Values; Stakeholders (including investors); People, Talent & Performance; Governance, Structure and Processes and Diversity, Inclusion & Culture. The biggest difference from middle management to C-Suite is stakeholder knowledge.
- Executives and organizations alike should be looking to fill future knowledge gaps in the C-Suite executive and building the attributes of great judgement, interpersonal skills and antennae.

Tiaras & Diamonds

- Executives should stop thinking of themselves as T-shaped executives and should consider themselves Tiara-shaped, a brighter and more interesting collection of skills and knowledge. The Tiara model illustrates the need for senior executives to have a broader general knowledge of the business.
- Technology is enabling departments to become smaller, changing their shapes from triangles to diamonds as the lower-value roles are automated. However, its implementation is often more challenging than anticipated as the people buy-in, rather than the tech is the critical success factor.

Structure & Fit

- Within organizations, you have departments at different levels of maturity and you can inherit or take over a reactive, proactive or world-class function. The leadership role and subsequent pressures will vary based on this maturity and certain stages better suit different types of leaders.
- Departments are structured differently and the executives and organization need to understand the difference and ensure the current structure is the best fit for the organization.
- Structure and power are intimately related and executives and organizations alike should not underestimate the challenges and impact of changes to the power structure. These conversations and negotiations need a lot of preparation.

Importance of Diversity & Line

- Having competent people in the role is key to the success of an organization and the alternative is dangerous. More diverse candidates and people in the role are likely to be more competent than the dominant group because of their behaviour and the environment that they have worked in.
- Line managers have an advantage over staff due to their frontline experience, strength of relationships and the size of business unit they have managed.
- To develop smart thinking more like an entrepreneur, you need to stay permanently curious, adding areas of knowledge and expertise to your CV.

3

Career Planning & Strategies

'Levelling the playing field with privileged kids'
John Jeffcock

In their book, *The 100-Year Life: Living and Working in an Age of Longevity,*[31] Lynda Gratton and Andrew Scott explain that half of the people who were born in and after 2007 will live to over 100. They predict that half the Japanese will on average live to 107 years of age, followed by the US, Canada, France and Italy at 104, the UK at 103 and Germany at 102. All over 100. There are some who also predict that the first person to live to 200 is alive today.

Gratton and Scott's work is important as a 100-year life is over 20 years longer than the average life expectancy was at the time of writing this book.[32] There is a very real personal economic impact of that life expectancy. Take the UK as an example: at the time of writing, the retirement age was 66 and average life expectancy 82 years of age, so a pension has to be big enough to pay out over 16 years. If you live to over 100 years and retire at the same time, your pension needs to last for over twice the length of time, nearly 40 years, so either your pension pot needs to be over twice the size or you save half of everything you earn. States are unlikely to be able to afford such a large retirement population and therefore

---

[31] http://www.100yearlife.com/the-challenge/
[32] https://www.macrotrends.net/countries/GBR/united-kingdom/life-expectancy

the other and most likely alternative, I am afraid, is that you will be working for longer, much longer. The latter is the more likely outcome for most of us and our working lives are going to increase from approximately 40 years to approximately 60 years. Feels like a lifetime, doesn't it? Well, it is, or at least was in the United States in 1935 and is still just longer than the average life expectancy in Nigeria today. So, we will be working for a lifetime, so we need to think about our working lives differently, no longer as an upward trajectory more an exciting journey.

I remember once rafting down the Grand Canyon in Arizona and being apprehensive as we approached the rapids, resting in the calmer waters and looking up all these beautiful valleys that I would have loved to have explored, had I the time and control of the raft. Well, now in your career the good news is that you will have much greater control and you will have enough time to explore, to go off up the beautiful valleys and become an actor, a social worker or a helicopter pilot for a while because we all have more time. So, start rethinking how you want to spend your time and your relationship with work. For many of us, the time of set working hours and retiring at a certain age is coming to an end.

But not everyone's working life is going to increase from 40 to 60 years and nation states will have to make compensations for different types of work. Blue-collar workers, those that have more manual work, may well be limited by their physical resilience and the wearing and ageing of their bodies. I remember once talking with a postman who walked miles every day on his hilly route, pulling and pushing a trolley. He explained to me the toll it had taken on his body, how office workers did not understand this as they worked in environmental-controlled places where the biggest strain on their bodies was probably walking to the coffee machine. It is not surprising that in 2007 the Communication Workers' Union created a 'Lighten the load' campaign specifically to support postmen.[33]

Similarly, science tells us that night workers such as nurses, due to disruptive sleep patterns, tend to suffer later in life. In 2009,

[33] https://www.unionsafety.eu/pdf_files/CWUHSGuideLightenLoad.pdf

Denmark was the first country in the world to pay government compensation to breast cancer sufferers[34] because of the connection it found to working nights for long periods. There is also a reason why in the military, the traditional retirement age was approximately ten years earlier at 55, the much often less communicated statistic as that former military personnel tend to also die younger and as a result, draw less on their pensions. We are still learning about the impact of different types of working environments but it is likely to become a reason for social tension as there is undoubtedly a correlation. The 100-year life projections at the beginning of this chapter were for 50 per cent of the population, so an important social consideration will be the life gap and its correlation with the wealth gap, and how the long-lifers look after or compensate the short-lifers.

There is also some good news for the short-lifers: as robotics is likely to replace a significant number of blue-collar roles, a large percentage of these people will increasingly live the lives of long-lifers. I am a huge advocate of social mobility and part of the purpose of this book is to enable social mobility and greater diversity into the C-Suite.

So, let's look at the impact of the 60-year career on long-lifers. In the mid-twentieth century, it used to be the norm to spend a lifetime with one organization and people who moved around were frowned upon, but now a CV where one person has worked in the same organization for over 20 years is a rarity and can be viewed as demonstrating a lack of initiative. Similarly, as working life extends from 40 to 60 years, it is likely that people in professions will transition into other fields, doctors may become accountants and marketers may become lawyers. The majority will need variety to maintain interest in what they do. Author Malcolm Gladwell, in his book *Outliers: The Story of Success*, popularized the idea that it takes 10,000 hours or close to five years of concentrated practice in order to possess a world-class skill in something so if you are working for 60 years, you have plenty of time to master multiple world-class skills. So how much time do you think we will spend

[34] https://www.medscape.com/viewarticle/590022

generating wealth, a tangible asset, and how much time will we spend retraining ourselves, an intangible asset?

At the early stages of Covid-19, back in March 2020, I proposed that while our tangible assets (property, money, etc.) plummet in value, there would be a surge in our intangible assets (love, relationships, etc.), something we have been needing for a while. I gave as examples family closeness, community cohesion and social responsibility. Family closeness, an intangible asset, was improving as fractured families were re-engaging with each other and even close families were getting closer. There were many jokes about the difficulties that may occur from families having to self-isolate but the truth is different. Having served in the army for eight years, I assured everyone that if you spend weeks in the same room as someone else, however much you may dislike them at the start, you do not come out the other side as enemies but more usually as life-long friends. Family bonds deepened during Covid-19 and simultaneously, communities grew closer and WhatsApp's user base jumped by 40 per cent as community and street groups formed and flourished.[35] We did not witness a collapse of communities but rather a rapid bonding of communities, with people creating online groups and making sure that those at risk or less advantaged were looked after. Neighbours helping neighbours who were once strangers. Meanwhile, across the world, social responsibility in corporates increased. The shift by organizations from being profit maximizers to value maximizers accelerated. Asda, for example, made a £5 million donation to FareShare[36] and The Trussell Trust, who collectively delivered 4 million meals to families in poverty. Corporates went through digital and social pivots concurrently and made their communities key stakeholders.

[35] https://techcrunch.com/2020/03/26/report-whatsapp-has-seen-a-40-increase-in-usage-due-to-covid-19-pandemic
[36] https://www.asda.com/creating-change-for-better/better-communities/fight-hunger/5million-donation

So, when you plan your 60-year career, you need to think about how much time you want to spend creating tangible assets and how much time creating intangible assets. Historically, there was a clear gender divide in this area; partly, a consequence of biology, where women worked on the majority of intangible assets and men the majority of tangible assets. But now the child-rearing time will be a comparatively much smaller percentage of a woman's career, so the number of women and the economic importance of women in the workplace will become even more important. Nonetheless, during the Covid pandemic when people switched to home working, women bore the brunt of the domestic chores, caring responsibilities, and home schooling. It pushed some women to resign from their jobs, led to heated conversations with partners and was a retrograde step for gender equality. Gender equality like the new corporate stakeholders are likely to suffer in times of duress for a while yet, however, hopefully the norms and debates held at the end of the twentieth century and beginning of the twenty-first century will be considered primitive by 2050.

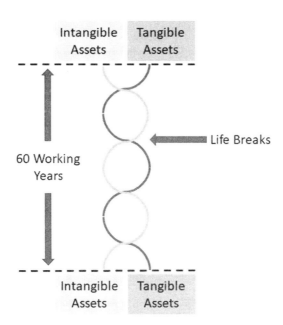

People in partnerships may go through high-earning tangible asset building phases and intangible asset-building phases, or may take it in turns, as illustrated by the above diagram. They may decide to take life breaks, to travel for a year, live in a remote cottage, repair a vintage car, work for a charity or just move to provide cover for their grandchildren for a while. So, as we start and travel along our career journey, we need to think about when we want to do things and how we want to spend our lives.

Some people may find the prospect of a 60-year career depressing but it becomes much less so if you consider it a meandering journey between tangible and intangible asset building. The last 20 years of our careers may, conversely to modern thinking, end up being the most creative. The average age of a Swedish Nobel Prize Winner is 65,[37] pretty much the same time as people retire today. Admittedly, their invention or great work may have occurred before this age but have we been unwittingly retiring people at the peak of their intellectual or creative ability, at the point when they have truly mastered their field, throwing away our greatest assets onto the greenways of golf courses, to hit a plastic ball into a hole? Will these additional career years be the greatest boost to human innovation in our history? Maybe 60-year careers will lead to a golden age of work-life balance and human achievement.

This book, through its focus on the C-Suite, is addressing a period of tangible asset creation during someone's life adventure. If we know that the average age of peak Nobel Prize Winners is 65, what is the average age of peak C-Suite? Wouldn't it be useful to know this to plan our career? Certainly, and it is highly likely that this is before 65, as former CEOs like Jack Welch of GE (General Electric) fame often cites the advantage of hindsight and how much they learnt in role. So, CEO and C-Suite peak wisdom, the thing of Nobel Prizes, will as a consequence happen after they have stepped down from their roles. The wisdom of reflection and hindsight makes them better and that is why so many business

[37] https://bigishdata.com/2015/06/07/whats-the-average-age-of-nobel-prize-winners/

leaders choose a mentor, so they can benefit from someone else's experiences and learnings.

PEAK EXECUTIVE POWER = MID-FIFTIES

The precise data varies slightly but my own research through Winmark showed that FTSE 100 CEOs are on average 54 years old and that average age has not changed by more than a year or two over the last 20 years. This data is supported by 2020 BoardEx data, which merges data from 30 European Indices,[38] including the FTSE (London), DAX (Frankfurt) and CAC (Paris) indices, shown in the table below and shows CEOs across Europe have an average age of 55. The average age of Fortune 500 and S&P 500 in 2017 and 2018 was 54, but it has been younger and older. In 2005, the average age for Fortune 500 and S&P 500 CEOs was 46 years old according to *Business Insider*,[39] but in 2019, this had gradually increased to 58. In 2020, BoardEx USA data shows that the average age of CEOs across 9 indices[40] including S&P, Dow Jones and Nasdaq, remained at 58 years of age.

In 2016, the Korn Ferry Institute[41] in Los Angeles conducted a study of the top 1,000 US companies by revenue and they came to the same answer of 58, with a variance to 55 for tech CEOs and up to 60 for financial services CEOs. So, I think we can safely say that

[38] Thirty EU Indices: AEX, AEX MID-CAP, ATX, BCN GLOBAL 100, BEL-20 INSTITUTIONAL, CAC 40, CAC ALL-TRADABLE, DAX, Euro Stoxx 50, EURONEXT 100, FTSE 100, FTSE 250, FTSE AIM, FTSE FLEDGLING, FTSE SMALL CAP, IBEX 35, IGBM, ISEQ OVERALL, LUXX, MDAX, OBX, OMX Helsinki 25, OMX Stockholm 30, PSI-20, RTS Index, SBF 120, SMI, Stoxx Europe 50, TecDAX and WIG 20

[39] https://www.businessinsider.in/strategy/news/corporate-america-is-seeing-a-spike-in-the-age-of-ceos-being-hired-and-yes-theyre-overwhelmingly-white-men/articleshow/71856494.cms

[40] Nine US Indices: BOVESPA, DOW JONES INDUSTRIAL AVG, NASDAQ 100, S&P 100, S&P 500, S&P MID CAP 400, S&P SMALL CAP 600, S&P/TSX 60 and S&P/TSX COMPOSITE

[41] https://www.kornferry.com/about-us/press/age-and-tenure-in-the-c-suite-korn-ferry-institute-study-reveals-trends-by-title-and-industry

CEOs are not getting younger and the CEO role, which is the peak of executive power, is usually achieved in your mid-fifties.

The same study by BoardEx on the six Asian Indices,[42] including the HANG SENG (Hong Kong), Nikkei (Tokyo) and BSE (Bombay, now Mumbai), showed an average age of 58 for CEOs – exactly the same as the US. The table below shows a breakdown of C-Suite ages from across the world and sourced from 45 different indices and thousands of companies.

C-Suite Role	US	EU	Asia	Average
CEO	58	55	58	57.0
CIO	55	53	55	54.3
COO	54	52	55	53.7
CLO	54	53	52	53.0
CFO	52	51	55	52.7
CHRO	54	52	52	52.7
CMO	53	51	52	52.0
Average	54	52	54	
Total Age	380	367	379	

What is notable from this table is that the average ages in the US and Asia are exactly the same, with Europe being slightly younger. If you total up the ages, you might argue that the average EU C-Suite executive has ten years less collective experience than their US and Asian counterparts. The C-Suite age table is organized in average age order and globally after their CEO – the CIO – is the second oldest at 54.3, then the COO at 53.7, CLO at 53 and the CFO and CHRO at an equal 52.7 and the youngest is the CMO at 52 years of age. The age difference across the globe for different C-Suite roles is pretty consistent, the one slight anomaly being that CFOs in Asia tend to be a little older than their Western counterparts. Interestingly, in Europe, CEOs tend to be three years

---

[42] Six Asian Indices: BSE 200 (Bombay, now Mumbai), HANG SENG (Hong Kong), Hang Seng China Enterprises, KOSPI 50, Nikkei 225 (Tokyo) and TOPIX Core 30

older than the average C-Suite age, whereas in the US and Asia, the gap is slightly larger at around five years. So, in the US and Asia, boards may expect a slightly longer tenure as a C-Suite executive before becoming a CEO. This is summarized visually in the bar chart below:

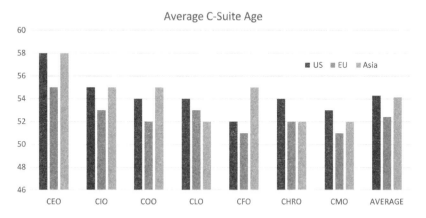

The average and often recommended tenure for a CEO is eight years, so that means they are going into the role in their early fifties and finishing at around 60 or soon after. It is interesting to note that C-Suite executives all tend to be a few years younger than the CEO.

In the same study, Korn Ferry also looked at tenure and found that CEOs stayed in the role the longest at eight years, CFO stayed for on average 5.1 years, CHRO for 4.6 years, CIOs for 4.3 years and CMOs for 4.1 years. Let me draw that data into a simple summary:

- CEOs and C-Suite Executives tend to be in their mid-fifties;
- CEOs tend to be a few years older than their average team age;
- CEOs are also in the role on average for eight years compared to four to five years for C-Suite executives;
- There are sector and role differences but for career planning purposes, these are minimal.

The other conclusion we can draw from this data is that it is possible to stay in the same C-Suite in the same company for over a decade. For example, a CFO after completing their 5.1-year tenure as CFO could be promoted to CEO, where they spend another eight years. This would give them a total of over 13 years, over a decade, in the same C-Suite. The last chapter of this book is aptly titled 'C-Suite Musical Chairs' and is about how to be successful and to stay in the C-Suite.

If we now put that peak age of executive power in a career time frame, from leaving university, we have around 30 years until our early fifties, slightly less time in some countries like Germany, Austria and Switzerland as graduates tend to spend a longer time in academia. Post-60, we will then have another 20 years of our career to use wisely. As the role of this book is to help you get into the C-Suite and be successful there, we need to look at those first 30 years of your career quite carefully. The importance of making it into the C-Suite executive or onto a board by the age of 54 is critical – once past 54, your chances diminish significantly. For example, unpublished research conducted by Dominick Sutton, Chief Data Officer, BoardEx identified that the probability of becoming the CEO at age 50 is 0.45 and by the age of 55, it drops to 0.21. So, we will make 54 to 55 our target age for this chapter.

LET'S START AT THE BEGINNING

Think of the C-Suite as a foreign country. It has its own etiquette, its own language, often meets somewhere else and even the laws are different. As you enter the C-Suite, you are exposed to new levels of governance responsibilities, the laws, you meet in a boardroom, a separately labelled room reserved just for your group, you talk a new language of stakeholders and governance, and the behaviour and etiquettes around the table are different to the informal team meetings you will have been used to. The advantage privilege has in this foreign country is that they will have more experience of it and experience in life can have many benefits.

The truth we all know is that the race is not an equal one – we are not born with equal talents, are not all given the same privileges and burdens, and are not all invested in and nurtured and mentored to the same degree. For many parents, their life focus is to give their children the opportunities they never had, to ensure that they are better equipped to be successful in the world. So, how can we level the playing field?

In 1990, Michael E. Porter wrote a famous book called *The Competitive Advantage of Nations*. Whereas this book is concerned with the 'Competitive Advantage of Rich Kids' and how to neutralize their advantage and ultimately become more successful. Nation states have natural advantages like better education systems, economics, resources and environments, but some nation states who start with much less still manage to be richer, healthier and more influential than others. So, if states can do it, with all their complexity, it cannot be that hard for individuals or can it?

All children, rich and poor, can suffer from neglect but in the round, rich kids have a number of what I will call 'ecosystem advantages'. Rich kids are not the only group to have natural advantages over those less advantaged, but they are a good illustration for the reasons given below:

- **The School Network** – Rich kids start developing their network from a very early age through both the schooling system and who they holiday with. Private schools are very expensive, Castilleja School in Palo Alto, California is $54,000[43] per year per child and Eton College in the UK is £42,501[44], which means all the parents are rich and the majority will be successful business people. The parent networks of private schools in their own right are powerful groups, which was illustrated by a fundraising activity at Knightsbridge School in London, where close to £1 million was raised for a charity in a single night.

[43] https://www.castilleja.org/admission/tuition-and-affordability
[44] https://www.etoncollege.com/admissions/fees/

These networks help children develop a broader view of
the world, give them greater access to opportunities and
money helps. The access includes access to power players,
through the parents' network – a group of people we will
discuss towards the end of this chapter.

- **The Education Privilege** – Higher-class parents speak
  more words, have a broader vocabulary and tend to have
  a higher expectation of their children. Private schools
  have less children in each class, better resources and tend
  to run an academic year ahead, in terms of education,
  than their state equivalents. As a result, pupils tend to
  get into better universities, which in turn have better
  resources, academics and peer networks, so the gap
  continues to widen. However, the expectations placed on
  rich kids can be beyond their talents and as a result, can
  have a significant detrimental impact on them, where
  they lose confidence and are made to feel, quite often
  unconsciously, like they are a disappointment to the
  family.
- **The Parents' View** – From a young age, all children like
  to listen to their parents' conversations and people talk
  about what they do and have done and their views on
  things. If parents are already successful, the children are
  most likely to get to listen to conversations about macro
  issues and how businesses and the world works. This is
  the 'news and business' vs 'reality TV' education dilemma.
  News and business parents spend more time explaining
  how things work to their children, whether they want
  to hear it or not, and sometimes encourage questioning.
  Through this sometimes unintentional immersion process,
  they are more likely to develop a broader view of the
  world and understanding of how it works.
- **Money Can Help** – Money helps, but not always. It can
  help in many ways, ranging from better, more interesting
  holidays to taking stress off students through elevating
  them from student debt and allowing them to focus

on their studies instead of having to work part-time to survive. However, business needs people with commercial brains, who work hard and understand money. If you have never worked and have little commercial experience through to your early twenties, this may actually be a life disadvantage to you. But smart rich parents, like Alfred Nobel, are alert to this and ensure their children get plenty of work experience in a variety of organizations and roles, often through the parent and school networks.

> I regard large inherited wealth as a misfortune, which merely serves to dull men's faculties. A man who possesses great wealth should, therefore, allow only a small portion to descend to his relatives. — Alfred Nobel

- **Aspiration & Confidence** – Private schools are good at putting children on a stage, getting them to read out loud, finding areas where they are strong and supporting their development. You can often spot the privately educated young adult when they walk into the room as they tend to be more confident, look you in the eye and are adept at talking with senior and older people. Through generations, children have been expected to grow up to do what their parents do – the son of a shoesmith was expected to become a shoesmith and so on. So often the aspiration is set by what the parent does. A well-known exception is first generation immigrants, whose parents often work long hours to fund their children through good schools with a view to giving them a leg-up from where they are. At the other end of the scale, I once heard a comment that gave me a huge amount of inner confidence. We were all potential officers at the Royal Military Academy Sandhurst (RMAS) and had just completed part of the course. To celebrate, we were having a few drinks in town with the training staff, who were typically ten years senior to us. In the back of the taxis, a

corporal, who we were all a bit scared of, turned around
to us and said, 'I love training you guys, one of you might
be Prime Minister one day.' The fact that this guy had
so much faith in us, we who had to date had achieved so
little, was an extraordinary boost.

• **Etiquette** – There is a thing about etiquette. RMA
  Sandhurst (UK), USMA WestPoint (USA) and ESM
  Saint-Cyr (France) all teach etiquette to their potential
  army officers. Why? How does this help them? Is this just
  elitist nonsense, a need to separate leaders from followers,
  a form of social discipline or skill or something different?
  At RMA Sandhurst, over 90 per cent of potential officers
  are *not* privately educated and when the etiquette lessons
  take place, you might be horrified to discover that
  privately educated potential officers used to be dismissed
  because they already knew the etiquette and behaviours.
  Army officers throughout the world are taught how to
  hold a knife and fork! The truth is it doesn't really matter
  why, what matters is that you know how to adapt your
  behaviour in different environments. Exposure to limited
  social diversity or a single homogenous group, whether
  at the top or bottom of society, can limit their social skill
  and progress. Every society in the world has a class system,
  whether we like it or not, and although these 'fake'
  boundaries are decreasing as social mobility improves for
  the moment they exist and therefore we need to know
  how to be successful in these environments.

  I remember once mentoring a young black man and
  I took him to meet an increasingly famous black leader,
  Cephas Williams, the originator of the 56 Black Men
  and Letter to Zion campaigns. I hoped it would give
  my mentee some much-needed confidence, would be a
  good connection for him and a fun and relaxing meeting.
  It was a cold spring day, we met at a fashionable coffee
  shop in the financial district. The young black guy I was
  mentoring was the only one of us not to take off his

jacket, to ask for the menu and somehow you could tell
that he saw the waitress as senior to him as she had a
job. I remember thinking it was a bit different but never
paid much attention to it. At the end of a productive
conversation, Cephas turned to him and said, 'Do you
mind if I give you some advice?'

'Sure,' said my mentee.

Then Cephas said: 'The white guy, John, did not down
you in front of me, that is good and many people will
down you to position themselves. You got to be resilient
to that and just take it. You're poor, aren't you? You asked
for the menu because you were looking for the cheapest
thing and you didn't take your jacket off because you
couldn't afford to lose it. Those two things tell this white
guy that you are poor and not part of his club. You got
to be wise to these things, it is those little behaviours that
will keep doors closed to you. Because we invited you
for the coffee, we were always going to pay – the person
who invites pays, you need to know that. Sometimes
people split bills but not often in business. We are in the
financial district, no one here is going to nick your jacket
and you look uncomfortable. That immediately makes us
conscious that you don't feel relaxed in this environment
and that you may not fit in. Fitting in is good and the
more different you come across, the less likely they are to
invite you back.'

We left the café slightly less energized than when we
arrived because a gap had been highlighted that we had
not previously felt and now we both felt a little awkward.

So, how do you overcome the 'Competitive Advantage of Rich
Kids'? Well, there is lots you can do and luckily we live in a time
when social mobility is encouraged and championed, so we must
seize the day as it is certainly not a guarantee that the world will
always be like this. The rich kids' escalator may have slowed down
for a while but rich kids are smart and in response are starting

to hide their early advantages. Why is this happening? The professionalization of HR and focus on equal opportunities has a lot to be thanked for. For example:

- Influential parents are now less able to secure internships and work placements, as HR now acts as a filter and select on merit, while actively looking for diversity.
- The awareness and training around unconscious bias and proven business case behind diversity all mean that the 'old boys' network' has been fragmented and only survives now in small pockets in old-fashioned sectors. These 'old-fashioned' sectors are now also being pushed into the margins by the 'information age', which creates meritocratic transparency.
- When equal CVs are presented, the less advantaged or more diverse background is now more likely to be selected. As a result, privately educated young adults have started to take their school off their CVs so the potential employer cannot see the advantage they started with.

In the earlier years of your career your focus should be on learning and building a network. This should be within but not limited to your own organization. Try and avoid poor managers and leaders and find people you can learn from who will support you in the future. As your career develops, this support will become more important and your personal visibility in and outside the organization becomes a form of third-party assurance.

It is also useful to identify who the key influencers are for certain roles and to make sure that you are positively known to them. You need internal and external ambassadors and you can do the same for others. You must know how to create a value, be able to evidence this and your organization and others must be aware of the value you have created. Do not hide your successes, instead promote them. Many leadership books talk about praising your team for successes and taking personal responsibilities for your losses and this is the right and admirable approach. But don't forget every time you praise your team, some of the fairy dust lands on you. And every time you protect your team and take responsibility, fellow leaders – who all also get things wrong – trust you a little more.

BOARD ADVICE TO THEIR OWN CHILDREN

As part of the research behind this book I interviewed a large number of board directors from a wide variety of sectors. Some of them were former CEOs, others were C-Suite executives and some had been top consultants in the world's leading consultancies. My questioning was focused not on their children at school or university, but rather those already in business. Most of these board directors were 50-plus in age and had adult children, and I was particularly interested in the advice they would give to their own kin, their children. I was on the hunt for hidden advice that they would give in private to a member of their family early on in their career. What was interesting was that they all reflected on their own careers and their advice was all variations around several common themes. This is what they said:

1. **Ambition Check** – First, you need to decide whether or not it is for you, you have to want it. Is being the CEO or part of the C-Suite executive what you really want, will this be your dent in the universe, is it important to you and when you honestly look at yourself, is it who you are? You will need to have the right skills to match your ambition and if you don't, you will usually get found out very quickly, so you need to be realistic. Also, remember that a lot of people hate being part of the executive team as it comes with material responsibility and with that material pressure. Do not back one horse, have a plan B and alternative route or career direction that you would also be happy with.
2. **Right Match** – You need to be extremely thoughtful on getting the right match, it helps to choose an area

where you have a natural passion. You will need a healthy self-knowledge and an honest view of yourself and must choose an environment where you would be most successful. Ensure that what you do is going to get you up every morning, motivate you and be enough to carry you through the tough times. If you don't know what you want to do, a place everyone has been, the advice is do something useful and sensible until the clarity comes.

3. **Agile & Resilient** – Executive roles are more complicated and tougher than they used to be, full of highs and lows. This means you have to be resilient and good at consistently motivating yourself and others in often difficult environments. You will need to be agile, adaptable and resilient.

4. **Enjoy, Don't Endure** – Don't confuse 'enjoy, don't endure' with not working well under pressure. No one can escape periods of significant pressure during their careers and it is important you push through these periods rather than give up. But if you are enduring something you don't like that is different and it's probably time to move on because you will never be at your best if you are in an enduring state of mind.

5. **Traps** – Don't fall into the trap of doing something because one of your parents did it or they wanted you to do something. Don't think because you qualified in something you need to do that all your life. Don't trap yourself in a life you don't want or that doesn't make you happy, which also means don't financially stretch yourself or apply excessive financial pressure on yourself so you are forced to stay in a job or role you do not enjoy.

6. **Stay Current** – It is important to stay current and push yourself to make sure your skills do not go out of date, keep looking for and learning new and different things, which sometimes means you may need to volunteer and be at the front of the queue for new opportunities. You

will need to be continuously reinventing yourself. A good example of this is Tangy C. Morgan, an American who came to live in the UK and while being a senior advisor to the Bank of England, at the age 54 she completed a Master's Degree in Business Continuity, Security & Risk Management at Boston University.

7. **Keep Moving & Learning** – This is not about always looking for a new role or jobs, but always looking for new experiences and challenges and ensuring that you are always progressing. Go back to school or go on courses when you have time. As Warren Buffett, Chairman and CEO of Berkshire Hathaway, puts it: 'One can best prepare themselves for the economic future by investing in your own education.' Look for change that needs to be led but be selective on what you choose to lead. Don't try and change things you can't but do change and improve what you can.

8. **Get Out There** – Do not wait for it to happen or for someone to notice you. Leading executive search people are often criticized by candidates who say, 'Why did you never approach me for that role?' The answer more often than not is 'I didn't know you, I cannot put you forward for a role if I do not know who you are. You have to be visible or to tell me you are looking for a role.'

9. **Outside In** – Always keep an ear out for your customers – they pay your salary. Try, where possible, to own or represent them. Whatever you do, always ensure you make your customers look good to their stakeholders and particularly their boss.

10. **Know-How** – Embed yourself in the knowledge of the company, understand what knowledge is unique and important, be a sponge and soak up knowledge whenever you can. Don't get too hung-up on how the tech works, instead care more about how it creates value for the customer and your organization. As a business leader, you will need to be a hybrid. These days, you need to be

tech-orientated and have the ability to adapt as different situations demand different behaviours from you.

11. **People & Management** – Organizations are groups of people that deliver a service or product to other people. Make sure you always respect members of your team and your customers as people with needs. You need to think about soft skills from a young age – management and particularly management skills are very useful things to develop and invest in. People talk about having a high EQ (Emotional Quotient), something we will look at later in this chapter.

12. **Judgement & Mistakes** – We all screw up occasionally, some a little more than others, but even the business stars get stuff wrong. Don't worry about making mistakes but don't make the same mistake twice. Don't be put off by your mistakes or by others: if you think you are right, stick with your gut feeling.

13. **Keep Building Your CV** – Keep building your CV and be conscious of what you have and can actually achieve. It is important you understand your value. This is not necessarily about looking for a new role or job but ensuring that you are always learning – if you stop learning, it is probably time to move on.

How Orgs and C-Suite Roles are Changing

As outlined in Chapter 1 (*see also* pp. 17–21), the external pressures on organizations are substantial. Not only do leadership teams need to deal with a fierce competitive environment, they must take that into account while operating in a changing geopolitical world. To help deal appropriately with this increased complexity, organizations have increasingly moved to find a common purpose, why they exist in the first place. They are moving to a broader group of stakeholders and as mentioned, they need to respond to significant governmental and societal pressures. This in turn impacts what they do and what they report on. For example, the multinational insurance giant Aviva, which has over 33 million customers globally, incentivizes management on areas such as well-being, social mobility, carbon reduction and corporate responsibility. They do this at all levels and like the retail group Kingfisher plc, which has over 1,300 stores, they have now aligned the stakeholders and their stakeholder interests with reporting and management incentives. This is done at multiple levels and as you would expect, measurement is easier in some areas than others. Regulators are keen to encourage more organizations on this journey and sometimes say that the only real power they have is to shine the light of transparency on an organization. Similarly, business schools and managers often say 'what gets measured, gets done'. Creating a measure and reporting on it is equivalent to shining a light on the area and as a result, it drives different and new behaviours in the leadership teams and ultimately throughout the organization.

In Chapter 2 (*see also* pp. 81–85), we talked about the end of department silos and T-shaped managers, the digitalization of the workplace, diamond-shaped functions and tiaras of knowledge. We highlighted the importance of governance, the need to have competent people in charge and the need to understand the core processes that run through your organization. Now we understand the external pressures, we should look at their internal impact and more specifically the impact on different business functions and C-Suite roles. Let's start with marketing.

Marketing functions have evolved rapidly in recent years and there seems no let-up in this transformation. Digital has enabled consumer feedback to become interactive and instantaneous, consumer behaviour to be monitored live and customer journeys to be tailored to the individual. Marketers have become data architects as they use analytics to improve engagement online and inform product development. Product development and innovation have become customer-led. The use of design thinking and behavioural science approaches have allowed rapid innovation and new streams of marketing, including neuromarketing, such as a new technology, installed on buses in Seoul in South Korea that released the aroma of Dunkin' Donuts coffee into the atmosphere for riders to inhale. Marketing has always been about influencing people's behaviours, getting them to buy your product or service and its accuracy has recently increased at a frightening pace. What has happened is that marketing has evolved from market segments to an individual viewpoint. Chief marketing officers are looking at a single customer view, which enables more accurate and targeted marketing, product development and reporting.

In good hands this is great news as it means we all receive a more tailored service addressing our specific personal needs closer. However, an extreme alternative example of this in action was the SCL Group, the behavioural research and communications company and the parent company of Cambridge Analytica, the corporate face of SGL. You may remember that SGL closed in 2018 as a result of the Facebook–Cambridge Analytica data scandal. Major clients of SGL were the US and UK Ministries of Defence. SGL were commissioned to discover the psychological triggers that drove the behavioural change of local people in Iraq and Afghanistan. Once they knew these triggers, they could test social media to identify the most effective methods of changing behaviour. However, when the same approach is used to influence a democratic election and benefit one particular party over another, you get a more mixed response. The winning party sometimes applauds and thanks the organization and the losing party starts to attack the behavioural research and communications company for unconsciously manipulating the voter. This scenario gets even worse when that behavioural research and communications company is actually a foreign nation state, trying to influence the politics of another nation state to benefit itself through aiding the election of certain politicians. Politicians who may favour them may have certain agendas that will benefit them or weaken the competitor on the global stage. So, was the Facebook–Cambridge Analytica scandal really about Facebook selling data without their users knowing about it, or was it more about people not knowing if they had been manipulated or not and being scared of the power an organization may have over them without them realizing? Either way, Facebook pumped billions of US dollars into public relations in a single week to protect itself from the scandal and SGL soon closed its doors on 1 May 2018.

What this tells us is that with the right data marketing, and as a result, chief marketing officers, can now be extraordinary powerful. As Virginia (Ginni) M. Rometty, chairman, president and CEO of IBM says, 'Big data will spell the death of customer segmentation and force the marketer to understand each customer as an individual within 18 months or risk being left in the dust.'[45] Yesterday, this level of research, analysis and communications was only accessible to the largest of organizations, such as state players and the digital giants, but today, it has become more available as the skills become more common and the tools cheaper and more accessible. This may sound to some like a scary science fiction future but like a virus, humans will increasingly develop immune systems to this type of manipulation, so its effectiveness is likely to grow and then slowly diminish over time. Research and communication methods are like products – they have lifecycles and become obsolete as they are replaced by the next and better approach. One thing we can be sure of though is that marketing and communications, if not already, will soon be entirely personalized. This personalization has to have supporting processes and fulfilment systems. To support this, the organizations processes need to be holistic and joined up through the organization. What this means for chief marketing officers is that they need to have a combination of soft skills, data analytics, creativity and innovation. In the new data-heavy world, the CMO must be at home with data, but not just make data-driven decisions.

[45] https://www.marketingmag.com.au/news-c/ibms-ceo-on-data-the-death-of-segmentation-and-the-18-month-deadline/

They need to understand data, quality and still provide creative solutions and opportunities.

The human resources function is on a similar journey to marketing, treating employees like customers, tailoring solutions to individuals and empowering their work. Once again, human resources is increasingly powered by data. I remember meeting the chief data scientist of a large insurance company in a wine bar near Victoria Station in London. He had recently joined them from the gaming division of Sony, where he had been instrumental in guiding the successful launches of new PlayStation consoles and their rapid adoption. The CEO wasn't quite sure what the data scientist was going to do and arranged to meet him a month after he arrived. During that month the data scientist utilized software that read every email in the business, who they were sent from and to and what was the tone of the communication. Simultaneously, he accessed the telephone system and looked at who was calling whom, for how long and at what frequency. He then combined the data to produce a report on who the 200 most powerful people were in the organization. When he met with the CEO, he handed over the list and explained his methodology. The CEO read the list with bulging eyes, astonished by its accuracy, but there were also people on the list who he would not have expected and in some cases did not know.

Data can be used by HR to do many things, including prioritize work, improve recruitment, increase performance and retention, identify leaver patterns and the interventions that stop them. Bundle this with the technology revolution and new working practices, including the huge amount of work being done in the area of diversity and inclusion, and employee psychological contracts and you have very busy CHROs. They are combining and aligning purpose, values, agile, flexible working and new contracts with tech and AI-backed robotics that can interview candidates, on-board new joiners and exit leavers, ensure compliance and use virtual reality and augmented reality to train staff. Much of this can now be managed through 'one-stop shop' HR software that can personalize benefit bundles and run engagement practices. Happiness is high on the agenda, sentiment tracking important and concepts such as stand-up meetings, no internal email (email locked for holidays), on boarding apps similar to what L'Oréal use, benefits inflation, remote and home working, digital campuses and apps such as mindfulness, meditation, mentors are just a few of the ideas that CHROs are evaluating and implementing.

This personalization in human resources and marketing has a huge impact on internal processes, the flow of data through an organization and how different parts of the business can now be joined up. The two roles working hard to knit the organization together are the chief operating and chief information officers. One mapping the organization and process flows while the other integrates the systems and enables the flow of information from its source to the place where it is needed most. Remembering that they are doing this while the departments and business units are simultaneously restructuring themselves. The model below summarizes these three factors and the result is a new business model.

Chief information officers oversee the technology and how it is changing sector dynamics, the competitor landscape and ultimately the way business models create value. In this environment, CIOs need to create an agile defendable governance model that provides a framework for controlled growth while reducing and mitigating corporate risk. This may require the establishment of an IT and Business Innovation Hub, where new ideas can be identified and managed; and investment in architecture that is scalable, agile and secure. This may mean looking at single platforms, new tech stacks, replacing legacy systems, cloud enablement, leveraging big data (including governance and interoperability)

and mitigating potentially crippling Cybersecurity threats. The new systems should be able to cater for growth, including mergers and acquisitions, innovation, data analytics and product development, while reducing the organization's cost base. To do this, IT departments will need to reskill their own people, raise the digital literacy of their organizations, recruit a more diverse and better-skilled and motivated team. The ability to attract, reward and recognize the necessary people will undoubtedly require significant investment but all this costs time and money and both those assets are already under stress, so how do you decide on where to invest?

One of the best approaches to this that I have seen was at Tullow Oil plc, a multinational exploration oil and gas company. In 2012 their CIO was Andrew Marks and he knew from experience that without aligning leaders of all function areas, it would be almost impossible to correctly prioritize where to spend finite funds so he used to create a heat map that balanced strategic value on one axis and ease of delivery on the other. The size of each investment 'bubble' combined with a sum of total investment on the page created a common language for comparing diverse investment ideas. Marks would then invite in the entire C-Suite and run a tech investment session. He would start off by explaining what his budgets were and what they gave him the capacity to do, while inviting department leads to present their own cases for each of the major initiatives, highlighting what share of funding and resources they required, in the context of change across the entire organization. He would then facilitate a debate, helping to bring out the optimum mix of risk, investment and value for an agreed budget. In the end, the whole C-Suite team agreed what would be best for the business – they all had buy in and had all been part of the decision making process. Of course, things came up and people had their pet projects, but they always knew that they had agreed to the plan that their CIO was implementing on their behalf.

Chief operating officers are mapping processes and addressing issues right across the value chain, seeking to achieve standardization at the same time as managing increased complexity. COOs are investigating a host of potential improvements impacting on their function, including client digital access (portals), virtual workplaces and meetings, enhanced collaboration and decision making, intrapreneurship, robotic warehousing systems and the usage of blockchain to securely manage inventory and financial flows in their supply chains. At the same time the COO role is looking to step away from the detailed operations of the business and spend more time anticipating upcoming trends and developments to focus on building the future business model.

In order to align this model to the Common Purpose and broader group of stakeholders, COOs need to have a clear understanding of ESG, CSR, diversity, inclusion and engagement requirements. It also requires a re-examination of the current business model and integrated systems thinking that can create the new underlying plan and economic model, leveraging data and tech to build a full vision. The process needs to be closely managed, driving the future culture, collaborating internally to create the supporting plans, creating quick wins through existing people resources and triggering the necessary future infrastructure and talent investments.

All new models include a shift from the Industrial Revolution 'pay for hours worked' approach to more flexible outcome-based management. Better tech, transparency and the ability to source, manage and validate richer data is a prerequisite for achieving this flexibility. For example, one of the largest chains of supermarkets in the UK appointed an insights director to the Board in 2020 to spearhead the effective management and utilization of data across the organization.

The **Chief Financial Officer**, as we know from the digitalization of the finance function example earlier, presides over a function that is one of the most obvious to digitalize. The impact of digital is enormous and includes everything from the Digitalization of Tax (state direct access) and Foreign Exchange (decentralized currency trend) to automated expenses, accounts and dynamic planning, budgeting and forecasting. Simultaneously, many functions are migrating to the cloud and regulators are pushing more responsibilities on to corporates, such as AML (anti-money laundering) compliance. As mentioned, this has already started to reshape finance functions from the historical triangle to a more diamond shape so now the primary focus is to shift the finance function from being a driver of cost control to a creator of capital value. Finance departments are starting to become the centre of all reporting data for governance, ranging from finance to environmental, and the annual audit and regulators are amongst those encouraging this transition. Some would argue that the chief finance officer role is morphing into a chief administrative officer role or starting to absorb parts of the chief operating officer role as the finance function shifts to include more reporting and measurement responsibilities.

As with CFOs, digital has presented substantial opportunities for **chief legal officers**. Digital has enabled the automation of litigation, case preparation and due diligence (e-disclosure). Contracts have been standardized, processes unbundled, templates created, obligations and risks mapped as legal teams become more embedded in the business. As repetitive work is automated, commercial lawyers can be redeployed onto more complex and value creating work. This automation has often led to a temporary increase in legal work as many uncovered issues float to the surface as the transparency of technology bears fruit. Legal departments are at the forefront of capital protection. They provide the legal protection behind nearly all assets and the enforcement ability behind contracts and resulting cash flow. They also play a key role in communications, reputation and ethics management and, as a result, governance. Most CLOs do not feel their organization has a clear, integrated view of risk and feel they are working hard to achieve this but are hampered by lack of investment.

CLOs, like CIOs and all the C-Suite, exist in a more complicated and faster-moving world and staying abreast of current regulations across multiple jurisdictions is a challenge on its own. Adding the digital aspects in one area as simple as remote work can be a nightmare – for example, where is the employee actually working and does this change over the course of the year or over time, is their employment contract appropriate at that place, which countries' employment rights are valid and to whom do they and the organization have tax obligations to.

THE LEADERSHIP MODEL

In Chapter 2 (*see also* pp. 68–73), we talked about knowledge at different levels and the types of knowledge that are important in middle management and to the C-Suite executive. We looked at how people start building expertise in their careers, then start running teams and then finally how they need to add value across the organization. We also in Chapter 1 (*see also* pp. 30–52) looked at the importance for staff leaders to gain line experience. And as you have probably already guessed, someone who has purely line or purely staff knowledge or experience has a limited view of the organization. This is why even line leaders also need to work on cross-company initiatives so they can see how the whole organization joins up and understand why things they may have considered petty are actually important. Earlier in this chapter, we looked at advice from board directors to their children (*see also* pp. 133–136) and one of the areas they repeatedly reinforce is the need to stay curious and keep learning. What they are less specific about is what you should learn. However, what we now know is that to manage your career, you need a mix of line and staff experience. Similar to the 100-year life, you need to weave a life of building tangible and intangible assets, and incorporate a career of line and staff experience. The length of time in each area will depend on your ability to learn and master the area and your ability to make the connections that will enable yourself and the organization you serve. As part of this, you need to be able to cover the knowledge areas reviewed in Chapter 2, but knowledge on its own will not give you the keys to the C-Suite, the room where it happens, you need to have more.

I remember on my Master of Business Administration (MBA) that we were asked to write an assignment on leadership. One of the dilemmas that most people found it hard to get their heads around was the issue of bad leaders. They were focusing their attention on the characteristics of what made a good leader rather than looking at what attributes make up a great leader. Like me, they were also looking at how much of what they achieved was due to something they were born with – nature – and how much was due to something they had learnt, nurture. Separately, I was trying to reflect on what do Nelson Mandela, Mahatma Gandhi, Adolf Hitler, Winston Churchill, Abraham Lincoln, Martin Luther King Jr, Saladin, Julius Caesar, Mao Zedong, George Washington, Alexander the Great and Napoleon Bonaparte all have in common. For me, the basics were obvious: they are all materially intelligent human beings with abundant energy and had a very clear purpose. I guess that's pretty similar to what makes a great organization, talented people, highly motivated and knowing where they are going.

Research across disciplines agrees on the heritability of intelligence, it even has been argued to be the most heritable of behavioural traits.[46] This genetic predisposition is then further supported by experiences in what psychologists call gene environment correlation. Just think about how many more hours of music the children of a concert pianist would have heard, how they would have met other musicians and sat at the piano themselves. So there is some truth in the saying that leaders are born and not made, but they need more. They need the right environment, to find their purpose and learn to become excellent communicators. I created the model below to summarize what I consider to be the makeup of great leaders.

The model below illustrates that the talents that leaders are mainly born with are material intelligence and abundant energy. What they learn on the way is their direction or purpose in life and how to communicate at a profound level that influences people.

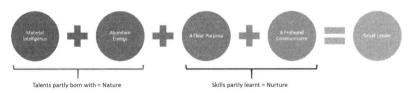

[46] (Mol Psychiatry. 2015 Feb; 20(1): 98–108. Published online 2014 Sep 16. doi: 10.1038/mp.2014.105 PMCID: PMC4270739 EMSID: EMS59747 PMID: 25224258 Genetics and intelligence differences: five special findings R Plomin1,* and I J Deary2,3)

Like a lot of things in life, few leaders score excellently in each of the four areas and like the flying carpet analogy, if one corner of the carpet is a bit ruffled, the carpet will still fly well. If two are a bit ruffled, you are starting to have serious flight problems and if three or more are ruffled, you will never get off the ground and should probably curtail your C-Suite ambitions. Steve Ballmer, who led Microsoft as their CEO from 2000 to 2014, is a corporate leader who clearly ticks all the four boxes. All you have to do is look at one of his presentations on YouTube and you will quickly see he has all the nature elements in place and is a profound communicator. In his case, the clear purpose was most likely a joint purpose with the founder of Microsoft, Bill Gates.

I did my MBA over 20 years ago now and what I had missed in the above model were two fundamental aspects I was just not aware of at the age of 26. You cannot run an organization, the government, a university or any other establishment if you don't fundamentally understand how it works – you have to have that breadth of understanding the officer element in CXO we talked about earlier gives you. People like to feel safe and to feel that way, it is essential that you have a competent leader. I always remember once going to a talk about the Arab uprisings in North Africa. It was explained to me that the uprisings were not Muslim uprisings but were instead uprisings against incompetent leadership. Libya, which was run by Colonel Gaddafi for 40 years after he led a successful revolution against King Idris I of the Senussi, was a textbook example with a relatively small population of approximately 7 million, significant oil reserves and a long coastline well located on the Mediterranean. It should have had schools, hospitals and universities on par with the best of Europe. Managed well, Libya could have been like Denmark and a beacon of what could be achieved. A competent leader without supporting people, their followers and powerful connections is not a leader, they are instead a lone voice amongst hundreds of lone voices.

So, I had missed the competence element, which finds its source in knowledge, and the people element, which finds its source in connections. Those two elements link closely with the profound ability to communicate and are each joined by different types of intelligence. The material intelligence in my first model can be broken down into three different elements – Intelligence Quotient (IQ), Emotional Quotient (EQ) and Political Quotient (PQ) and we know from science that these can be improved with training.

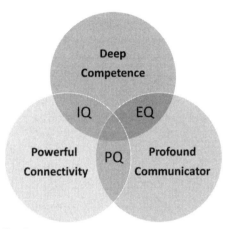

Copyright: John Jeffcock, 2020

The Deep Competence is based on knowledge and experience and has been covered already in the previous chapter (*see also* pp. 68–85), but we must remember that it is permanently evolving so we need to continuously update, challenge and retain this understanding. A 35-year-old chief marketing officer of a multinational financial services company expressed concern to her CEO that she did not have as much experience as some of her peers might have doing the same role in other competing organizations. The CEO responded by saying that old world marketing experience was not relevant today and that she had more new world marketing experience than anyone else he knew. So, he told her not to worry about it and to get back to delivering value. This is a good illustration of how knowledge can become redundant and how age is not always the best indicator of relevant experience.

The profound communication is something we can learn, go on courses to develop and be coached or mentored to improve on. It is a social skill that takes lots of practice and even the most senior of business leaders always practises. My sister was a personal assistant at one of the top global consultancies and she said that her boss who was managing partner always used to get nervous before speeches and go to the bathroom beforehand. After over ten years, she discovered that he went to the bathroom to practise his speeches – even leaver speeches, something he regularly did – and she said that the leaver speech he gave for her was amazing. In it, he said that if he had had a daughter, he would have wanted her to be like my sister. In terms of a compliment, you cannot get much better than that.

The powerful connectivity like knowledge builds over time and will be the focus for the latter half of this chapter, so for the moment let's look at the different types of intelligence quotas: Intelligence Quotient (IQ), Emotional Quotient (EQ) and Political Quotient (PQ). These are placed in the above diagram, where they are most prevalent but the brain is plastic and as a result, the measurement of each quotient will include elements of the other quotients.

IQ or Intelligence Quotient was coined in 1912 by the German psychologist William Stern for the term *Intelligenzquotient*. IQ does not measure knowledge and wisdom as most people think, instead, it measures quickness of mental comprehension or mental agility and is therefore particularly relevant in the speed you pick up knowledge and make connections. That is why in the diagram above it sits between Deep Competence and Powerful Connectivity.

EQ or Emotional Quotient was first mentioned in 1964 by the American psychologists Joel Robert Davitz and Michael Beldoch. EQ is the capability to recognize the emotions of others and manage your own behaviour accordingly. Therefore, EQ starts with self-awareness, then evolves into self-regulation or self-management. Having empathy for others is a key element and when you combine empathy with appropriate self-regulation and management, you get to social skill so business leaders need to be exceptional at self-regulation and adept at social skill, which can be more demanding than you might think. I used to work with a senior consultant who was incredibly empathetic, great at understanding others, adapting herself to the person and environment. But occasionally, she found the manipulation of herself to be that person exhausting and she used to call me up to get it off her chest. We had some very entertaining calls!

PQ or Political Quotient was coined in 2007 by the British author and social entrepreneur Jo Owen. PQ is not just about tact and courtesy, it is about understanding the power structure of the organization and how to plot your path through it. Owen advises people to use the system and not fight it, to work your way up to the top, from where you are more likely to be able to make changes. Once you understand the politics, which can be complicated even in smaller organizations, you can start to have greater influence and you need influence to get stuff done. This is not about being manipulative but rather utilizing the political environment to achieve the tasks at hand.

So, IQ is about understanding the workings of the organization and making the right connections, PQ is about operating successfully in that environment to get things done through influencing people and EQ enables you to understand and motivate the team and bring them with you on the journey.

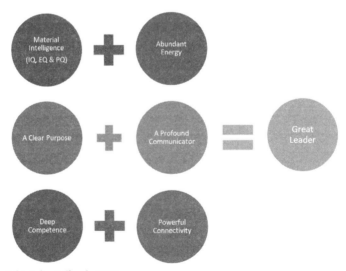

Copyright: John Jeffcock, 2020

If you combine these six elements together – intelligence, energy, purpose, communication, competence and connectivity – you have all the ingredients to make a great leader, as the above model illustrates. The trick is following the instructions well or having a career plan and then getting your timings right, and in timings, there is always an element of luck. As mentioned, some C-Suite executive teams have a one in, one out policy, so it may take some time before a space becomes available and you will need to be the right person at that point in time. And to have a career plan, we must start by looking at career options.

CAREER CHOICES

The careers advice from senior business leaders is to always keep learning and challenging yourself. And once you are at middle management stage, the advice is to broaden rather than deepen your knowledge and experience. This means that the way up may be to move sideways. A lateral move will give you experience and knowledge in a new area and will show the organization that you have the capability to be successful in different environments. As illustrated in the diagram below, this new area can be a similar role in a different organization or a different role in the same organization. The advantage of a lateral move is that because you have carried out a similar role before, you are likely to perform even better this time around and thereby improve your chances of a promotion. Both experiences also increase your knowledge and connectivity and as a result, make you more valuable and promotion-ready.

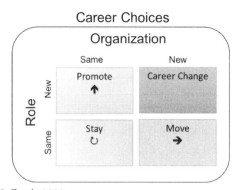

Copyright: John Jeffcock, 2020

I remember a former CEO of Barclays Bank explaining how he had turned down a pay rise and promotion within the retail bank to make a lateral move into the strategy department. At the time he felt that this would give him a broader view and experience of the bank. He was exactly right and whether he consciously or unconsciously realized the full importance of this move at the time is not important. What is important is that he added strategy to his already strong operational experience and this is important as when looking for new CEOs, executive search companies look for people with both operational and strategic capabilities: you can be stronger in one or the other, but you always need to have both. These strategic capabilities do not have to come from joining the strategy function, they can also come from mergers and acquisition experience, running the innovation labs or think tank, or running the research and product development operations. The key is to have both operational, today capabilities, and forward-looking tomorrow capabilities. Later, while still at Barclays, he turned down another promotion to opt instead for international experience in Africa, learning about different cultures, how to manage corruption and what it's like to be a leader from a different culture. On both occasions he felt that these decisions that were painful at the time would ultimately take his career further and now as CEO of another bank, he puts much of his success down to these lateral moves and says that they have paid back many times over.

As discussed in the previous chapter, we already know that being appointed to lead a team you were originally in can be challenging, but if you were to go and work in another area for a period of time and then return to your old team, taking up a leadership role can be much easier. So, your career rather than looking like a vertical trajectory may well resemble a ladder, with lateral moves leading to a promotion, then another lateral move leading to another promotion and so on, as illustrated in the model below. The key is to identify early on which roles you need to be moving into by what age so you can plan your moves and promotions accordingly. For example, in the automobile industry to get to the C-Suite you may need to be a country manager by the age of 35, so you need to review where those country opportunities may arise and make a lateral move so you are in the best position to be promoted into it. This is where an internal mentor may be able to help as they can give you advice about where the opportunities may arise, help you position yourself effectively and when the opportunity arises can act as an internal ambassador to help you secure the role.

Career Moves

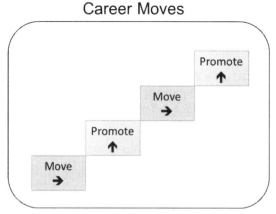

Copyright: John Jeffcock, 2020

In Chapter 1 (*see also* p. 54), we identified that 90 per cent of S&P CEOs had been promoted to CEO from line rather than staff management roles and we also talked about the gender implications of this. What this tells us is that boards and businesses value line experience over staff experience 90 per cent of the time. That is a massive difference and cannot be ignored in anyone's career or succession planning. Clearly, line not staff is the key to the CEO role. This illustrates the need for everyone to gain material line experience during their career so a key career move for a staff manager is likely to be a lateral move into line management.

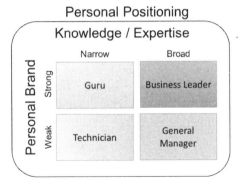

When looking at personally positioning yourself, there are two obvious routes to go down, one being the technical route where you become a guru in a particular area, have narrow expertise but great depth in it. The other route is to follow a general management route, where you have less depth in a specific area and instead build a broader expertise, as illustrated by the above model. The guru route is an equally admirable path to take but it is a staff route only and therefore limiting in terms of career. If your personal plan is to join the C-Suite executive, the guru route is a higher-risk route. When a gap appears in the C-Suite executive, if the knowledge and experience match your guru area, you may have a significant advantage over others. However, as you will have specialized the chance of the gap being in the area of your expertise is less likely and someone who has taken the general management approach may as a result have a better chance of a knowledge and experience match, albeit weaker than a guru in that area. The general manager route also takes into account the need to cover for multiple areas and as a result, the safety in technical knowledge is offset by the safety in management experience. In summary, a general management key acts as a master key and is more likely to fit the door to the C-Suite than a technical guru key, which is likely to open fewer doors.

This need for breadth and different experiences is well described in David Epstein's 2019 book, *Range: How Generalists Triumph in a Specialized World*. Epstein advises us to start our careers with sampling, doing lots of different things; this is how we find out what we are good at, most like and could be most successful at. For example, Roger Federer, the world record-holding Swiss tennis player who has to date won 20 Grand Slams, played many ball sports as a child and he puts his hand-eye co-ordination and success down to this. Many professional services get this right: for example, trainee lawyers are rotated through different legal practices to learn what a law firm does. At the same time the trainee lawyer and the firm can see what they are most adept at. So, diversity in training is important, allowing graduates to then specialize. Specialization, as Epstein explains in his book, works well in simple domains like chess or golf, a place where a single expertise may prevail for the long term but in complex environments like business breadth is key. Epstein explains that late specializers tend to be more common on the success tables than intense specialization, although the specializers tend to do well to begin with, as being great at their X gives them an early head start. However, in the long run, the generalist is more useful in C and O roles. How can you be expected to manage multiple areas if you have only ever specialized or worked in one? Epstein also supports the idea of lateral moves, saying that changing direction may be worth it. He admits it takes time to make the change and you may start slow, but the older you are, the more likely you are to be successful.

Automation is also more a threat to specialists than generalists as specialists have a narrow knowledge or skills source, these chunks of knowledge and skills are easier to automate as they can be captured and are often linear whereas generalists pull on many different knowledges and skills, assembling and reassembling chunks, and are therefore very complicated to automate. Generalists can also co-ordinate specialist chunks to win, but the leader must be a generalist. Imagine two people competing for the CEO role: one is a deep expert in one area, say manufacturing or accounting, you choose. The other is trained in many business areas, so who do you think would win? Why do you think that? Probably because a generalist does better in a variety of environments so it may be better in life to have four Master's degrees than one PHD in order to avoid cognitive entrenchment.

INTERNAL VS EXTERNAL

It is useful to look at the pros and cons of being an internal or external candidate through the prism of the Johari window. The Johari window is named after the psychologists Joseph Luft and Harrington Ingham, Johari being a combination of their first names, and it was created to help people understand their relationship with themselves and others. Johari's window looks at what you know and don't know about yourself and what others know and don't know about you. The idea being that the space where you know yourself and others know about you is safe space where you can talk about a range of things comfortably. You can enlarge that safe space through learning more about each other and the danger area is the space which is unknown to yourself and unknown to others.

A good way of illustrating this is, for example, if someone in a group shares personal knowledge about themselves that others would not otherwise have known. For example, if they were to say that 'We had our child through IVF.' This comment suddenly gives everyone permission to talk about IVF (In-Vitro Fertilization) and feel comfortable talking about it. So, a very private issue that might have been a dangerous sensitive issue to touch on is now okay to talk about, so the safe space has just grown. People increase the size of the safe space by taking a risk in conversations. Using the Johari window as a template to approach a company's knowledge of a candidate you can immediately see the knowledge pros and cons of being an internal or external candidate:

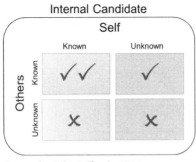 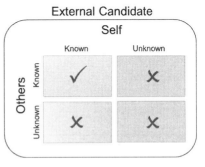

Copyright: John Jeffcock, 2020

As the left- and right-hand models illustrate, organizations will tend to know at least three times more about an internal candidate than an external one, so an internal candidate is always a safer bet if the two candidates are equal. The recruiting or promoting organization may assume that the external candidate is at least average in the Unknown areas and may even place their idealized version of what the perfect candidate would look like on the external candidate. As a result, if the internal candidate is weak, the external candidate – if on par – may have an advantage. Conversely, if the internal candidate is strong, the external candidate is more likely to be a benchmarking exercise than a real opportunity for them. So, if you have baggage in the organization that may damage your chances of promotion, it will be worth you considering a lateral external move to get a promotion as the other organization is unlikely even through references to be able to learn about your baggage. This means they will assume average performance or better and that may trump the internal candidate, if there is one. You may intuitively know this and have realized that some people move more often to escape their baggage. This is why some recruiters are naturally suspicious of people who move roles too frequently.

For higher-pressure or high-profile roles such as CEO, safety may be the overriding criteria. This was clearly illustrated during the height of the Covid-19 pandemic when many leadership roles whose terms had come to an end were extended to ensure continuity and to reduce further stress on the organization. At the same time, around a quarter of CEOs were replaced, as organizations need different CEOs for different phases of their journey. LinkedIn research on 12,000 CEOs who employed more than 50 people showed that 80 per cent had been externally recruited.[47] This indicates that smaller organizations who do not have succession planning in place are more likely to go external. Therefore, a jump down in size of organization may offer more C-Suite and CEO opportunities for tenured executives and equally ambitious executives in smaller organizations either need to grow with the company or will be promoted over.

I remember speaking with the executive search lead on the new Director-General of the BBC. She was looking for a new CEO who was particularly good at pulling teams together and creating a positive culture. The reason for this is that the previous Director-General had been brought in specifically to restructure the organization and to reduce costs. They had done a good job but restructuring director-generals are rarely good cultural and team builders and therefore they needed another person at the helm with a different skill set. When you are looking for a new CEO, the Board will be thinking rigorously about the job specification and will be asking themselves three questions that can be applied to most C-Suite roles, as follows:

- What are you specifically asking them to do?
- What specific skills might they need?
- What personal qualities would benefit the organization most at this time?

We look at the first 100 days for a CEO in Chapter 4 (*see also* pp. 186–189), where we will see that internal and external candidates may need to have different approaches to how they establish themselves in role. Internal candidates may look at symbolic actions to illustrate the change, show a freshness of approach, and will spend some time talking to people and learning how to do the job. For a period, internal promotions have 'permission to be a newbie again'. External candidates should also have a 100-day plan and may also choose to make symbolic actions. Symbolic actions for new CEOs and C-Suite executives can be very important and new CEOs can use them to establish a new direction or values. These can work exceptionally well but can also go wrong and create the wrong image that can be difficult and sometimes impossible to shake off. As they say, first impressions count.

Let me give you two opposing examples: the new CEOs of Lloyds of London and new CEO of BT (British Telecom). The new

CEO of Lloyds of London wanted to show a fresh start and arrived on his first day on a Harley-Davidson motorcycle, which he revved and then parked at the entrance. I do not need to tell you what the team thought of him and the descriptive language they used would not be appropriate for this book! On the flip side, the new CEO of BT arrived and on his first day he noticed a separate lift for managers that went to a separate managers' canteen and restaurant. Within an hour of walking through the front door, he had taped the lift closed and ordered the managers' canteen and restaurant to be closed. In doing so, he achieved a very different response and people knew positive changes were coming.

One of my favourite business leaders is David Lister, former chief information officer of National Grid, a FTSE 100 company with annual profits of around $3 billion. Why I am so impressed by him is because nine of his former direct reports have also become FTSE 100 chief information officers, which is an impressive legacy. So, what does he do when he arrives in a new role for the first time? The first thing he does is he conducts a review and decides on what the department needs to look like in five years' time. Once he knows that, he interviews the top 100 or so people in his department. What is interesting about his approach is that he does not care so much about their past, instead he is entirely focused on whether they fit with the five-year plan of the future. This means he cuts through internal politics and old power structures and gives some people a clean slate. He then makes the changes and implements a transition plan to ensure the right people are in place and know what they are doing. For him, the worst nightmare is being asked by your CEO, 'Why does my computer not work?', and he is keen to be perceived as the owner and deliverer of the IT strategy, not IT support. Therefore, the other thing he does is to recruit the best IT services lead he can find in the country in which he is working. He makes sure he has a brilliant second-in-command and he looks after that person.

External candidates have a steeper hill to climb in terms of establishing their reputations and the first few days can be very important. They need to understand the business model, how the organization makes money, who the key stakeholders are, how decisions get made and they also need to get to know and, like our friend at National Grid, sometimes need to make changes to their own top team. Internal networks can be incredibly important as they tell you what is going on and who to reach out to, to know what is going on or how to do something. This is obviously harder for people coming from external organization as these networks can take some time to develop and are not always easy to master. So, now let us look at the mastering of career and business networks.

CAREER & BUSINESS NETWORKING

INSEAD espouse that 'the alternative to networking is to fail', while Harvard thinks MBAs should cover it as – 'more business decisions occur over lunch and dinner than any other time'. Harvard Business School estimate that 65 to 85 per cent of jobs are found through networking and therefore commend students to spend 80 per cent of their search time doing this.[48] In China, they talk about 'Guanxi', and in the West, we use the term 'Social Capital' to denote the value of informal relationships. The UK newspaper *The Times* even published a list of the best networked people and in Hollywood there is a game where players challenge each other to find the shortest path between an actor and Hollywood megastar Kevin Bacon. However, networking without purpose is a waste of time.

Recently, a large financial Public Relations company took a call from a government department, who had lost a significant amount of personal financial information in the post. So, the PR wheels rolled, the communications team were crashed out to work through the weekend to be prepared for the media onslaught that would inevitably come the following Monday. At the same time the chief executive of the PR company picked up the phone and called the chairman of the mail company who had lost the package. He explained what had happened and asked the Chair

[48] https://www.alumni.hbs.edu/careers/connect-and-network/Pages/career-networking.aspx

for the name of his head of risk and permission to contact them. The Chair gave him the name and said, 'Give me five minutes and I will tell him to expect your call.' The CEO of the PR company called the Head of Risk and said, 'A package has been sent from this place to this place, it has fallen off a shelf somewhere,' and strongly suggested that he find it. Sure enough, within four hours the data was found, the crisis adverted and all the stakeholders thought the PR company CEO was a star. So, the question is, how did he know the Chair of the mail company, how did he get close enough for the Chair to ensure he picked up his call, amongst all the other priorities, late on a Friday afternoon?

The journey is a simple one of networking and social debt but the approach he took was slightly unique. Several years before the PR chief was offered a non-executive director (NED) role for a City club, which was remunerated but not by much. It was something that some people would have turned their noses up, but he jumped at the opportunity and said that he didn't want to be paid. What he did ask for though was for the club to host a breakfast for him of around 40 people once a quarter. The club quickly agreed as the people he would invite would be potential members of the club and the total cost would be less than the NED pay they had offered him. Then once a quarter, he would organize a breakfast, which he subtly branded and he invited to each breakfast every FTSE 100 chair every time.

He kindly invited me to one of these breakfasts, where the Head of the Secret Service was speaking, and it was astonishing to see who was turning up and the power in the room. One of those people was the Chair of the mail company, who through the breakfast was now slightly indebted to the PR chief. It is important to recognize at this point that he achieved this coup with an external, not an internal, network. Herminia Ibarra, Chaired Professor of Organizational Behaviour, INSEAD says, 'As a manager moves into a leadership role, his or her network must reorient itself externally and toward the future.'

Broadly speaking, most careers follow a similar trajectory: you start off as a junior executive or analyst, an X, move up to being a senior executive or manager, that is the C, and then become a partner and director, which is where the O starts. As you go up the organization, as illustrated by the diagram below, the number of people doing the same role tends to decrease and your network tends to increase, becoming more outward focused the more senior you become. We must also remember that the glass ceiling, as previously discussed at the close of Chapter 2 is between the C and the O and exists for a combination of reasons.

We started this chapter looking at the length of people's careers and how they may peak in their mid-fifties, with people probably joining the C-Suite executive just before or at around 50 years of age. If we put that in an age time frame, as illustrated by the model below, most people will spend their twenties learning their X, their thirties becoming a manager and learning about leadership, their C, and then in their forties, they should be building their O and this is where they get stuck:

20–30 years of age – learn your X
30–40 years of age – learn your C
40+ years of age – build your O

However, sometimes in life people present opportunities for you to leapfrog forward. The key is to recognize this and not let them pass. Such opportunities occur rarely and have a lot to do with good timing and luck. Like the man in the hotel who found the Chinese medical supplier, the PR chief who knew the Chair of the mailing company, you need to see and recognize the opportunity. This recognizing of opportunities is something serial entrepreneurs can be exceptional at.

My break was when a friend of mine suggested I meet a senior entrepreneurial chair. I agreed to meet him, invented a reason and went to meet him in his private office. He completely ignored my suggestion and started talking about another company which he chaired and in which he was an investor. To be honest, I only understood about half of what he was talking about. While he talked, he explained to me that he would be firing the CFO the following day and asked me whether I wanted to be the new CEO, so I just said 'yes', thinking in the back of my mind, 'I can always get myself out of this later.' I then put my MBA hat on and said that I wanted to meet the Board, visit the company and see the accountants, while still not understanding what the company actually did. Within a few months I had taken over the company and appointed someone else to be their CEO and appointed myself as deputy chair. The company was a network of chief information officers and that meeting ultimately enabled me to buy my first house and has led to me writing this book many years later. So, a big thank you to the investor, David Williams, and to Andrew Cumming, who made the introduction.

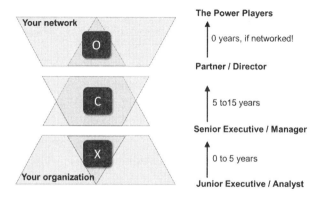

Your network or how you get along with people is an absolute key component of your career and we will now look at this in detail. In the end, it is a people thing so as Theodore Roosevelt, the youngest ever President of the US once said: 'The most important single ingredient in the formula of success is knowing how to get along with people.'

As illustrated in the diagram below, at the beginning of your career you network to learn from people with more experience, with different skill sets and from contemporaries in other organizations. You are continuously looking to build your own expertise, your X. So, your friends are the people in essential services, people in Human Resources, Marketing, Finance, Tech and all the support functions. Your clients are internal directors and partners, those you report directly to, and your role is to become your contemporary lighthouse. You don't have to be the brightest person from your school or university, instead you need to be the one who organizes a gang of friends to meet up regularly, who all joined the same sector or type of organization. In doing so, you learn what your contemporaries are learning and over time, you become a source of that learning and a lighthouse of knowledge for your contemporaries. If your contemporaries start to come to you for career advice, you know you are heading in the right direction.

	X	C	O
	Junior to Senior Exec	Partner Director	Business Leaders
Your Customers	Directors / Partners	Clients	Stakeholders
Your Friends	Essential Services	Leading Peers	Power Players
Your Role	Contemporary 'lighthouse'	Sector 'lighthouse'	Your 'brand'

As you move into management, your personal brand needs to be increasingly recognized by clients, your leading peers and the industry in which you operate. Your network externalizes and you start networking to improve your personal effectiveness and reputation, to get onto committees, take responsibility and win business. While building this influence, you still need to learn from others and this learning becomes increasingly focused on your role and specialism. Your friends should be the best people who do what you do and it is highly unlikely that they all work for your organization. It is like playing any sport: if you play with people at the top of their game, you will learn and develop faster and that is now what you need to do. As you get older, your personal commitments tend to grow and with that comes more bills, so you need to earn more and so does everyone else. So, the competition for roles gets fiercer and the people who fall behind are usually those who are slow to recognize this.

In senior management and as you enter the C-Suite executive, your personal brand should already be in place and you should have built relationships with the power players in your industry, related media, the City and Government. You need to be a deal maker or have assets and know people with both. You also need to understand how to leverage these external connections to benefit your organization and to have the will and skill to make it happen. And as mentioned earlier, you also need to know and be practiced in working with key stakeholders.

If you work in the field of marketing or advertising in the UK, there is a good chance you read a magazine called *Campaign*. As an executive or X, you would most likely subscribe and read the magazine and as you progress and become a successful partner, director or chief, you may well know the editor. Knowing the editor is good news – they cannot be seen to favour you but every other year, they may drop in an article about you, your organization or something you wrote. Most people see that as the pinnacle of their careers but there is a whole level above this and that is the O again. The question you should be asking yourself is who publishes *Campaign* and the answer is Haymarket Media, which is a well-known and respected publishing house. The next question is who owns Haymarket and you will find out that it is owned by the Heseltine family. Similarly, this book is being published by Bloomsbury, which was founded by Nigel Newton in 1986 with three other partners. O level executives will know the family and that makes a huge difference. In reality, the editor is in a position of influence and the owners hold genuine power, so we need to look in detail at the power players and who they are.

POWER PLAYERS

Power players know each other, not everyone but a healthy number of other power players. They are invited to the same occasions, are sat at the same tables, become genuine friends and many actively support each other. Tesla founder and internet entrepreneur Elon Musk says, 'Instead of baby showers, let's host business showers. When a friend starts a business, we all come together, congratulate them and bring resource for their business.' Power players can create power showers, turning on the taps to support a campaign or initiative. What can look like a deluge of unconnected people, supporting a worthy cause, may in fact be the WhatsApp group of a single power player creating a power shower. As power players are particularly alert to the important link between their reputations and their influence, they are more cautious in what they put their name to. These power showers are important as they act as a multiplier effects and their impact in turn becomes even greater. Sometimes we see this acted out in the media – for example, Marcus Rashford MBE, who plays football for Manchester United, campaigned for free school meals for children and to end child food poverty and many celebrities quickly moved to support him in his campaign.

This is the point when some people think networking starts to become manipulative but the truth is knowing people who hold legitimate power will help you achieve things. Apple founder Steve Jobs often spoke about 'What is your dent in the universe going to be' and that doesn't have to be corporate – in fact, you may have a far happier life if it is not corporate. You may decide that your dent in the universe is to be the best parent, a head teacher, someone who starts a charity or looks after a group of people or animals. It doesn't really matter: what matters is that you need to decide. You have limited time and senses and the eye for example is a hungry sense in terms of brain resource, so you need to focus it. If you know where you want to go, you will start to see the way there, not because of some mystical experience but because your brain will be tuned to pick up on things that will help you on the journey. Once you have decided on your path, which for many may take years to discover, you need to focus your networking as time is precious. Power players are key and you don't need to know all of them but you are likely to need to know some. Even if you decide that the corporate world is not for you and instead launch your own charity, you are probably going to need to have a launch party. Who is going to host that? Are you going to pay for a venue, or do you know a powerful person who can lend you a venue free of charge? So, understanding who these power players are and how they might be useful may be the difference between success and failure in achieving your dent in the universe.

Power players can be divided into four groups, which are the Owners' Club, Media Moguls, Leading Performers and the Ministers.

The Owners' Club has legitimate and reward power and it includes old and new money. If you want to know who sits in it, read the Sunday Times Rich List. The key to remember is that old money is passed on and each generation is considered a guardian of it for the next generation, so there is not a huge amount of flexibility in how they spend it. Often these people are burdened with big houses and expensive assets that take considerable investment to maintain so it is better to know new money and most of that is in the hands of entrepreneurs.

Wealth managers will say that they have lots of bankers as clients who have done extraordinarily well but their richest clients are nearly always people who have built and sold businesses. I have a friend who is a lawyer and when you ask him what he does, he explains that he spends most of his time working with untalented children, squabbling over money made by a very talented grandfather or mother. The grandparents were the new money and the great thing about money you made yourself is that you can spend it on anything you want. Family businesses sit between old and new money, as they were often founded by people now long dead and have taken several generations to build. There are exceptions, particularly with the digital giants in the

United States, but as the table below illustrates, the majority take
generations to build.

Rank	Company Name	Family Owner(s)	Country	Revenues 2018 US$ million
I	Walmart Inc.	Walton	United States	500,343.00
2	Volkswagen AG	Porsche and Piech	Germany	270,035.50
3	Berkshire Hathaway Inc.	Buffet	United States	247,537.00
4	Exor N.V.	Agnelli	Netherlands	163,012.40
5	Ford Motor Company	Ford	United States	160,338.00
6	Schwarz-Group	Schwarz	Germany	117,760.00
7	Cargill, Incorporated	Cargill	United States	114,695.00
8	Bayerische Motoren Werke AG	Quandt and Klatten	Germany	111,609.80
9	Tata Sons Private Ltd	Tata	India	110,700.00
10	Koch Industries, Inc.	Koch and Marshall	United States	110,000.00
11	ALDI Group	Albrecht and Heister	Germany	106,175.00
12	Comcast Corporation	Robert	United States	94,507.00

The World's Top 750 Family Businesses Ranking[49]

The Owners' Club also includes people who own a rare or unique
asset, like a vintage car or a collection of impressionist artists'
paintings, or a club or rare building – anything that others may

[49] https://www.famcap.com/the-worlds-750-biggest-family-businesses/

want. As in this case, it is the ownership of the asset that is their source of power.

The next group is the **Media Moguls**, who have legitimate and referent power and it includes people with followers, media stars and controllers. I live quite near to the Battersea Dogs & Cats Home. One of the oldest animal rescue centres in the UK, it moved to Battersea in 1871. The home exists between a couple of railway lines, behind which there was an acre or so of redundant land and the home wanted to make use of the land so that it could expand its good works. The land behind was managed by Transport for London and an innovative chair of the home managed to acquire the usage of the land for free, so how did they do it?

The first thing they did was to invite the property lead from Transport for London (TfL) for a free personal tour of the home, an invitation gladly accepted. This occurred in 2012 at the same time as the presenter and comedian Paul O'Grady was creating a seven-part series called 'Paul O'Grady: For the Love of Dogs' for ITV. The ambush was set and the introduction made. The TfL property lead was generously greeted and their personal tour commenced. As they travelled around the centre, they kept on bumping into the TV crew and each time the redundant land issue was raised. A little while later, land permission had been given and the power of the media had played its unsuspecting role in this.[50]

On social media they openly recognize this power and even call them by their power type, 'influencers'. They use platforms like Facebook, Instagram, TikTok, Twitter, WeChat, WhatsApp and YouTube. Social media influencers like Kylie Jenner, who has 118.5 million followers, can be paid as much as $1 million per Instagram post.[51] Singers, politicians and famous sports stars can all have huge social media followings, as can TV personalities such as Oprah Winfrey, news anchors and stars of TV series

---

[50] https://www.london.gov.uk/sites/default/files/public%3A/public%3A/PAWS/media_id_81753/battersea_dogs_report.pdf

[51] https://www.influencer.yrcharisma.com/highest-paid-influencers/

like *Game of Thrones*. In April 2021 on Twitter the former US President Barack Obama led with 130.3 million followers, closely followed by the singer Justin Bieber at 114.4 million and singer-songwriter Katy Perry with 110 million followers.[52] The group more regularly overlooked is the controllers and creatives, those who control what people see and hear – these are the King and Queen makers of today. The good news is that these people permanently need experts to talk about things on the news and they hold lists of such experts. So, you need to get on the lists and when they have the need, programme makers will call down the list until someone answers and hopefully that person will be you and that call may be a life-shaping event.

The third group of power players is the **Leading Performers**, who have legitimate and expert power, and this includes the Chiefs – the people who this book is about – the people in the C-Suite, who are the holders of significant power and budgets. Every Fortune and listed company C-Suite executive in the world sits in this group. Hopefully, this book can do its little bit in helping you enter the C-Suite to become a power player. Leading Performers also includes Nobel Prize Winners such as Malala Yousafzai, Al Gore and more controversial figures like Aung San Suu Kyi; Olympians such as Michael Phelps, Usain Bolt, Steve Redgrave and Nadia Comaneci; famous authors including JK Rowling and Paulo Coelho, and this list goes on. If they are the top person at what they do in your country, they are by definition a leading performer. In this group it is important to consider their personal assistants, who as we described earlier are the gatekeepers of power.

The final power player group and often the most criticized are what we call **The Ministers**. These people have legitimate and coercive power and include political and religious leaders, ruling classes and social orders and influential groups. All presidents, prime ministers and government department leaders, current and former, are powerful, whether or not you voted for them. This

---

[52] https://www.brandwatch.com/blog/most-twitter-followers/

does not include all politicians but does include all politicians of note – for example, Jacinda Ardern, the youngest female prime minister of New Zealand and Kamala Harris, the first female and first Asian-American and the first African-American Vice-President of the United States.

Alongside the politicians, you have the religious leaders of our time, such as the Dalai Lama and Pope Francis, but this extends to all their cardinals and more senior bishops. We still have class systems and 44 of the 200 or so nation states still have monarchs, even in republics such as Germany and the US, old families hold social status and their names can be brands in their own right. Alongside this you have social orders such as Nobel Prize Winners and the Order of St John, and influential and pressure groups such as the World Economic Forum, Extinction Rebellion and Greenpeace, and passionate champions of the environment, such as Greta Thunberg and Sir David Attenborough.

If you want to quickly test to see whether someone is a power player, check to see if they are listed in Wikipedia. Some power players are not listed but the majority are. The other more personal test is the dinner party test: if you sat next to them at dinner, would you tell a friend the following day? If you would, they hold influence over you. It may be small but you are more likely to do what they ask of you than others. So, the question is, how do you network into this group? The answer is the same answer to how do hedgehogs make love? – carefully!

NETWORKING WITH POWER

First, it is important to acknowledge that this will take some time and a minimum of five years. As by now, you have already decided on your direction, you need to start identifying people of power who can help you on your journey. One way of doing this is to jump forward five years and imagine yourself where you want to be. Have a good look around and think about who your new friends are, then look back and understand who would have been important to you on that journey. Start by writing down a list of the people or roles of power that you need to know. For example, one might be CEO of an institute, another a politician who sits on a relevant committee and another may be someone internal, who you never liked but have now realized you need to get on with. Try and limit the number to 12 people – this is called the Disciples Theory – and the idea is that we can probably only influence a maximum of 12 people at any one time. Once you have this list of people, you may also have a list of your stakeholders. Now write down next to each of them what you think they want from you, not what you want from them. What you want from them comes next, is less important and is the second column. The third and final column in your stakeholder table is your mini plan. For example, if you have not met them, how are you going to meet them? Are they speaking at a conference, a friend of a friend or are you going to start by approaching them direct on social media like LinkedIn? The good news is that whatever the media says, these people tend to be good, hardworking folk, trying to do what is right for the organizations they serve. That means they are always on the lookout for talent, deeply conscious of the need for diversity and always on the lookout for succession too. If you have never met them before and say they are a conference speaker, go up to them afterwards, introduce yourself and thank them for the great speech, then walk away. If you push a card on them at this moment, you will probably get a negative reaction.

Why you always look at what they want from you first is because in networking, your first aim is to create social debt – called 'reciprocity' – with them. Like the Chair of the mail company, you need to find a way to help them, so they in turn want to help you. This could be an invitation to an event, an interesting introduction or a snippet of knowledge that you think might help them. Once they have accepted this, they have started to be in your network.

A self-test to see whether they are in your network is how comfortable do you feel giving them a call? At one of the big four global accounting firms it is reported that some people have to bring their new contacts, a list of 12, to their appraisals. At their appraisal, the appraiser passes them a phone and says to call one as a test to see how real the list is. Not sure how true this story is, but it would certainly work as an approach. As you move along your life journey, your guides and stakeholders should change as your needs and ambitions evolve, so this is an area you should continually nurture. This is where rich kids have a potential advantage as they may be a child of a power player or will know the children of power players. Therefore, they have both access to the network and built-in reciprocity. Power players sometimes find it is politically easier to help the children of friends rather than their own as they are more likely to carry another name.

One of the problems you may face is being remembered and in being remembered, it is helpful to be somehow different, to have something about you that is unique or interesting. My unique thing is poetry – I have written one book of poetry and edited another and that makes me different. I know a tax director who also flies aeroplanes and that makes him different, an executive who fosters children from other families that need care and another executive who just wears particularly loud waistcoats. You may be funny, beautiful … again, it doesn't really matter, what you need to remember is that power players are approached by hundreds of people, find it hard to remember everyone, so need a trigger to remember you. My only advice is make it interesting and definitely non-commercial. If you are a purely commercial person, you might be pigeon-holed into the group of people who only care about money and that is not good or helpful in networking. If you have a friend in the communications industry, ask their advice on how you might increase your profile and this may well lead to extra learning for you, such as vocal or speech coaching.

So, to network with power players, first you need to start with a list, then start by helping them first and nurture and evolve your network regularly, and somehow find a way, a good way, of standing out from the crowd. Most importantly, power players all tend to be really interesting people, so stay curious and enjoy the journey!

Key Learnings from Chapter 3

Age & Career Planning

- Working life is rising from 40 to 60 years and individuals will need to find a balance between creating tangible and intangible assets, create a life journey plan and potentially use mentors as guides.
- Executive power peaks in your mid- to late-fifties, so this or a little before is the target age for your career planning and you can spend over a decade in the C-Suite. CEOs tend to be a few years older than their average team age and are in the role for eight years as opposed to the four to five years for C-Suite executives. There are sector and role differences but for career planning purposes, these are minimal.
- You need to spend your twenties learning your X, your thirties learning about leadership, your C, and then in your forties, building your O. However, if an opportunity arrives that enables you to leapfrog forward, take it. Opportunities like this are rare and may only happen once in your career.

Behaviour & Fit

- Learning how people think and behave at the top of business – and that includes etiquette – is important if you want to be considered for the C-Suite. Levelling the playing field with rich kids includes building a network fast, identifying people who can help you like personal ambassadors and mentors, looking to work for good managers and making sure that people know of your good work. Be humble and known.
- Leadership behaviours and business models are changing and that means your chosen area of ambition will not be the same in years to come. Therefore, to choose your area of ambition, you need to understand where your chosen area

is heading. For example, Marketing and Human Resources: is it becoming more personalized and data-heavy? You then need to adapt yourself accordingly or adapt your ambition.

- From university to the C-Suite, you have approximately 30 years and in those years you need to decide on your direction or ambition, make sure it is yours, not your parents, find an area that suits you or you are passionate about, learn how to become agile and resilient, know when to stick things out and when to move on, stay current and keep learning, gaining new experiences and building your CV. You need to have an external profile and represent and know your customers and how your business works in depth; you have got to be good with people and able to make mistakes and learn from them.

Leadership & Purpose

- If you are lucky enough to be born with a high intelligence and level of energy, you are en route to becoming a leader. Then you need to convert your ambition into purpose and learn to become a profound communicator. You also need to have a deep understanding of the area you are leading, you need to be competent and have the right people connections to make changes. These ingredients of natural and learnt attributes are partially enabled through your intelligent, emotional and political quotient.
- Once your purpose or dent in the universe is clear, you need to identify the power players who can help you and these will fall into four categories: the owners' club, media moguls, leading performers and the ministers.
- Think forward around five years, create a list of your top 12 stakeholders and start networking by helping them first – start the reciprocity process. Find and nurture something different about yourself so you can stand out from the crowd and make sure it is not commercial.

Breadth & Lateral Moves

- When choosing between a technical or a general management career route, remember that a general management route is more likely to get you into the C-Suite.
- Lateral moves give you more experience and connectivity and another opportunity to prove yourself. As a result, your career may look more like stairs, lateral move, promotion, lateral move promotion than a straight trajectory.
- Breadth of experience is more important than technical depth; ensure you have both operational business unit experience and forward-looking experience such as strategy, research and development or innovation. You need to be able to add value today and in the future.

Corporate Careers

- You need to start off being a contemporary lighthouse, then a sector lighthouse and then a brand in your own right. Over this time, your customers move from being internal to being clients to being stakeholders and your friends become increasingly powerful until they are power players.
- Internal candidates have an advantage over external – if they are on a par – but if you are the internal candidate and have negative baggage, it may be better to make a move as your baggage may act against you. If you move, it is effectively cleaned off your known CV, but moving too often will count against you.
- When applying for a new role you must know what is needed of you, what skills would be involved and what supporting qualities would be the best fit for the role.
- Enjoy the journey!

4

Chief Executive Officer (CEO)

'Stop dreaming and start being a CEO.'
John Jeffcock

As you will now already be aware, once in the C-Suite there is still further progression you can make. You can become more influential in the group and then there is the top role, the role of CEO – unquestionably the most powerful role in any organization. This chapter is focused on CEO leadership, the role of a CEO and how they create value. The role is tough and the lessons gleaned from it are useful for every senior business person regardless of role. The chapter starts by looking at the CXO methodology and its application, then looks at how to start in the CEO role and shares wisdom that pulls learnings from a wide range of mainly Fortune and FTSE CEOs, including FTSE 100 legends like Justin King, former CEO of Sainsbury's. There is also technical depth, looking at what works and how it can realistically be managed. It presents an enhanced version of leadership theorist John Adair's famous and enduring 'leader, team, task' model. Again, useful for all potential and existing business leaders, including CEOs who may want to reflect or reset their roles.

The CEO role is incredibly important as it is entirely linked to value creation for the stakeholders. If a company goes bankrupt and into administration, the Chief Financial Officer can always say that they did what they could to save the company but the strategy was wrong, the Chief Marketing Officer can say that they did amazing marketing but the product fulfilment was never good enough, the Chief HR Officer can excuse themselves by saying the leadership team was not competent enough or the wrong one was in place. However, the CEO has no excuses: they can be unlucky but ultimately, they are responsible and as a result, the level of personal responsibility and exposure is significantly higher than the other C-Suite roles. That is why many who get close to a CEO when they get into the C-Suite realize that they don't want the top job. They witness first-hand what the role of the CEO involves and decide that it's not for them. This is usually for a combination of reasons including personal capabilities, resilience and personal/family reasons.

The difference between the role of CEO and other C-Suite roles is often underestimated. This is well illustrated by a friend of mine, who was CFO of a large business park. He had been a good friend and trusted advisor to the CEO and they used to go out for lunch weekly at different restaurants in the business park. The CFO would often raise finance issues with the CEO, who never seemed quite as interested as the CFO thought he should be. Then one day for personal reasons, the CEO decided to step down and they began their search for a new CEO.

While the search was underway, the CFO was appointed interim CEO and he thought he'd take this opportunity to increase the awareness of finance in the organization. On his first day as interim CEO, he sat back in his new CEO chair, smiled to himself and took a deep breath before starting the day's work. Just as he leant forward, the phone rang and it was the site manager calling to say the main tower building was on fire. That day, he realized two things: first, the CEO role was different to what he thought it had been and that he was a very good CFO, wanted to stay as CFO and did not want to be a CEO. Everything you learn on your career path to being a CEO will have helped qualify you to be a CEO, but don't expect to be prepared for the role: truly understanding a CEO role is hard-earned through exposure.

The role of a CEO is broad and covers many aspects yet can be summarized in six words. As a lot of the governance books say, the role of a CEO is 'to create, propose and implement the strategy'. They create the strategy with input from many sources and support from the C-Suite executive and then make their proposals to the Board, who provide wise counsel and rigour in the process. Then comes the 'executive' part of their role, the implementation of the strategy. They are called the Chief Executive Officer as the majority of their role is focused on strategy execution. The word 'executive' comes from the Latin *Executivus*, which means to carry out and accomplish so the Chief Executive is a person of action, the centre of organization decision making and is responsible for achieving the strategy. This is easy to say, but rarely as easy to achieve in practice.

THE CEO AND THE CXO METHOD

So, how does the CEO role fit into the CXO model? This is simple, with an important nuance: the CFO, CMO, CHRO and all the other C-Suite roles report into the C or Chief element of the CEO as the CEO is the Chief of the C-Suite, and through the C-Suite, the Chief of the entire organization. Execution is the CEO's expertise and the main focus of their role is to execute the strategy – or is it? Now we need to stop here for a moment and take stock. Remember, strategy is aligned to the purpose of the organization and the execution of the strategy is to create value for the stakeholders in line with the purpose. This is important because in the same way as management thinker Peter Drucker famously said that 'culture eats strategy for breakfast' so does 'purpose trump strategy'. So, the purpose of a CEO is to achieve the purpose of the organization and the strategic execution is the means through which they achieve this. As a leader, the CEO will need to regularly remind themselves, their team and organization of their purpose and keep tweaking the strategy to ensure alignment.

There is the now legendary story of President John F. Kennedy visiting the NASA headquarters in 1961. While touring the facility, he introduced himself to a janitor who was mopping the floor and asked what he did at NASA. The janitor replied, 'I'm helping put a man on the moon!' Purpose gives everyone in the organization a guiding direction for everything they do and every decision they make, all those decisions and actions collectively have a significant impact. The O for a CEO is not about adding value across the organization as it is for the rest of the C-Suite, as this is covered by the E of executive, the O for a CEO is all about external stakeholders and influences. External stakeholders, as indicated earlier, are likely to include shareholders, investors, customers, bankers, suppliers, society, environment and even lobbying groups. As a result, CEOs will spend much of their time externally facing. In Chapter 2, we talked about knowledge and the importance of stakeholders (*see also* pp. 68–112) and this is where the CEO is front and centre and the lead actor, alongside the Chair, whose role we shall look at later in this chapter.

So, for a CEO, the C is for running the C-Suite to which they hold the keys, the E is for executing the strategy to achieve the purpose and the O is for representing the organization to all interested parties.

UNDERSTANDING THE ENVIRONMENT

As a former infantry officer, the key thing to know before launching any form of initiative was to understand the ground you were about to cover. You start by analysing the purpose of the initiative and by reviewing the resources you have at hand, then look at the ground, asking yourself where is the dead ground you can move through unnoticed, where are the vantage points from which you can dominate ground and where is the enemy most likely to be and what traps or obstacles are they likely to have put in your path.

Similarly, in business before taking up the role of CEO, you need to understand what the lay of the land looks like today and what it may look like in the future. You need to know what the board, Chair and stakeholders want, to have a view of the top team you will be inheriting and understand the organization as a whole. You also need a clear understanding of the external environment. So, let's start outside in and look at the external environment first.

The first thing to consider is that although a focus on process and product improvement is important, the unpredictability of the external environment means that adaptability, innovation and disruption are now more important. Wyndham Worldwide is the biggest hotel chain in the world by the number of hotels, operating in nearly 95 countries, with 8,900 hotels and 797,000 rooms.[53] It can trace its origins back to 1990 but in 2019, Wyndham Hotels had revenues of $2.05 billion[54] half Airbnb's $4.81 billion,[55] a company created in 2012, that can boast 5 million places to stay in 191 countries, twice as many as Wyndham. So, why did the CEO of Wyndham not build an Airbnb equivalent? Probably for the same reason that Mattel, Inc. – who own Barbie – didn't build Bratz, or for the same reason the UK accounting software giant Sage did not buy Xero, its New Zealand challenger brand. Maybe they were all too inward-looking, trying to improve their own business model or focusing on other areas while not recognizing the existential threat on the horizon.

Public Interest & the Media

The second thing to consider is whether there is a public interest in the organization and what it does. This is important as public interest has an impact on the media and government interest, and if you or the organization are of interest, it may be the biggest factor in shaping the CEO's role. A quick test is, if the organization failed under your watch as CEO, would the media report on it? The scale of how much you would expect them to report is likely to be the scale of public interest you should expect. I remember talking to the Chair of the UK tax authority, which is a significant role but usually low-profile and few would know

---

[53] https://corporate.wyndhamhotels.com/news-media/media-fact-sheet/

[54] https://www.macrotrends.net/stocks/charts/WH/wyndham-hotels-resorts/revenue

[55] https://craft.co/airbnb/revenue

the name of the Chair or CEO. He took up the role soon after the 2007 credit crunch and a government representative advised him to look at the escalating national debt and explained that it would make tax a top priority for government for many years to come. If tax was going to be a priority, the tax authority would become much higher-profile and the media attention would be relentless, the two people in the firing line being the CEO and the Chair. Historically, printed media news cycles were 24 hours. Google Trends now reports that top media stories trend for around seven days[56] and major geopolitical stories such as the Trump–Biden election of 2020 trended for longer.

Sector & Competitive Advantage
Soon-to-be-appointed CEOs also need to understand the sector, whether it is growing or restructuring, and where the organization is. Is it a pioneer, a specialist, a unique or tired brand, a disruptor or laggard, and where is it on its lifecycle? Is it in a growth or reduction phase? Is it time to leverage its brand or assets, a time to focus or a time to turnaround existing operations? Is it a good fit with the market, how sticky are its customers and how fierce is the competition? The brutal truth, as we will look at later, is that CEOs have a shelf life after which their energy and ideas tend to wither. Five to ten years being the norm, with five years being short to achieve significant change. This means any prior preparation CEOs can do, so they can hit the ground running when they start, is hugely important. Boards recognize this, which is why out-of-sector appointments in large organizations are rare and internal appointments are again favoured.

Part of the role of the Board is to help the CEO understand what it and the stakeholders want, so they have an educational role. However, on occasion the Board is not able to do this because they are not the right board.

When a potential CEO of TT Electronics plc, a global manufacturer of electronic components, was being interviewed,

---

[56] https://www.newslifespan.com/

the Chair asked what he would like to see happen if he was to take up the CEO role. The potential CEO boldly replied that he would not accept the role unless the entire board resigned. Arguably a high-risk approach, asking his potential employer to resign. He then explained that TT Electronics had become a global supply chain organization and no one on the Board had any global supply chain experience. The Chair reflected, discussed with the other board members and they admirably agreed with him. So, all the Board stood down and the Chair remained in the role for a short period while the new board directors were brought up to speed and then he in turn stood down. The CEO took the appointment and the share price went up. In this and all cases, the Board needs to be clear about the framework in which the CEO should operate and collectively, the Board and CEO need to get the Board and the C-Suite executives focused on the same goals. This approach avoids unnecessary future potential conflicts and can be achieved through things like strategy away days.

C-Suite Maturity

The maturity of the top team, the C-Suite executive, is important as again this changes the role of the CEO. Using the Tuckman[57] stages of team development – Forming, Norming, Storming, Performing and Adjourning – is useful. During the team Forming phase, the CEO needs to be a director; during the Storming stage, a coach; during the Norming stage, a participant and during the Performing stage, a steward. If board directors or C-Suite executives are behind the curve, what can be done to bring them up to speed? Similarly, it is important to remember that the Board is the CEO's line manager. If the CEO gets too big for their boots, they need to be reined in. So again, how a CEO behaves has to flex to meet and be successful in the environment in which they operate.

[57] https://en.wikipedia.org/wiki/Tuckman's_stages_of_group_development

If a change needs substantial action, the Board must assess whether the CEO is able and willing to make the changes. If not, it is probably easier for the Board to replace the CEO. Alternatively, the CEO may need more support in the form of mentoring, training or consultancy. CEOs who have problems with the Board are usually focused on themselves and not the strategy. Good CEOs share experiences with each other through their own private and external networks. CEOs need to think about how they are going to work with the Board and manage the relationship. Similarly, executives wanting to get into the C-Suite can benefit from a mentor and those within the C-Suite wanting the CEO role may benefit from a CEO or chair mentor.

Getting Started as CEO

The problem you have as a CEO is encapsulated by Justin King, former CEO, J. Sainsbury plc, when he said, 'The further you go up an organization, the less truthful feedback becomes.' For a CEO to make effective decisions, they must understand what both staff and customers really think. This is why most CEOs on joining a new organization spend their first 100 days visiting lots of places and talking to staff at all levels, customers in different segments and stakeholders and influencers. This internal people orientation should help ensure everyone buys into the CEO's proposed journey and the external customer orientation ensures it is real and sustainable.

CEOs are expensive and therefore have their own return on investment, so at the end of their first 100 days, they are expected to start implementing the way forward. If you can start this research phase before you start in the role, it can give you more time and/or enable you to start the implementation process earlier. This often includes significant people, operational or customer interventions and usually starts like all good change management with a clear vision of the future and a new sense of urgency without panic. Bill Gates, when chairman of Microsoft, is well known for reinforcing this urgency through comments like 'At any time, Microsoft is just two years away from bankruptcy.'

In 2005, Pierre Danon took over as COO of Capgemini, a French headquartered consultancy and tech firm with sales of around Euro 14 billion, and he was sent to the US to turn around what was an ailing organization. He had a view that professional services have to be growing or people start to walk. In 2005, Capgemini had 8,000 employees in the US and was making an annual loss of $150 million. As a result, the French were making incremental cost reductions on the US operation and this was building to become an American–French cultural clash. Danon had the advantage of being able to start his review in January and was not being formally appointed until March. What he found was that they had a great and happy client base and that the service being provided was good. In March, he took up the role and put in place what he called a significant cost reduction framework. What was interesting about this is that he did not tell his team how to do it but he did tell them what they needed to achieve and by when. He reduced the number of offices from 43 to 13 – nine was the original objective and there was a fight over the last four that ended up remaining. He also made every VP who was not client-facing redundant and that was about one in three. The astonishing fact is that he achieved this in three months and in June of the same year, Capgemini USA reached breakeven and in September, it reported its first quarterly profit. Danon had a view that cost reduction in people businesses needs to be fast or you lose your good people.

At a large Swiss bank, a new CEO came on board and gave a directive to reduce the risk, compliance and governance costs by 40 per cent. That seems a lot but after considerable initial push back, was achieved with no impact on the organization. Why? Because individuals typically grow up in an organization trying to grow their empire rather than improve performance and as a result, build in non-essential resource. Then when they get to the top team, their role changes to focus on reducing the size of empires as it focuses more on efficiency and performance of the business model.

So, how do we motivate them earlier to ensure efficiency and performance? Currently, all the financial benefits of efficiency are passed on to shareholders or to a cost reduction consultancy who are paid by a percentage of savings made. One way this could be done is through sharing the rewards of the savings made with the people who made them.

When Lee Kun-Hee took up the role of CEO of Samsung Electronics, he created a sense of urgency through stating that Samsung was suffering from 'terminal cancer'. He refocused on design, innovation and marketing, and spent over $100 million on educating management in the best business schools in the US and Europe. Justin King, CEO, Sainsbury's, warned investors, 'the level of profitability you have previously expected is not a realistic reflection of what this business is in a position to deliver'. Then he wrote to one million customers, of whom 250,000 replied. He also put together one of the best retailing teams and launched a campaign, 'Making Sainsbury's Great Again'.

CEOs often encourage their managers to do the same, to talk to customers. Mark Wilson, former CEO of Aviva plc, had a meeting of his top 300 executives at which he asked all those present to stand up and then he asked a series of questions. He asked everyone who had not seen a customer in the last six months to sit down – half the people sat down. He then went to three months, a month and finally, a week, at which point five people were left standing. A clear policy of Aviva's was to be customer-centric and this simple action highlighted the fact that the voice of the customer was not being listened to.

CEO Derailers

In Elena Botelho and Kim Powell's 2018 book, *The CEO Next Door: The 4 Behaviors That Transform Ordinary People Into World-Class Leaders*, they identify that most people who become CEO didn't plan to do so at an early stage, are not Ivy League graduates, some don't even have degrees and few have a flawless curriculum vitae, but they all tend to share four key behaviours that can be learnt. All CEOs are decisive, relentlessly reliable, adapt boldly and engage with stakeholders without shying away from conflict. The big derailers that knock CEOs off track in their early days are:

- Jumping to decisions too early;
- Doing nothing;
- Forgetting key relationships;
- Making it too complicated;
- Losing your personal balance;
- Losing touch with yourself (your humanity).

Source: Patrick Macdonald, Chair School for
CEOs & Institute of Directors

Lessons from Experienced CEOs

At the C-Suite networking company, Winmark, where I was CEO, we ran an annual event with our CEO network, 'What I wish I knew before I became CEO'. This was always a very popular event and we heard from CEOs from a variety of sectors, including retail, chemicals, financial services and real estate. The organizations ranged in size from several hundred employees to tens of thousands but the themes were often similar. These words of wisdom have been captured below under the CEO's CXO approach, but in this case we have changed the order from CXO to OXC as we need to start outside in, so it runs OEC, not CEO. Before sharing the wisdom under the OXC approach, we have summarized the key elements of the CEO role. As the CEO role is broad, multifaceted, complicated and widely impacted by the environment the organization finds itself in, summarizing the role into three clear and succinct areas is useful.

O for representing the organization
Within the O of CEO there are three main elements: external stakeholders, the Board and the purpose and strategy of the

organization. The O is mainly focused on the 'where' question, the organization's direction of travel, and as a result, it needs to include all the stakeholders, especially the Board, and include the key elements of establishing the destination.

The role of the CEO with all stakeholders is to rally them around a common purpose, the 'why?' question. To achieve this, the CEO needs to prioritize different stakeholders and proactively build relationships that can weather the most difficult of storms, as the CEO needs to know that they and the organization will be supported through good and the bad times. The CEO needs to commit to making a positive social impact that aligns to the purpose of the organization.

Similarly, with the Board, the CEO needs to develop positive, effective and forward-looking relationships with each board member. These relationships will undoubtedly extend beyond the boardroom meetings, are likely to be developed in business and social environments and will take into account the capabilities and connections of each board member. To align these stakeholders, the first task is to set the purpose of the organization and many would include as part of this process a vision and a mission statement, may be also a strapline, followed closely by some core objectives, a stretching five-year plan and a detailed one-year plan with initiatives that develop over years.

Leaving the planning aside for a moment, as that is covered in the E of CEO, let's focus on the purpose, vision and mission. Personally, I think that is too much. An old consultancy trick when visiting a client is to ask the receptionist as they enter the building what the vision statement is. If they don't know, the consultant uses this to tell the CEO that their organization is not aligned. So what should the receptionist tell them: the purpose, the vision, the mission statement or the company's strapline? Should employees be remembering all four or is it most likely they will be confused and remember none? Will your janitor be able to say, 'I'm helping put a man on the moon!' or will they remain quiet for fear of getting it wrong? My advice would be to keep it simple, have a good concise purpose that is also your strapline and one directional statement. Whether you call it your vision or mission statement is not really important, but it is good to have one. Once you have rallied the stakeholders, the Board, the C-Suite and the organization around your purpose and vision or mission statement, you have done well.

Now let's look at the words of wisdom of the CEOs who have gone before us and whose experience we can leverage to improve our own.

- Keep your friends close and your funders closer. Respect and listen to your funders but don't forget to balance financial success with delivering to your societal purpose.
- Know how to navigate local and national political systems. It takes time to master politics and governance, so invest in this area of self-learning. Appoint team members to interface with some stakeholders such as the regulators so you can become the point of escalation.
- Be media-savvy: Learn how to engage effectively with the media, ensure your team can do the same, train yourself and them or keep them out of sight. Practise the top team in crisis management, role play so when the inevitable happens, whether a cyber-attack or rogue employee, you are prepared and your stakeholders stay with you.
- Be consistent: communications are key, particularly internal. Communications focus on values, culture and alignment around a sustainable ethical purpose that will protect the organization and help it be a leader in its fields.
- Ensure you have time to connect within and outside the sector, do your own horizon scans and check your developing hypothesis with others, who will give you honest views.
- Engage your fiercest critics and listen to their fair and unfair messages, this will help understanding and

trust. Remember, feedback from happy customers
will not improve what you do, whereas feedback from
disappointed customers will teach you how to do things
better, so you need to talk with them.

- Lonely CEOs are lonely because they lock themselves
in their rooms and don't talk to people. Customers pay
your wages, employees do all the work, stakeholders
genuinely care, so go talk with them. The CEO must
always sit on the same side as the customer, know what
frontline staff are thinking and feeling, and should get
the organization to do the same. Running customer
and employee forums can help you keep your finger
on the pulse, clear out blockers and find good ideas
that work.

- Use evidence and multiple data sources – for example,
a global accountancy firm discovered a direct
relationship when tracked over time between employee
satisfaction measured by human resources, customer
satisfaction measured by the marketing department and
profitability measured by the finance department. But
treat the evidence as guidance and if your gut feeling
still says otherwise, trust it.

- Always be clear, transparent and honest, ensuring your
values are adhered to. Values should be communicated
and demonstrated relentlessly. Be prepared to stand up
against the Board and to be in the minority if they are not
aligned to the company values. If right, stick to your guns.
Create alignment with the Board, not power blocks, to get
things done.

- Observe cultural differences and accustom yourself to
different ways of doing business early on. Remember,
in the end you have to bring all stakeholders from all
cultures on the journey with you.

- Being popular will be important, particularly when we
look at capability planning. Being popular enables even

mature industries to attract the next generation, who look at the organization's ethics as they want to be proud of where they work.

E for Executing the Strategy
Now we have answered the 'Why and where?' question, we need to answer the 'How' question and this is where the detail and hard work really starts. We need more than five- and one-year plans as we need to bring them to life and make it happen. The CEO should set stretching and achievable objectives and will need to be able to explain why they are objectives and how they fit with the purpose of the organization and the strategic direction.

'The less objectives the better and three is ideal,' said Douglas McCormick, when he was CEO, WYG plc and CEOs would generally advise to not go over six, over ten being definitely too many. Once the objectives are agreed and in place, the CEO may make multiple bold moves to build energy and momentum behind the new focus and objectives. These moves reinforce the strategy and make the direction of travel clear to everyone.

The C-Suite will need to be a 'high-performing team' 100 per cent behind these moves, with no traitors or moaners in the group. They would have been instrumental in creating the objectives and supporting moves, and their diversity of skills and competencies should be aligned to the task at hand. On the journey, they will need to trust and respect each other and always feel free to speak their truth. For multisite and multinational organizations, the CEO may want to move the regular C-Suite meetings around to different offices to encourage a 'one organization' feeling. The C-Suite help the CEO and entire organization corral around the new future. The alignment model below may remind some of John Adair's Action-Centred Leadership model, which includes three core management responsibilities, achieving the task, managing the team or group and managing individuals.

Behind this sits the business model, the organization's core processes or platforms and the people themselves. The role of the CEO is to permanently test the business model, ensuring that it is fit for purpose, and then to identify and nurture the core processes or platforms until they are excellent and outperform those of the competition. It is about having the best business model, that has the best market fit and the best processes behind it. Making all this work is the people themselves and the CEO's role is to permanently strengthen the team and its teamwork, ensuring the very best people available are in the key roles and that the organization has a stable and mature pipeline for succession. The key output of these people is obviously their behaviours, skills and knowledge and resulting actions; the task of the CEO and C-Suite is to energize these, ensure a disciplined focus, the appropriate level of autonomy and the right rewards and recognitions. Or, as one chief HR officer once said to me, 'to ensure the right people are in the right roles doing the right things'. In summary, to execute the E, CEOs need to focus on three streams of activity:

Purpose: Strategy → Objectives → Tasks
Process: Core processes → Excellence → Performance
People: Values → Culture → Behaviours

So, what can we learn from seasoned CEOs on this, the execution element of the CEO's role? What drives the engine of your organization? This is what they say:

- Have a well-evidenced and clear purpose, a rigorous commitment to sticking to it and a small number of core objectives that enable it. When making decisions in line with the purpose, make the decision and do not hesitate because of the potential negative outcomes.
- Get the tough stuff out of the way early. Make the tough decisions, particularly the people ones, and demonstrate your values and standards.
- Make sure your personal ambition is aligned to the organization's purpose and ambitions, and don't accept the job if it is not. Work with the remuneration committee to ensure that this alignment is reflected in your remuneration. At HSBC, everyone has a 'behavioural conduct' element to their scorecard. This runs all the way through the organization and you need to score over a certain amount to qualify for your bonus.
- When the business is failing, don't kick it. Instead, create a positive future and lead people on that journey. When a business is arrogant, that is the time to kick it.
- Imagine your back is against the wall and you have to act now: what would you do? Do that now and you will be impressed by what can be achieved. It is not surprising that organizations often make the changes they want and need to only when under duress. Alternatively, if you are an outsider taking on a CEO role in a new organization, imagine you just bought the company – what would you

do with it? What would your plan be and what would you want to see happen in the next 100 days?

- Ensure customers buy in to the service or product, your purpose and ethical stance. It needs substance and depth and it should be easy to communicate to create loyalty in an increasingly fickle world.

- Remain agile and be prepared to make daily tactical adjustments to refine the strategy and achieve the purpose. But don't get lost in the detail or allow your diary to be overtaken by meetings of limited value.

- Look for the 'Velcro Effect' – what makes customers sticky, why should a customer come to you rather than a competitor. Never feel content, stay alert and keep testing the business model. Disruptors often appear when you least expect them: remember, recessions are the hotbeds of start-ups.

- Be prepared for systemic change, to evolve your business model, as advances in technology have broad and sweeping impacts and these need to be managed exceptionally well. Being the lead architect of these changes is a key CEO role.

- Tech-up and embrace technology before your competitors do and have a clear vision of the organization's technology future. Leveraging data and utilizing artificial intelligence (AI) is usually expensive and will inevitably lead to cultural change, which may be difficult to manage. Be real with people, engage them in the journey and be honest about its implementation and impact. Their worries will be real and personal. Remember that the tech side of a technology transformation is the easy part, the hard part is when it touches people and behaviours need to change.

- CEOs that moan about their organization should take a long good look at themselves because they are probably the problem.

- Adjust your tone and attire when engaging with different communities, such as investors and blue-collar workers, but always remain authentic. Find the person or persons stopping the organization from performing, then either train them or manage them out.

C for Running the C-Suite
Now we know 'why' we exist, our purpose, 'where' we are going, our strategic ambition and 'how' we are going to get there, the detailed strategic plan and execution. The final element is 'who', or as the children's game puts it, 'Who's on the boat and who's off the boat.' So, who are you taking with you on the journey and who is not invited?

I remember a new CEO in the Midlands who went into role and one of her first actions was to fire several senior people. They were all important client-facing people but none of them were abiding by company processes and they were all running independent chiefdoms, so her bold move was to jettison these people and seven years later, others still thanked her for doing this.

In the CEO network, we had a fascinating session called 'Managing Your Gorillas'. The gorillas tended to be male and 50-plus in age, and spent a lot of their time telling everyone how important they were. As a result, no one ever touched them. Over time, these people had become more and more independent and some had gone so rogue, they were impossible to turnaround. In the meeting, the former CEO of the largest law firm in the world, as it was at the time, confessed that he used to be a gorilla and no one dared touch him but he always found that when you fired a gorilla, the client impact was much less than you might have expected. So, one of the best things you can do as a new CEO is to jettison rogue employees and unprofitable business units. These two simple actions can free a huge amount of C-Suite and management time to focus on the stuff that works and fits with the organization's purpose and ambitions.

The immediate team to address will be your C-Suite, through whom the CEO leads the organization. But the 'who' may also include other key people in your ecosystem, such as a major supplier, a key investor or strategic partner, such as a bank or distributor. You need to decide who is on your boat and who you are taking with you. As Jim Collins, author of the 2001 bestseller, *Good to Great: Why Some Companies Make the Leap… and Others Don't*, puts it, 'Look, I don't really know where we should take this bus. But I know this much: If we get the right people on the bus, the right people in the right seats, and the wrong people off the bus, then we'll figure out how to take it someplace great.' He goes on to say that the old adage, 'People are your most important asset', turns out to be wrong – people are not your most important asset, the *right people* are. So, you begin with who should be in your C-Suite, rather than what, because if the C-Suite are part of deciding the direction, they will not need motivating to get behind it and if you need to change direction, they will be more adaptable as they joined because of the team, not the strategy.

Once your C-Suite is in place, encourage them to do the same reviews of their own teams and make sure that your and their succession is in place. As a C-Suite team, you will also need to decide on a common set of values, ethics and conventions, so people across the organization know what good behaviour looks like and can copy it. Sharing this across the organization may involve authentic storytelling and symbolic leadership that connects with the purpose and busts a few old beliefs.

Again, how do experienced CEOs capture these people elements? What is their wisdom?

- Surround yourself with the right people, trusted guards who will give you honest feedback on what to improve. Remember, the higher you are in an organization, the less truthful feedback becomes. A US General in Afghanistan, concerned that officers may only tell him good news, took his rank off his shoulders and asks for the truth in the first half of every meeting, however painful it may be, then puts it back on for the second half and says what will now happen.

- Remember, a team member who you wanted to leave, who should have been in performance management and who resigns is an opportunity to reinforce your culture missed. You must be in control of who joins and leaves the team.
- Be ready to depart with senior team members who are not willing to buy into the culture and strategy. Keep in the team those that reinforce the culture and put the company before themselves – for example, funding a staff party instead of a pay rise for themselves.
- Don't be afraid of paying for the best talent and make sure that the people around you are great at what they do; delegate to them or you will end up doing their job. In a mergers and acquisitions environment, a ruthless analysis of skills may be needed to decide who stays.
- Great CEOs have confidence and humility and saying 'I don't know' occasionally can be a powerful thing. When things go wrong, ask 'How did this happen?' not 'Why?' as that is looking for blame. Let them explain their role and when you are wrong, admit it, so they can also admit mistakes.
- Treasure diversity as diverse teams produce better outcomes and are more fun. Look for more than gender and ethnic diversity, include competencies, personalities and breadth of experience. Diversity breaks down silos (areas of the business that operate in isolation) and fosters cross-business solutions.
- Be able to name every member of staff, their partners and children – 'Know enough to care, care enough to know.' Demonstrate your loyalty through covering for them when things go wrong, so they in turn will have your back when you need it.
- Pull the whole organization together at least every six months and always thank people for their contributions at these sessions.
- Try the two-meeting rule to ensure buy in, float the idea or initiative past the team at the first meeting and close

down on agreement and implementation at the second
meeting.
- Never fill a vacancy with someone who is not amazing,
  recruit for the future. Ask the Mars question 'Could they
  be CEO one day?' and don't promote people on time
  served – 'If they are good enough, they are old enough.'
- Make better decisions than your competitors based on
  values, not finances. Don't accept consensus in the early
  stage of an idea, better decisions get made when they
  are challenged. Be prepared to take decisions without
  complete information. Foster inclusive discussion, achieve
  collective responsibility, but never confuse being a CEO
  with being democratic.
- Listen to people and ensure they are heard or they will go
  out and moan. Explain why decisions are taken to nullify
  their reasons to complain. Make yourself available to
  employees and their enquiries, have an 'open-door' policy
  and be real. Be visible, be seen walking the floors, visit
  sites and talk to people.

Help & Thanks

Every CEO will experience the role differently and as a result,
independent external trusted advisors and support like a coach or
mentor may be helpful from the start or during different phases
of the role. The Chair should help the CEO in identifying when
this type of support would be useful. The CEO role is broad and
as a result, it is unlikely that any new CEO will have experience
in all the areas they will need to oversee. Again, this is somewhere
personal external support may be useful to help develop a CEO.
Good learning, like joy, is usually the result of hard work and it
stays with you for a long time, whereas easy learning, like pleasure,
can be fleeting. There is a book called *Letters to a Young Poet*. It
is a collection of ten letters written by the famous Austrian poet
Rainer Maria Rilke to Franz Xaver Kappus, a 19-year-old officer
cadet. One letter that has always stayed with me is when Rilke

replies to the admiring Kappus, who had wished to be as wise as he was. Rilke's response is, 'And if there is one more thing that I must say to you, it is this: Don't think that the person who is trying to comfort you now lives untroubled among the simple and quiet words that sometimes give you much pleasure. His life has much trouble and sadness, and remains far behind yours. If it were otherwise, he would never have been able to find those words.' There is wisdom and comfort that can come from people with appropriate experience that it can be wise to tap into.

Remember, if you make it all the way to CEO in an organization many people will have helped you on your way. It is always important to acknowledge their help and to give back to others who may be following you on the journey. I remember once being at one of those inspirational talks at a law firm. They had a Paralympian talking about their journey and I remember clearly his very moving story. The Paralympian was a very promising young swimmer who developed cancer in his arm; it was spotted late and in the end his arm close to withered away. He gave up swimming, his dreams and would not go near a swimming pool. Slowly, he withdrew into himself. However, he was gradually persuaded by his friends and family to start swimming again and was immediately spotted by a Paralympic swimming coach. The coach invited him to take part in trials for the Paralympics selection. He refused, saying his competitive swimming was over. The coach persisted but he kept on refusing. The coach then persuaded him to at least come and have a look. What he witnessed was swimmers, many of whom had worse physical disabilities than himself, and they were all swimming, all competing, and all looked like they had a purpose in their lives – something he was missing.

He got back in the pool and started swimming again. Although he struggled to begin with, he was taught new techniques and once again rose to the top of his group. He competed at the London Olympics of 2012 and his hard work and resilience was recognized by an Olympic medal. To celebrate, he invited all the people who had helped him throughout his swimming career. Around 60 people helped him win that Olympic medal, one of whom was a middle-aged woman who had woken up early every day for months on end to unlock the swimming pool so he could train before it opened. He acknowledged that without her support, he would never had been able to train and would never have won the medal. He brought her up to the stage to a round of applause.

Once you have made it to the pinnacle of your career, you have a duty to recognize the help you received from others and in turn to help others on their journey.

Capability Planning & Talent Ecosystems

Traditionally, in most organizations there is a group of people who look at the leadership succession. This is either a dedicated human resources team and/or a nominations committee. These groups look at senior executive succession and their role is to ensure that in the event of change there is at worst, temporary cover and at best, a promotion-ready replacement. The numbers vary but usually there are two to three levels of succession planning.

The first level is focused on the CEO and C-Suite Executive, then behind that you may have a group of 20 to 30 people and behind that in large organizations, a group of several hundred. The idea is that you have immediate succession already in place, which mitigates the risk of planned and unplanned changes, and then after that, you have a healthy pipeline, looking at those who may be ready in three years' time. In the three years ahead group, you have what are known as 'stretch candidates', who are assessed based on their aptitude and historical performance. Each of these different groups are given extra development to help get them ready for the new leadership roles. However, succession is not always linear and what makes someone successful today is unlikely to be what tomorrow's company needs. Skills become out of date, job descriptions evolve and at worst, experience can sometimes breed overconfidence and resulting incompetence.

In the last chapter we talked about the 100-year life that the majority of people born today will now live (*see also* pp. 117–123). We mentioned that people might work a 60-year career, working until they are 80, and that their corporate career may peak in their late fifties. We talked about the building of tangible and intangible assets, the importance of lateral moves and how people need to stop thinking about linear careers and think more about life journeys. Similarly, ambitious executives need to start thinking about portfolio career development and life plans, organizations need to stop thinking about succession planning and start adopting capability planning. 'Resource Planning' that looked out around one budget year and filling current vacancies while building a talent pipeline was replaced by 'Succession Planning', which typically looks at one to three years and focuses on continuity and stable leadership whereas 'Capability Planning' looks out across three horizons, the immediate need and then mid- and long-term horizons. Because of this longer-term view, it needs to anticipate the business changes that will be necessary to flourish in evolving markets that we only have half an idea of today: what future capabilities will be needed and where and how can they be developed or sourced. This modern approach is not likely to be good news for your traditional loyal executive as it will be more difficult for them to accumulate the spectrum of capabilities needed for tomorrow's company.

The difficulties organizations face is to align strategic workforce planning with portfolio career expectations. Half of CEOs say that one of their biggest interventions was to move people around their organization more regularly. However, the truth is that a lot less than half of organizations actually do this. The barriers are numerous, ranging from personal resistance from people reluctant to change due to the cost of handovers and the courage of organizations to actually make it happen. Interestingly, many successful organizations have this built into their culture and as a result, suffer from much less internal resistance. Another issue you have with long-term succession planning is that the vast majority of millennials expect to change jobs every three years and as a result, over their careers they may have 15 to 20 different employers. Half of employers also privately admit that they do not have the right people and skills in place to succeed in a digital age. Research published by Dell Technologies in 2017 quoted experts that attended an Institute for the Future (IFF)[58] workshop, where it was estimated that around 85 per cent of the jobs that today's learners will be doing in 2030 (13 years later) haven't been invented yet. Although this figure is unlikely, it does illustrate why organizations need a capability plan in this environment, where people and skills like Lego blocks keep on moving.

STAFF ON DEMAND

To start with, organizations need to think about what they will look like in the future and what type of skills and capabilities will be necessary. They must consider when old skills will become redundant and where the new skills will come from and how will they be acquired. They will also need to look at how they embrace rather than resist external secondments to build experience, as well as revisiting their alumni networks – employees who change careers frequently may well return and they need to balance the alumni spend with the spend on graduate development and executive search. Alumni have the unique advantage of already knowing the organization and what it does and are therefore able to hit the ground running and potentially offer a greater return on their investment.

For example, Chief Digital Officers (CDOs) are creating what they call 'contingent resource' grouped into practices, good people they can call upon when they need it, people they trust, who in between working for them gain new experiences. These agile teams can assemble quickly and already know the business and how people work. Tech companies like Airbnb, Amazon, Netflix, Spotify and Uber call this approach 'Staff on Demand'. As an organization they would rather outsource tasks and bring in contractors as required, avoiding where possible a large, full-time workforce.

Organizations are moving to a smaller core workforce with a larger and more regularly accessed talent ecosystem (TE), as illustrated by the diagram below. In the diagram, the old world

[58] SR1940_IFTFforDellTechnologies_Human-Machine_070517_readerhigh-res.pdf

organization has mainly full-time executives (FTE) and a small group of part-time executives (PT) that may consist of consultants and contractors. In the new world, the number of full-time executives is under half the size but the total talent accessible is twice the size. Obviously, automation is playing a significant factor in reducing the fixed cost of FTE but the total cost of talent may not be decreasing as contractors can be expensive and may be used regularly. So, although there are cost benefits, these are not the main drivers for this approach. Instead, CEOs in the new world approach are looking for flexibility, resilience, specialist skills, ideas, innovation, speed of adaptation and many other factors that enable their organizations to be more agile, competitive and sustainable.

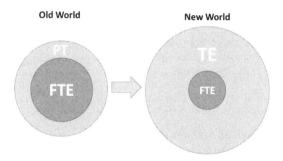

We may also find that although people may change more frequently, they may be staying in the same talent ecosystem and changing within the same small pool of organizations. Organizations will need to invest in, upskill and support line management so they are able to manage effectively in this more transient talent ecosystem. Like football teams, corporates will work with or develop their own talent scouts, who develop networks to identify people with potential to take on the bigger or key roles. Then there will be the brokers who use their knowledge of individuals and of future likely vacancies to suggest internal and external candidates, who may not be the obvious contenders. Organizations will also need loyal mentors and coaches who build relationships with high-potential individuals in their business area, meet with them regularly to discuss their aspirations, development opportunities and potential career moves.

What all this means for the executive wanting to be considered and to perform well in the C-Suite is that they need to have an external profile and to be connected into the evolving talent ecosystem. This connectivity should not be limited to recruitment and search companies, it will now need to include mentors and coaches, consultants, trusted advisors, networks, school and university alumni and key sector and power players. Their external profile should not be limited to LinkedIn; there needs to be articles demonstrating their capabilities and recognized awards that celebrate their achievements. In short, people who move around more need to be much better at marketing and selling themselves just to be considered. They also need to be highly skilful at learning and their ability to embed themselves into a new organization rapidly and add material value may also become a key point of hiring differentiation.

THE CEO & TENURE

In Casandra Frango's 2018 book *Crack the C-Suite Code: How Successful Leaders Make It to the Top*, she proposes that there are four routes to the corner office and these are the Tenured Executive, The Free Agent, The Leap Frog Leader and The Founder. Ignore the Founder route as anyone can start a company or organization and appoint themselves as CEO but much fewer are successful and even fewer ever make it past the $2 million revenue point. If you want to know how easy it is to register a new company, google it and you will find that in under three hours with less than $100 you can have your company up and running in many countries, including the UK, with you as the newly appointed CEO. Every start-up is launched this way, with a single or handful of founders and an idea but probably no clients.

I remember talking with the Chair of a large Anglo-American education company who explained to me that every company that ever existed had a single client to start with and for many, that first client is their venture capital. Then the role of the founder is to win more customers to dilute their dependency on their founding customer. The dilemma that founders often face is whether to be 'King' or 'Rich'. Those who want to be rich seek external finance earlier, tend to scale faster and put in place the talent or more specifically the leadership to build wealth. These are the real entrepreneurs of our time, who over their lifetime build multiple companies and leave when the time is right, cashing in as they go. The Kings or Queens enjoy the CEO title a little too much – in fact, they cherish it and as a result, can become the blocker to the company's growth. So, the idea is if you are a founder and want to be rich, you probably have to give up the CEO title and role and let someone else more suitable for that environment and point in time take up the reins. Many founders are experienced corporate executives who break away from their career trajectory to start up new businesses. Founding CEOs that are not seasoned executives may not always respond as a professional might expect, therefore being close to other C-Suite executives in these environments may be particularly useful.

Frango's Tenured Executive and The Free Agent routes are similar, both with experienced high-performing executives, except the Tenured Executive is internally recruited and the Free Agent externally recruited. So, The Free Agent is reminiscent of the lateral moves introduced in the previous chapter (*see also* pp. 151–153) and these moves can take many forms. For the reasons given in the previous chapter, we also already know that currently the majority of CEOs and C-Suite appointments are internal for good reason. In fact, the statistics are between two-thirds to four-fifths of all C-Suite appoints are internal. This presents a dilemma for someone now starting out in their executive career, because historical evidence tells us that tenure wins in the majority of cases against free agents but future research on millennials tells us that they as a group will move much more often. So, will Free Agents be in the majority at 2035 when the millennials start to take over the C-Suite? Will companies be able to offer the breadth of experience needed to be a modern CEO and will they be able to effectively manage the transitions in and out of the organizations?

The Leap Frog Leader[59] was proposed originally by Boston Consulting Group as someone who was elevated to be CEO from below the second layer of management. BCG gives Marissa Mayer (37) appointment of CEO of Yahoo!, Daniel Schwartz (33) to CEO of Burger King and Andrew Wilson (39) as CEO of Electronic Arts as examples. Leap Frog appointments tend to be most prevalent when the leadership or organization appears to have plateaued or is not making as much progress as the Chair, Board, investors or stakeholders want. An environment where the obvious successors are expected to deliver more of the same and that is not what is wanted.

History is littered with Leap Frog leaders, individuals picked from seemingly nowhere to lead their organizations and countries, because they were the right people at the right time or simply because of the recognition of a need for a new direction or vision. To be considered for Leap Frog opportunities, you need to have several things in place: you must have a clear vision of the future and people need to know that you have this, you need to have had that sizable line management and profit and loss responsibility, you need board experience almost inevitably of another organization and it is useful for you to be known to at least some of the stakeholders. Undoubtedly, at least some of the people you will leapfrog will be bitter or resistant to the appointment and ensuring management and stakeholder alignment will need to be a top priority on appointment. The talent scouts of good organizations focused on capability planning should have already spotted you and you should ensure you are already known to them. Your leap may fall short of the first hurdle if the leadership's advisors cannot reference you, but once in the role you are given a window of opportunity to make your name.

[59] https://www.bcg.com/publications/2014/people-organization-leadership-talent-leap frog-succession-a-new-trend-in-appointing-ceos

Fellow Spencer Stuart consultants conducted a review of The Best-Performing CEOs in the World through researching 747 S&P 500 chief executives. Their article 'The CEO Life Cycle' by James M. Citrin, Claudius A. Hildebrand and Robert J. Stark was published in the *Harvard Business Review* in 2019.[60] In their review, they identified five stages of the CEO value creation:

- *Year 1: The Honeymoon* – This is where the new CEO brings a new purpose and energy to the organization, aligning all the key stakeholders, the C-Suite Executive and organization. Also, it can too often be a period where too-higher expectations are placed on the CEO and the reality of the business environment is looked at through rose-tinted glasses.
- *Year 2: The Sophomore Slump* – This is when things have not progressed quite as fast as was hoped and the rose-tinted glasses have been removed. Stakeholders may move from supporters to critics and it is key for CEOs to minimize this dip as its perception will linger. This can be done by dampening expectations in the first year and by communicating honestly and consistently with stakeholders.
- *Years 3–5: The Recovery Phase* – This is when the new purpose from the honeymoon phase and the hard work of making it happen in Year 2 start to materialize in results. The hard slump second year will also have bonded the team and now the high-performing organization is showing what it can achieve. For some, the slump may last longer and for others, the recovery may come earlier and stakeholders will need to be managed accordingly.

Let's hold here for a moment and reflect on career planning and make one big assumption. Let's assume all career appointments follow a similar path to the CEO – they start with a honeymoon

[60] hbr_ceo_lifecycle_spencerstuart.pdf

period with great hopes of the new person, they then slump as the hard work of change takes place and expectations are recalibrated and then they recover as the hard work and new direction starts to show results. If millennials are changing role every two to three years, they are not fully entering the recovery phase and benefitting from its upside or are they bailing out too early? Earlier in this chapter, we talked about the Tuckman stages of team development: Forming, Norming, Storming, Performing and Adjourning (*see also* p. 185). This process can be quite rapid in a small team but for a whole organization or a business unit, it would take longer and although the team may be performing very well in Year 2, its results are not seen until later.

Remember, the Chair and Board has a huge impact on how the CEO personally feels on a daily basis. In an organization run well, generating a healthy profit, the CEO typically has good support from the Board. However, when things go wrong and profitability drops, a CEO has less freedom of choice, typically feels less able to take risks and support is less forthcoming. As a result, CEO personal confidence can drop, creativity stifles and they may need to reach out quickly for help.

The last Chair I spoke with said that the tenure of a CEO should be around five to eight years, so after the recovery phase has born its fruits. People normally say around seven years is ideal and many would cap the CEO's tenure at ten years. The team at Spencer Stuart consultants go on to say that there are two more phases:

- *Years 6–10: The Complacency Trap* – This is when the CEO is firmly ensconced and may pull his or her foot off the accelerator a bit, become a little less daring or may get too absorbed in external activities, such as talking at conferences and joining charity boards. They may also be held back from further necessary developments by a board that enjoys the success, is tired of the continuous change and rests on the phrase 'If it ain't broke, don't fix it.' In short, their energy and focus, whether board- or CEO-led, wanes or is distracted.

- I used to work with a FTSE 250 chair who sat on the board of a company which won Public Company of the Year. To my surprise, rather than celebrate he sold his stock and left the Board. Sometime later, he bought back into the company at one tenth of the price and then took the company back to its peak share price, making millions in the process. He explained to me that the leadership teams of public companies that start winning awards tend to sit back and lose grip and nearly always as a result fare less well than they could do. Maybe the Board and CEO get trapped in the 'King or Rich?' dilemma and move unconsciously from focusing their energy from wealth creation to self-promotion.

- The Board needs to ask itself the question, 'Has the CEO run out of momentum, do we need to make a painful change or do we need to back the CEO?' At Winmark, the C-Suite network company I had the honour to serve as CEO, we always encouraged C-Suite executives to take up non-executive director roles and to increase their profiles and helped many in doing this. However, have you ever wondered about all those senior executives on the 'speaker circuit' – you know, the ones that appear again and again – and wondered how they find time to do their roles? The truth is, so did we and now we both know that they are in the 'Complacency Trap' and arguably should be doing more for their own organizations.

- *Years 11–15: The Golden Years* – Not every CEO makes it to this period and those that do tend to be exceptional. As a result, you would expect good results. Long-term plans that initially might have failed and had to be reworked can flourish in later years. The CEO may run out of ideas but the organization may have them in abundance, so the CEOs that have longevity tend to be those that are best at harnessing their teams and keeping stakeholders on side. Incoming CEOs rarely admit that their early success is a result of benefitting from the work of their predecessors so it can sometimes be difficult to attribute the success of an organization. Succession after a long-tenure CEO can be difficult, so maybe it is better to let a new CEO benefit from the Golden Years of another.

Ultimately, the Chair decides with the Board when the CEO should go and when they should be supported and stay. In the US, where the CEO and Chair can be the same role, active stakeholders may take the place of the Chair in persuading the CEO that now is the time for them to be considering different options.

Chair of the Board

We started this book with an example of corporate governance gone wrong, a story of a too-powerful CEO and weak chair, the resulting problems and the impact of them that rippled dangerously on through the organization. The Chair and CEO relationship is critical to the success of the organization and their roles should be clearly defined and known from the very start. The relationship should be one of mutual respect, strong rapport and healthy questioning, tough but empathetic, and there may need to be an appointed adjudicator if the relationship starts to go astray. As organizations and environments evolve, the Chair, like the CEO, needs to adapt and respond effectively. For a chair to be effective, they need to understand the CEO role, the individual and the environment they operate in. Likewise, for a CEO to be effective, they need to understand the Chair role, the individual and the environment they operate in. The majority of the Chair's time will be spent on stakeholder management, running the board, supervising the CEO, being their counsel and helping the business manage external relationships.

There are many factors changing the Chair's environment and these vary from place to place. The frequency of environmental changes also appears to be on the rise and here we will use a FTSE 100 UK Listed company chair as an example. There are six primary environmental changes impacting the FTSE Chair's role and they are the Corporate Governance Code, scope of transparent reporting, erosion of trust, investor approaches, new stakeholders and engagement and social media and its speed. Each are explained briefly below:

1. **Corporate Governance Code:** In the UK, there are continuous changes to the UK Corporate Governance Code, as illustrated in the table below. A change on average occurs every two years and four months and more recently, this has become more frequent with a change every year and a half. This means that the current codes tend not to have the longevity, estimated to be around five years, to test their effectiveness before the next change.

Year	Report/Review	Year	Report/Review
1992	Cadbury Report	2010	The UK Corporate Governance Code
1995	Greenbury Report	2012	Boardroom Diversity
1998	Hampel Report	2014	Risk & Viability
1999	Turnbull Committee	2016	Audit Updates
2003	Higgs Review	2017	Comprehensive Code Review
2005	Revised Turnbull Guidance	2018	New UK Corporate Governance Code

This means that someone, most likely the Chair supported by the Chief Legal officer or Company Secretary, needs to adapt the governance of the organization to ensure ongoing compliance. The CEO needs to be conscious of these and understand the limitations and opportunities they may present.

2. **Scope of Transparent Reporting:** The breadth of areas that need to be reported on appears to be continuously increasing and may impact the competitiveness of

the organization. The scope already includes financial performance, pay and diversity and risk. The perennial issue of executive pay has expanded into the environment, the organization's carbon footprint and will increasingly be looking at the social impact of the organization. CEOs can help their chairs and company reputation through producing better data than their competition to satisfy demand without giving away too much. We have also seen a trend in the CFO picking up on the role of chief reporting officer, the consolidator of company information.

3. **Erosion of Trust:** Driven by politics and the media, there is a negative cycle of erosion of trust. Something at one of thousands of companies goes wrong, the media attacks and politicians then in turn respond as they want to be seen to be doing something, so another expensive review takes place, leading to new regulation. This political response can often damage years of good intelligent work on the interpretation and creation of new legislation or codes for short-term political gain. Instead, an understanding should be established that public companies will fail every year and that is an acceptable level of risk. In the meantime, the Chair and CEO need to ensure that they are on the same page, telling the same story, so the media cannot prize open gaps that do not exist.

4. **Investor Approaches:** Shareholders, shareholder forums and activists have asserted themselves more in recent years. Activists are more numerous and more diverse than they were in the past, both in their agendas and their methods. This can rub up against the societal demand for broader stakeholder engagement and reinforces the need for management, with the Board's oversight and guidance, to engage with shareholders proactively and to be prepared for friendly and confrontational activists. Boards need to have a stakeholder map and base their shareholder engagement strategies and long-term shareholder engagement on a thorough analysis of the motivations,

expected behaviours and rights of shareholders. For example, in the UK, a shareholder with 10 per cent of the equity or more has the right to demand a poll, at 25 per cent has the right to block resolutions and at 50 per cent has the right to block ordinary resolutions. It is also essential for the Chair, CEO and Board to consciously establish their roles in this potentially tricky area, where the Board has a dual role of representing shareholders and advising the CEO and C-Suite Executive.

5. **New Stakeholders & Engagement:** The traditional capitalist ownership model is changing from being a profit maximizer to a value maximizer with more holistic returns for a broader range of stakeholders, including society, the environment and political interest groups. Internally, employee equity, the full range of diversity and board representation are the most obvious examples of this, which all add to the task of the Chair in developing the Board into an effective body. Externally, you have the social and environmental impact of what the organization does and the resulting broader stakeholders. Even individuals with no direct stake in the organization can be very vocal antagonists via social media and in turn all need to be addressed. So, the time a Chair and potentially a CEO has to spend communicating to these different groups has risen significantly and appears to be still increasing.

6. **Social Media & Speed:** Social media demands or appears to demand immediate and very fast responses. In disasters and crisis situations the public response is live at around 30 seconds and corporates need a response framework like the example below:

15 mins	Acknowledgment of issue
30 mins	Confirming the issue, some detail and notification of a press conference
60 mins	Press conference
90 mins	The response

Normally, the press conference will have taken place and response started before the true facts are fully known and so this need for speed can lead to poor communications and decisions unless the board is already trained. As a result, boards need an increased level of preparedness for a wider variety of situations and tasks need to be pre-allocated, for example:

	Investors	Clients	Staff	Media
What they want	No surprises	Reassurance	Reassurance	A scoop
Who does it?	Chair	CEO & team	Line managers	Comms team

Their role is to deliver concise messages and reassurances, calmly and warmly reminding each stakeholder group of their value.

The governance knowledge, transparent reporting and sheer number of interested parties have all been increasing, while trust appears to have been decreasing. This means that boards, particularly the Chair and CEO, need to dedicate more time to governance, be better prepared for a wider variety of situations, be closer aligned than ever before and spend more time communicating and engaging with stakeholders. The list below of approaches a chair may take with support from the CEO is not exhaustive and is designed to enable them to operate in this dynamic and sometimes hostile-feeling environment.

- **Board Agenda & Time** – Chairs backed by the CEO need to be ruthless in managing the agenda, ensuring that value adding opportunities are not pushed out by compliance. It is about getting the right balance. What goes on the agenda is also a signal to the organization about what is important, so the CEO must have a say in this. Where possible, people should not be left waiting outside a boardroom and then have their time cut from 30 to 5 minutes. If this, for example, was the Health & Safety presentation, what message does that send? For chairs of privately held companies, their priorities are slightly different and this will impact priorities and therefore the allocation of time. For example, private equity firms are less interested in governance and tend to want either a narrow niche specialist or an experienced generalist. Private equity is after a chair who can help find buyers for exit, improve the exit price and act as a mediator between stakeholders, the CEO, management and investors. They are also after a chair who can act as a sounding board to the CEO, giving them an outside and sometimes consultant's view. They are after chairs who bring tangible value to the table and the skill of running an effective board meeting is low down on the investors' priority list of essential chair capabilities.

• **Task Delegation** – To help manage the workload and focus on important issues it can be appropriate to allocate to a committee, create a bespoke committee or delegate to the executive. If delegated, the Chair and CEO need to know everything is in place to have assurance that a good job is being done and that the committees have enough time to deal with their delegated work. A balance of trust, competencies, measures and priorities needs to be weighed up and no single solution will work for all organizations.

• **Risk Appetite & Cyber** – The Board needs to decide on what is right for their company and their environment. Where do you have zero tolerance and where do you need to take a more measured, risk-based approach for the organization? Cyber is like all risks in that its likeliness and impact will vary dramatically and resources should be allocated proportionally by the CEO, with guidance from the Board and Chair.

- **Fit for Purpose** – The question addressed earlier in this chapter is whether the CEO and Board is fit for purpose. They may have done a great job but that does not mean that they are the best people for the next five years. The CEO is appraised by the Chair, the Chair by the Senior Independent Director (SID) on an annual basis and the other non-executive directors (NEDs) by the Chair. Which places the Chair in a powerful place and illustrates the importance of the SID, who is not allowed to replace the Chair, which ensures their independence. Knowing when to stand down is often the most difficult of decisions and as a result, these conversations are often multiple and usually difficult as change is the only certainty.

- **Chair Influence** – Although chairs are not executives, they have a long shadow over the tone at the top and culture of the organization. This is one of the reasons why chairs enjoy their role so much. Chairs tend to find their roles more fulfilling because they have more influence, can set the agenda and thereby the priorities of the organization and as a result of this and the time spent with the organization, they are more involved than your average non-executive board member. In privately and Private Equity (PE) owned organizations, the line between executive and non-executive is more fluid because value creation is a priority over governance.

Chairs need absolute transparency and honesty from their CEOs, they hate surprises. They like CEOs who build legacies for the next generation and who play the long game and think about where the business will be in ten years' time.

Key Learnings from Chapter 4

The CEO Role

- The purpose of a CEO is to achieve the purpose of the organization and their role is 'to create, propose and implement the strategy'. The majority of their role being focused on strategy execution, thus the name chief *executive* officer.
- When applying the CXO method to a CEO, the C is for running the C-Suite to which they hold the keys, the E is for executing the strategy to achieve the purpose and the O is for representing the organization to all interested parties.
- The O of CEO is focused on getting the stakeholders rallied around a common purpose, the 'why' question and answering the 'where' question, your vision or mission. Achieving alignment of stakeholders on the answers to these simple questions is a significant accomplishment.
- E for executing the strategy and answering the 'how' question. Supported by detailed planning, the CEO should set few objectives and then make bold moves to achieve momentum and demonstrate the new direction of travel. The C-Suite should be aligned to this, detractors removed, the business model and core processes realigned and the right people should be in the right roles doing the right things.
- C for running the C-Suite and who is in the team. You will need to jettison rogue employees – the impact is often less than expected and the management time it saves is significant. Surround yourself with a group of great and honest, diverse people and be prepared to pay for them. Don't forget to thank those who helped you on your journey.

CEO Role & Time

- Before taking up the role of CEO, you need to understand what you are undertaking, where the organization is on its journey and in its market, the maturity of the organization and its key teams, what opportunity the future presents, the innovation and disruption landscape and whether the organization is of public interest. You then need to reflect honestly on whether you are the right person to be CEO at this point in time.
- As a new CEO you should spend your first 100 days learning and speaking with lots of people, in and outside the organization. This helps ensure the new direction is real and customer orientated. Many CEOs start their second 100 days with a state of the nation speech to all staff and stakeholders. This reality check is done to reset expectations and to try and avoid the Sophomore Slump (*see also* p. 209). Then the new direction comes, which should be clear and should come with a renewed sense of energy.
- Simultaneously, during their second 100 days, CEOs tend to focus on sorting out the governance and top team, corralling the new stakeholders and team around a common purpose, dropping baggage such as unprofitable business lines and aligning the cost base to ensure a profitable business.
- CEOs tend to have a honeymoon first year, a slump in the second as the strategy is executed and a recovery in the third to fifth years. After this, they or the Board may become distracted, complacent and lose their focus and energy for several years. Then if they survive they may be lucky enough to have a second wind after the ten-year point, where the more long-term initiatives start to bear fruit.

CEO Words of Wisdom

- Always be honest, stand up for the company values and engage with your most unhappy customers, your fiercest critics and keep your funders close. Master governance, the media, your data, while being adept to working with diversity.
- Imagine your back is against the wall and you are a new investor, what would you do? Ensure your processes, technology and customer attractiveness is always better than your competition. Remain agile to your environment, both internally and externally.
- Business leaders should stop stating their headcount as a measure of success and instead measure their talent ecosystem. Likewise, Human Resources should stop thinking full-time investment and start thinking talent ecosystem investment.
- Capability planning looking out over three horizons is key in winning the war for talent in a time of more frequent job changes. It includes moving people around the organization, catering for jobs that do not yet exist, employing talent scouts and having talent ecosystems, with many branches in touch with different capabilities.
- Executives on the move need to be fast learners, have great networks and a managed profile, so they can be found and put to use quickly. This on-the-move group currently represents around a fifth of the senior executive pool but is expected to at least double over the next 15 years. As a result, more senior executives are likely to be overtaken by external candidates leapfrogging ahead.
- If you want to leapfrog in an organization, have a clear vision of the future, find an environment and leadership that is stagnant and put your hand up as someone who can give a new focus and energy.

- The CEO and Chair relationship is key to the organization and needs to be healthy but not always easy. The Chair is ultimately the CEO's line manager and decides how long they stay for.
- The governance knowledge required, demand for transparent reporting and number of interested parties have been increasing, while trust appears to have been decreasing. This means that the Chair and CEO need to dedicate more time to governance, be better prepared for a wider variety of situations, be closer aligned than ever before and spend more time communicating and engaging with stakeholders.

5

World-Class & Future C-Suites

'Being your best, not an imposter'

John Jeffcock

This chapter is focused on how effective world-class C-Suites work and what future C-Suites may look like. It starts at a personal level and then looks at different types of organizations and some of the issues the C-Suite may face. Stakeholder and governance issues are addressed and then the focus is on how each C-Suite role is evolving.

VALUES & ATTRIBUTES

If you have been on the Institute of Management Development (IMD) Master of Business Administration (MBA) programme in Lausanne, Switzerland, you may well have been asked to write an essay about what happens on your 70th birthday. Do you wake up on your own or with a partner you love? Do you have children that ring you up and say they can't make it or have they already arrived? Are you living in the city, a leafy suburb or some remote hideaway? Do you have hope in abundance or is the weight of your regrets holding you down?

The reason they ask students to answer the question is to help them establish and confirm a set of values which can guide them through their life and take them to the place where they would like to be. Too many business leaders have prioritized work over their families too often and left behind fractured and unhappy families. Decision making can be much easier and faster if it comes from a clear values framework. Howard Schultz, CEO, Starbucks wanted to create 'a company with soul' so it was easy for him to decide that every employee working over 20 hours a week should get healthcare and that coffee growers should receive a fair price. He is reputed as saying 'compromise everything but your core values'. What is more important is that everyone at Starbucks bought into the company with the soul and values story and they have in turn passed it on to many other people, including me and now you. The economic decisions that Schultz made were not stressful decisions as they came from a values framework so having good personal values and living by them can make your life much easier.

When I give talks at business schools, I sometimes put forward a business scenario that tries to highlight the importance of values. The scenario is a real one that was shared with me by a board director who had been a site manager when the 2008 financial crisis hit. He had been running a site employing approximately 600 builders when he received a text message from headquarters, telling him to shut the site down. It would take about two months to shut down the site, cover the steel, etc., and he needed to hang onto the majority of staff for that period and each builder was on just one week's notice. So, the big management question is, when do you tell them?

I ask students to shout out what they think. Some try to be smart, others honest and others manipulative – the audience of students is always and inevitably split. I then tell them what the site manager did. He pulled everyone on the site together and told them immediately. He had the advantage that the other sites were closing down as well, so their options of moving on were limited, but more importantly, he told them because they all had families and families need to make plans if a major money earner is about to lose their job and a week's notice is not long enough. He then sat in the canteen for three hours, where they called him all sorts of names and he answered what questions he could. He said it felt like being continuously punched in the face by everyone but that is what a site manage does. And because he told them, they trusted him and the majority stayed to get the job done. Again, his decision was easier as it was based on values and it meant when things got better, the same people would work for him again.

Leo Tolstoy's 1877 novel *Anna Karenina* starts with the line, 'All happy families are alike; each unhappy family is unhappy in its own way.' Similarly, all great C-Suites look and feel the same and all dysfunctional C-Suites are dysfunctional in their own unique way. You already know what a great C-Suite looks like, most probably you just haven't written it down before. Think for a minute what was the best team you have ever been in, whether work or play. Take yourself back to that time and start to list down the attributes of that team. My guess is your list will be pretty similar to the one below:

- Collaborative;
- Committed;
- Fun;
- Innovative;
- Dynamic;
- Confident;
- Honest, had integrity;
- Diverse group of able people;
- Complementary skills;
- Challenging;
- Successful;
- Safe, had your back;
- Loyal, trusted everyone;
- Common purpose;
- Competent leader.

The above list was the result of asking a group of 12 business leaders exactly the same question but it could have been asked of any group of people, from head teachers to chefs, and the list is always similar. An attribute is a quality or characteristic that draws on a principle or type of behaviour, so much of the above list of attributes is underpinned by common values held by the individual team members. So, to build your world-class C-Suite, you need to first find the people with the right values and skills and then collectively, you need to create the above environment.

MATURITY & SIZE

Research by Booz & Company's Gary L. Neilson and Harvard Business School Professor Julie Wulf[61] shows that the number of C-Suite Executives has been slowly growing. In the 1980s, the number of C-Suite executives in Fortune 500 companies reporting to the CEO was around five and this has slowly risen to almost ten. Four out of five of these additional people are department leads, which is good news from the C-Suite roles that are not guaranteed a seat on top table, such as marketing, technology, legal and compliance, risk, communications, strategy, research and development and supply and procurement. Although as mentioned in Chapter 1 (*see also* pp. 35–43), in FTSE 100 companies, the number has settled at around eight direct reports, so nine if you were to include the CEO.

New CEOs in their honeymoon period as they learn more about the organization tend to have larger C-Suite executives and then over time they review and reduce the number of people as they are clearer on what is needed and who the real star performers are. Therefore, a new CEO presents an opportunity for new C-Suite vacancies but these may change over time. In unicorn companies – privately-held start-ups valued at over $1 billion – the C-Suite changes approximately three times every ten years as different teams lead the organization through different phases of growth. So, C-Suite teams may appear stable but the reality is that they flex and adapt regularly to the changing needs of the organization, environment and leadership. A successful C-Suite executive running a mature and effective C-Suite function may fall out of the C-Suite

---

[61] https://hbr.org/2012/04/how-many-direct-reports

as the CEO may have confidence that they are self-running and are not needed in the room whereas they may promote up into the C-Suite a key strategic area that needs a greater focus. Who a CEO decides sits in the C-Suite sends a very clear message to the organization. If, for example, Health & Safety has a seat, everyone in the organization knows that the CEO considers it important. CEOs when deciding who is on top table need to reflect back on their role to achieve the purpose of the organization and create and implement the strategy. Who therefore should be in the C-Suite and do each of the core objectives talked about in the previous chapter have an owner at the table? They also need to reflect on their own strengths and weaknesses and avoid micromanaging areas they know well and ensure areas where they are weaker have strong leads.

The former CFO of Standard Chartered Bank advised fellow CFOs to have the Strategy Department reporting into them as that gives them control of the future view of the organization and as a result, potentially significant influence. Equally, this could be seen as a landgrab to secure their role in the C-Suite and a landgrab may be a very sensible approach to keeping a seat at the table. In Chapter 1 (*see also* pp. 35–43), we identified 45 C-named roles, five of whom are in the C-Suite, with the remaining 40 reporting in. Now is the time to think about which ones should report in through you. The more strategically important they are, the more secure your seat at the table but maybe they also present a threat of leapfrogging out of your control into the C-Suite, thereby depowering your C-Suite role. So, the unusual dual roles we previously identified, such as being chief legal & procurement officer or chief HR & information officer, may enable the tenure of an individual in the C-Suite to be much longer, even if their role and title may change over time.

Chief legal officers or general counsels often have the additional role of company secretary, which means that they sit on many committees and may attend many meetings. This can help them be the eyes and ears for a CEO, gives them cross-organizational insights and positions them as a trusted advisor. However, if they are not adding value in the meetings they should consider their breadth and time and may want to refine it to the more important areas and deputize the less important ones. Alexia J. Maas, Senior Vice President, General Counsel at Volvo Financial Services, located in North Carolina, United States, describes her role as being a mile wide and an inch deep. She refers back to the time when the big accounting and law firms were merging and calling themselves multi-disciplinary practices or MDPs, saying that her role is to effectively lead a multi-disciplinary function. Her role went from legal and compliance to then include data and now cyber, so she has lawyers and techies from across the globe reporting to her. She enjoys this diversity of role and says it has breathed new life into her day.

CEOs are keen to ensure that their C-Suite continues to learn and stay fresh and as a result, as mentioned in Chapter 1 (*see also* p. 43), they often give them exposure to other functions, shadowing each other, being appointed as cover for each other and presenting each other's work to the Board or Company. Some CEOs go further than this and give their C-Suite executives specific initiatives to run, like a merger or a new geography and may even rotate their roles within the C-Suite – for example, making the Chief Marketing Officer (CMO) the Chief Financial Officer (CFO) for a year.

In Chapter 2 (*see also* pp. 75–78 & 99–100), we talked about department structure and maturity and this again has an impact on how the C-Suite is structured. A mature department means that the lead is freer to do other things, it is easier for the CXO to rotate and they are more able to take up other responsibilities whereas an immature department will need more management attention and therefore the lead may not get into the C-Suite until the department is sorted or may be too heavily involved to take on other commitments. For the decentralized organizations, like conglomerates or organizations with disbursed businesses, the C-Suite may be six or less people. The reason is that headquarters of organizations of this nature typically do not have day-to-day management involvement – they are hands-off and instead decide on where to invest time, money and resources.

Like a private equity house, they may convene people to aid cross-organization learning and co-operation, but they do not need to have CIOs or CMOs reporting into them as these roles are in the operating businesses. In organizations of this nature, a C-Suite executive in each business may be appointed as a lead across the group – for example, a CMO in one business may be appointed the lead across all businesses but typically, this is an influence rather than a line reporting role and their job, like the private equity house, is to convene, share and co-operate.

I remember once a very senior and established C-Suite executive and department head in the oil and gas industry, who was starting to think about what he should do next, coming up to me and asking if I knew anyone who worked in private equity. The question perplexed me, because I had assumed that everybody at his level would know a broad selection of financiers and the fact that he didn't and that he thought that I would be better networked in this space was obviously a compliment, but it also came as a surprise to me.

He had been in the C-Suite for over five years and the company had a beautifully designed floor of a city building, full of dining rooms with five-star catering. It had clearly never crossed his mind to utilize that to further his network, to host an event where he invited in his peers from their top accounts or invite in finance friends, who could bring a guest. This for me was a very real example of siloed thinking and a huge lost opportunity for him personally. We will come on to what your career may look like post C-Suite later, but for the moment it is worth thinking about stakeholders again and the impact of siloed thinking and behaviours.

Siloes & Bridges

Organizations that have siloes have parts of their business that are isolated from other parts of the organization and the customer. It is difficult to make judgements on whether one department or another is likely to be more siloed in their behaviour. This is because the behaviours of the department leader have such a material impact and a simple change in leader can turn a department from being open to closed or closed to open. Some say culture is what happens when the CEO leaves the room, so a good question to ask is how collegiate is your C-Suite when the CEO is not present?

Most board directors would happily verify that a significant C-Suite problem is that 'C-Suite Executives are not trained' and no one shows them how it all works together as most people, even CEOs, sometimes do not know. C-Suite executives can lose face by asking for guidance and as a result, assumed knowledge may not always exist and presents a hidden risk for the organization. For example, CFOs may complain about CHROs because they do not understand the tax implications of staff mobility, while CHROs may complain about the CFO as they do not understand the motivational impact of different remuneration approaches. Some say that the more technical a profession, the more likely they are to hang out with each other, have their own language and by fruition, the more likely they are to unconsciously create siloes. Creatives in a marketing department, for example, may find the techies in the IT department sometimes difficult to understand and the techies in turn may find the analysts in the finance department equally mysterious – the siloes arise when these difficulties become gaps.

Experience also indicates that organizations with large manufacturing basis or fast-moving consumer goods (FMCG) tend to be more siloed. The gap exists between the people who talk daily with lots of customers or work on a manufactory floor, with their counterparts who sit in offices. This is one of the reasons why new CEOs tend to always spend the first few months visiting shops and manufacturing plants and talking to customers: it gets them closer to the reality of how the business creates and delivers value. Interestingly, non-executive directors new into role typically follow a very similar process.

In Chapter 1 (*see also* pp. 35–38), our research showed that the departments represented most frequently in the C-Suite are finance, legal, human resources, technology and marketing or communications. So, a good question to ask might be how technical or broad is the qualifying training for each of these professions? Is a lawyer, for example, taught more management than an accountant or vice versa? To address this, I looked at the main qualifying courses on offer at their top respective institutes for each profession and simply counted the percentage of modules on their syllabus that were technical focused and the percentage more general management focused. There is a lot of snobbery between professions – which is better or harder, which is technically more useful, who adds more value to the organization or commands a better salary – but this research was not concerned with that.

What I discovered is illustrated in the diagram over the page, which visually demonstrates the depth and breadth of training. I discovered that lawyers and technologist have no management or broader business skills training in their qualifications at all. Therefore, lawyers and technologist have 100 per cent technical training. Accountants and marketing professionals are both 65 per cent technical and 35 per cent general management, while human resources experts are the broadest, with approximately 40 per cent of their training focused on general management and 60 per cent on technical. Cynics may say that those professions that benefit from broader management training do so because their skills area is less technical and they may or may not be right, but that is not the issue being addressed.

If we relate this back to our CXO model (*see also* pp. 64–73), we can safely say that lawyers and technologists start with a strong X and that may even enable them to command a better earlier salary. Graduate lawyers starting at the top law firms in the world command salaries of over $50,000 in their first year and software engineers starting at Google start on basics of over $100,000. However, does this strong X and weak broader management training, a weaker C, become a disadvantage to them compared to accountant, marketing and human resource professionals as their careers develop? Are they more likely to have knowledge holes when they become more senior and more likely to preside over siloed departments as they are less able to partner other business units effectively?

THE TECHNICAL DEPTH & BREADTH OF PROFESSIONAL QUALIFICATIONS

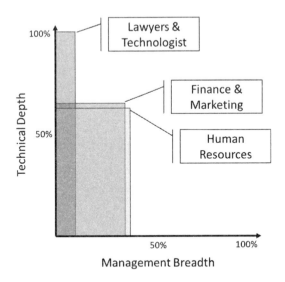

Management Breadth

Research by LinkedIn, looking at the background of 12,000 CEOs[62] who employ more than 50 people, partly reinforces and partly debunks this hypothesis. In order, the most common first degree of CEOs is computer science, followed by economics, business, banking & finance, electrical engineering and then accounting, followed by marketing. So, if you take out tech, the hypothesis would stand up, but the importance of tech today means that it trumps all other professions regardless. Using the same LinkedIn data source, the most common first job functions of CEOs were overwhelmingly business development and sales, once again followed by technology. Collectively, this would imply that we should all be advising our children to do a technology degree, start in business development and then gain their breadth through doing an MBA or equivalent broader management training.

[62] https://www.linkedin.com/business/talent/blog/talent-strategy/what-12000-ceos-have -in-common

The problem with siloes is that one rogue person in the C-Suite who is focused on building their silo and power base, or is just highly technical and not interested in other areas, tends to create another. As siloed individuals and areas do not respond well to communications, other business leaders and areas can withdraw from them – 'It's not worth the hassle' – and then the negative cycle of communication begins. Nearly all modern organizations require a collegiate culture to operate effectively and the less collegiate leaders who are creating siloes need to be removed or demoted. Good leaders build bridges to eliminate siloes and these bridges can take many different forms but may be categorized into two main groups, different business area experiences and business partnering.

I remember conducting research with a large professional service and the overriding question was, is it better to have your business development centralized and all doing things the same way with hard reporting lines, or to have your business development resource located with and embedded into the business units with dual reporting lines? What we discovered was that people who had grown up in a business unit could be centralized for long periods and still operate effectively. However, those who had business development experience but no experience of the business unit needed to be located with the business unit. But after a period of time, typically around three years, they tended to go native, be less adherent to central processes and needed to be recalled back into the central team. So, the answer to the question was that you need to rotate your business development resource in and out of the business units to ensure that they were central enough to follow central processes and local enough to tailor their activities to maximum impact. Similarly, different departments and business units can attach members of staff to different business areas and offices for temporary periods, so they can think central and act local. So, what they do is within the organization's agreed framework and also tailored effectively to the local need.

BUSINESS PARTNERING

We have already discussed the many ways that C-Suite executives can learn about their organizations and these methods can be equally applied to their own teams. Business partnering is another effective means of avoiding silos and joining up the business through creating multiple bridges. To start with, the department must have the data to understand what the internal client wants, be curious in its approach to uncover issues and have a genuine desire to help. With this in place, they can build partnership bridges in three key areas:

- **Shared Services & Portals** – This is where the day-to-day routine transactional part of the business takes place and is the area most open to automation. It is the bottom of the diamond-shaped department talked about in Chapter 2 (*see also* pp. 94–97) and typically, the first port of call for help. Portals can enable business units to reach into departments to access standard templates, contract agreements, guidance documents and automated advice. Currently, HR, Legal and Marketing all tend to have their own portals but in time, these are likely to merge into a single shared service portal that bridges all functions.
- **Centres of excellence** – This could be a social media product launch team, a legal contract negotiation team, a budget or business case training team or specialized HR advisors. These centres of excellence can be hosted internally and externally and can support new initiatives, instigate their own interventions and in many ways act as niche consulting businesses.
- **Business partners** – Every major and minor business unit needs to have an allocated business partner, a type of expert account manager who knows their business area well and how to get things done. These people work closely with the business units, act as bridges between business areas and can often mitigate potential

risks as they arise and provide interventions that enable the business units to perform better. They need to be mapped well onto the business unit, ensuring a good fit of skills and characters. Their job ultimately is to make the business unit they serve more successful and they can experience significant demands for their services.

Business partnering should be aligned to the organization's purpose, structure and objectives and is necessary when an organization follows a shared services approach. When combined with a collegiate leadership and a proactive approach to gaining broad experiences, including line and staff experiences, it is almost impossible for siloes to exist.

STAKEHOLDER RELATIONSHIPS

We have discussed stakeholders in every chapter of this book. In Chapter 1 (*see also* pp. 17–21), we identified the increased breadth of stakeholders and the impact of the new stakeholders on governance. In Chapter 2 (*see also* pp. 68–75), we looked at the knowledge gap between middle managers and C-Suite executives and identified stakeholder management and connectivity as one of the biggest gaps. In Chapter 3 (*see also* pp. 160–174), we looked at stakeholders in relation to career planning and in Chapter 4 (*see also* pp. 183 & 189–193), we talked about the CEO's role and stakeholders.

Once you have joined the C-Suite and have got through your first year and honeymoon period, you need to rethink who your key stakeholders are for your current role and should start to think about who will be important to you in the future. For your current role, they will be all the stakeholders previously identified, ranging from bankers to customers. However, you need to drill into this a little bit deeper. For example, you need to know who your key customers are and should know your counterparts at those customers well – at least well enough to call them up and chat about the last time you met. This may be a crucial inroad that may save or double the account one day.

When I was second-in-command of the northern cordon around Sarajevo during the 1992 to 1995 Bosnian War, at one point the formal UN and Serb relationships broke down. However, on the frontline we were working on, there was a bridge point: this was a small UN position of around five soldiers on a Serb frontline. Although a high-risk position, it gave the UN a back channel of communication direct with the Serbs and vice versa. In life, you need to create these bridge heads, strategic contacts that may be of material importance to the organization you serve. Which means you need to know someone senior at your regulators, at each key account, at your bank, at the asset managers and in each stakeholder group. Someone who, if things break down, you can approach and learn what can be done and someone who may be able to influence subtly or not the other camp. The power players we talked about in the network part of this book are usually exceptional at developing and accessing these people. However, if you do not already have the bridge point in place when the need appears, you need to create it quickly. A great example of this is the former Chief Financial Officer of the investment bank Schroders. I always remember him telling me that if he read something in the newspaper that could be important to Schroders, he would pick up the phone that morning and give his counterpart and fellow CFO a call. He concluded by saying that everybody at Schroders is in the sales team and that includes the C-Suite.

So, how do you physically do this and is this just another distraction that helps create the Complacency Trap? No, this is important: all C-Suite executives should be meeting a customer at least once a month face to face, you cannot build a relationship by email. These meetings and the people you are meeting become part of your strategic antennae and the information you gain may be material in many ways, some of which will be unexpected. I remember meeting one of our non-executive director network members once at a global firm of auditors. In passing, during the meeting the NED turned around to the Audit Partner and said, 'I hear you are pitching to Black & Decker, the $11 billion power tools company, tomorrow.' The Partner sat back in his chair with his mouth agape and said, 'How on earth do you know that?' The NED said, 'The guy you are pitching to is an old friend of mine and we had dinner last night.' He then gave the Audit Partner advice on what his potential client's major concerns were to help him win the pitch. This connectivity should also include the other stakeholders, such as the regulator, lobbying groups and bank, and once again, you should be meeting one of these every month. You should find the time to have one of these external meetings every other week. If you are heading into the C-Suite or moving on from it, this connectivity will help provide a lift to your promotions and a post C-Suite connection to other opportunities.

Lesley Titcomb CBE, a former regulator CEO at the School for CEOs, introduced me to a simple way of mapping your stakeholders: through classifying them according to their power over your organization or area and their interest in it. The model is an adaptation from similar account management approaches and is called the Power/Interest Grid. A further adaption of this is illustrated below and allows you to prioritize stakeholders:

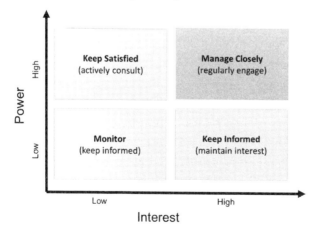

C-Suite antennae must also be innovation focused for their own area and for the sector in which their organization operates. Chief human resources officers, for example, must know what processes their department operates and how much can be automated, what data can be collected to improve performance and what the state-of-the-art looks like. The innovation leaps are likely to come from out of sector, so visit non-competing peers in other sectors and ask providers and consultancies to share their thinking and capabilities. Similarly, C-Suite executives should look at attending the disruptor forums and start-up and early-stage fundraising events. Silicon Valley Bank, the California based high-tech commercial bank, which has helped fund more than 30,000 start-ups, runs sector-based fundraising events like Biotech, Fintech, Proptech and Edtech. Typically, at each event, five start-ups and five early stage founders present their ideas and ask for funding from venture capital and private equity houses. You may be a potential investor, acquirer or even one of their first clients, either way you gain an insight into the type and direction of innovation in your sector.

Effective Governance

When I first drafted the contents of this book I had quite a comprehensive section planned for governance. As identified in Chapter 1 (*see also* pp. 16–25), governance is one of those 'boring, but important' issues because it can be critical to the success and reputation of the CEO and C-Suite. However, as the governance of organizations can vary considerably based on the type of organization and the rules and codes of the national jurisdiction in which it operates, diving into the details of what the numerous roles and responsibilities of different committees are seems inappropriate. Instead, I thought a better approach would be to pull out the key governance issues that boards considered to be really important as nearly all of these pertain to all organizations regardless of their governance structure or environment. However, the first point all boards make is that the CEO and C-Suite executive need to have read and absorbed the relevant codes and regulations for their organization and sector:

- **Purpose & MTPs** – Vision has been replaced by purpose and exponential organizations like unicorn companies need to have a Massive Transformative Purpose (MTP), a concept first captured by the Singularity University.[63] For example, Elon Musk, founder of Tesla and SpaceX, says that Tesla is not about making cars but rather about 'accelerating the world's transition to sustainable energy' and for SpaceX, it is about 'enabling people to live on other planets'. TED's MTP is 'ideas worth spreading', Google's is to 'organize the world's information' and Winmark's is to 'inspire the global C-Suite to create value for all'.
- **Board Frequency** – It is generally agreed that every board needs a strategy away day preceded by a social evening to allow people to get to know each other. Then there should be around eight board meetings, with six being too few and ten too many.
- **Time & Focus** – Meetings should take around four hours and the governance must flex to the business need and time must be spent on the key issues of the moment. This can be tested by asking at the end of each meeting whether the right amount of time was spent on each issue.
- **Speed vs. Rigour** – Many directors say in hindsight that we should have moved faster and things go wrong when they have not been thoughtful enough. This is the board dilemma, speed vs rigour in decision making, and this is also where cognitive bias may enter the room. Directors must be conscious of the risks and opportunities and take collective responsibility.
- **Planning & Dashboards** – The time of three-year budget plans has gone, most organizations are now moving

[63] https://su.org/about/

towards having a three- or five-year plan, a detailed one-year operating plan with supporting budgets and the appropriate measures. Reporting and connected dashboards have become real time and as a result, even one-year budgets are looked upon as flexible working plans.

- **Sub Committees** should be utilized to address material issues that would otherwise consume too much board time and should be given power to act. They typically meet quarterly or less and can be ongoing committees such as remuneration or risk or be pop-up committees to deal with material issues such as fraud, a cyber attack or major investment.

- **No Executives** – Once or twice a year, the Board should meet without the executives to talk about the Executive, the Board and future priorities and meetings.

- **Board packs** should always start with the objectives of that company or the business area presenting – this keeps them focused. The pack should include and start with the CEO paper, around six pages, focused on the organization's priorities and any major challenges, and should always start with the customer or people paper not the finance paper. After the customer metrics, people should be next, followed by trading and supply chain, technology, property, strategic projects and then finances last.

- **Board papers** should collectively be kept short by putting non-essential information in appendices. They should be concise – less is more – each area offering a one- to two-page summary, which is easy to read, highlighting the key issues. They should not be read out in the meeting, but rather brought to life asking for the decision or advice that is needed. It useful to have a single and secure place to access all board-relayed papers and organizations like Diligence and Board intelligence provide these.

- **Meeting Frequency** – Typically, meetings are more frequent for new teams as they get to know each other and for organizations going through transitions. As teams mature, the meetings may be more spaced, moving from weekly to monthly. In times of crisis, such as during Covid-19, teams may be meeting daily face to face or virtually.
- **Clean Decision Making** – Have an agreed proposer, an adjudicator and an allocated antagonist, who ensures that there is rigour in the proposed decision. Bring the red team concept into C-Suite meetings, where a group responds to a potential decision to test its viability and success as if they are the competition. Then once the good decision is made at the right time, even without all the information being available, ensure you have the capabilities to implement it and someone at the table is accountable for making it happen. When companies go wrong, it tends to be because of poor judgement, the decisions were not as good as they thought and they had unanticipated consequences. Decisions will also be judged by your successors, who may undo or improve them.
- **Diversity & Alignment** – You need diversity in people and alignment in values. In decision making, sometimes you need to go with the Board majority as you have collective and joint responsibility. If it goes wrong, you will go to court together. If your values are not aligned, you can end up with a toxic environment and the agreed values should be reflected throughout the organization and its supply chain.
- **Business for Good** – Issues like sustainability, stakeholders, the environment and business impact should be kept in the agenda and in the minds of all attendees. The Board should pretend that the regulator is in the room, the walls are transparent and everything said will eventually be known to the public, including

favoured stakeholders. Investors want to own a good
business.
- **Cognitive Bias** – Every member of the C-Suite and Board
  needs to be conscious of cognitive bias. This is where
  people or a group may deviate from a rational decision
  due to a bias that they may or may not be conscious of.
  There are many types of bias, including confirmation,
  conformity, authority, loss-aversion, false causality, action,
  self-serving, framing, ambiguity, bandwagon, projecting,
  anchoring, the halo effect and numerous others. Members
  of the Board and C-Suite need to know what these are, be
  able to recognize them and call them out when witnessing
  them first-hand.

What boards want from new C-Suite members is discussed in the
next chapter, C-Suite Musical Chairs, *see also* pp. 275–278.

THE FUTURE C-SUITE

The innovative forward-thinking CEOs of tomorrow are likely to
edge towards smaller C-Suites with fixed and rotating seats. Their
C-Suite will reflect closer the talent ecosystem of their organization,
as discussed in the previous chapter (*see also* pp. 204–206). Like
kings and politicians, their core group may be small, but they will
tap into the broader talent ecosystem to access people who can
successfully guide the organization to the next level. CEOs will
engage with special advisors, subject matter gurus and may include
them in the C-Suite. Today, we talk about around a third of the
C-Suite being line and two-thirds being staff; tomorrow, we may
talk about a third of the C-Suite rotating, with special advisors
included more frequently.

So, the question is, who will remain and what will their roles
look like? We now take a look at each of the typical C-Suite
roles and how they are evolving. This includes the COO, CFO,
CMO, CLO, CHRO, CDO and the two CIOs, information and
innovation.

Chief Operating Officer (COO)
Professor Nate Bennett of Georgia State University says that there are seven types of COO but he cannot tell you who the COO should be until he knows who the CEO is. The role of COO is significantly impacted by the needs of the CEO, the organization and evolving strategic priorities. As a result, the focus of COOs varies from managing staff leads, managing business units to managing a strategic priority.

Investors see COOs as people who get things done today, people who understand and excel at the execution of core processes and use their cross-organization influence to simplify, standardize and improve processes and infrastructure wherever possible. Their role being to minimize risk, optimize return on operations and adapt and transition seamlessly to changing operating models and environments.

To achieve this in an increasing complex environment, they need to deeply understand the value chain and business model, be able to unbundle processes, decentralize where appropriate and outsource non-core areas to free the company to focus on where it creates value. This can involve bringing the production process to the customer. For example, you can walk into a branch of Metro Bank and leave with a new bank account, your new card and cheque book printed and in hand as they are produced on site. A faster and better service, with no transport costs, ensuring local jobs and minimizing the environmental impact.

COOs are investigating a host of potential improvements, including shared digital portals for all C-Suite functions, a single gateway through which you can access all the organization's templates, policies and documents. They are also investigating virtual workplaces and meetings, enhanced collaboration and decision making, intrapreneurship, the internet of things, robotic warehousing systems and the use of blockchain to securely manage inventory and financial flows on their supply chains. All this in an environment where employees are increasingly wanting to enjoy 'hangout' spaces and work in flexible 'WeWork'-type environments.

However, tomorrow's COO should be looking to step away from the detailed operations of the business, putting in place a strong number two so that they can keep a close eye on the external environment and be more futurologist. Spending more time anticipating upcoming trends and developments, tech solutions and well-being, and focus on building the future business model and new work environment. They need to permanently re-examine the business model, have a close eye on the evolving competition and a clear understanding of the impact of decisions on society, their carbon footprint and the environment. Utilizing tools like integrated systems thinking that can create the new underlying plan and economic model, leveraging data and tech to build and support the purpose. The process needs to be closely managed, driving the future culture, collaborating internally to create the supporting plans, creating quick wins through existing people resources and triggering the necessary future infrastructure and talent investments.

Chief Financial Officer (CFO)

Almost every aspect of finance is being impacted by digital and the investment of the big four accounting firms into technology runs into billions of dollars. The impact scope is enormous and includes everything from the Digitalization of Tax (state direct access) and Foreign Exchange (decentralized currency trend) to crowdfunding and lending, to automated expenses, accounts and agile and dynamic planning, budgeting and forecasting. Invoices are now emailed, not posted, read by a machine, not a person, filed automatically and factored into automated payment schedules and cashflow forecasts. No one actually sees the invoice, which was probably created and mailed by a customer relationship management (CRM) system in the first place.

Simultaneously, finance departments have migrated to the cloud and regulators are pushing more responsibilities on to corporates, such as AML (anti-money laundering) compliance. As discussed in Chapter 2 (*see also* pp. 94–97), this has already started to reshape finance functions from the historical triangle to a more diamond shape and results in significant job losses and reskilling of teams. With finance departments like banks becoming tech businesses, there are two expected routes for the departments and CFO to take.

Deloitte's four faces of the CFO are strategist, catalyst, steward and operator. The control or stewardship area was historically linked to finance and the operator to efficiency, with the strategist and catalyst being common responsibilities or capabilities of all C-Suite executives. Based on the unique elements of control and efficiency, it is expected that the CFO and COO roles and their departments merge, shifting the finance function from being a driver of cost control to a creator of capital or the CFO also becomes the Chief Reporting Officer.

The digitalization of the workplace has enabled a merging of finance and operations, where the focus is on the current and future economic business model. This inward-facing C-Suite executive is responsible for ensuring the business model is as effective, relevant and sustainable as possible. So, CFOs may need to learn more about operations and COOs more about finance if they want to stay in the C-Suite. CFOs may also find that their COO counterpart would rather merge with the CIO and tech department than finance.

The Chief Reporting Officer or CRO route has already been underway for some time, with finance functions boosting their data analytics capabilities, but CFOs have kept their CFO titles even though their roles may have fundamentally changed.

CFOs have for some time been not just reporting on finance and their scope is likely to increase further to include customer, process, employee and environmental reporting. This centralization of reporting has many benefits, including:

1. **Strategic Focus** – It ensures that all the key performance indicators (KPIs) support the strategic purpose and objectives of the organization and together, they give you a holistic, honest and free-of-bias view of the organization.
2. **Central Dashboards** – A central dashboard can be created, consisting of a concise portfolio of the

material KPIs, to ensure the best decisions are made and taking into account the legitimate interests of all stakeholders.

3. **Causal Relationships** – Centralized data enables the identification of the relationships between different data points, such as customer feedback, employee satisfaction and revenue. Therefore, it can offer light-bulb moments and be empowering for the leadership and organization. As a result, Data and KPIs must be compared from across the organization and tracked over time.

4. **Intelligent Benchmarking** – KPIs can be usefully benchmarked against competition as snapshots and as trends, but single points may not tell the full story. For example, in one organization, there may be more people in HR for every person in sales and that could be seen as over-resourcing in HR. But sales people retention may be higher as a result and therefore the investment in HR may have a higher return.

5. **Time & Cost** – Collective data can be better at projecting and identifying trends, predicting behaviours and enabling the C-Suite to make competitively better decisions. Centralizing the resource, which would be a combination of technology and information analysts, reduces the cost of duplication in each department.

6. **Data Visualization** – Visualization can ensure data is easily understood by multiple stakeholders, and meaningful, especially to non-experts. Data visualization can be a key tool, illustrating importance and in achieving those light-bulb moments.

CFOs that go down this route will need to become excellent at understanding and managing data, and may have a chief data officer reporting into them. It is not a coincidence that the last CFO I recruited, qualified and trained as an accountant but his previous role was as a data consultant.

Chief Marketing Officer (CMO)

The Chief Marketing Officer (CMO) represents the customer in the C-Suite, in the boardroom and to the other stakeholders, whose trust they need to secure. Should the CMO be repositioned and renamed to Chief Customer Officer or CCO to illustrate this focus or the Chief Experience Officer, another CXO title, to represent what they aim to deliver? This is important to keep in mind when considering the responsibilities of the role and its reach into people's homes and lives.

Investors want marketers who have an obsession about customers, driving and capturing customer value and positioning the organization to capture further market share. They like organizations with good and sustainable reputations, with high customer retention rates and a superior competitive ecosystem of suppliers, distributors and strategic relationships.

In this environment, marketing departments continue to evolve rapidly and there seems no let-up in this transformation. As their supplier base polarizes into tech and creative agencies, they will need to be able to understand the data, leverage the new marketing technologies and still maintain their creative edge. Marketers have become data architects as they use analytics to improve engagement online and inform product development. Finding people in this data-heavy world who can get the right balance between the data approach and the creative engaging solutions will not be easy. CMOs who have strategic mindsets and are great tactical operators, who perform well in the digital and creative arenas while staying on purpose, will be in high demand. Others who find it more difficult to achieve the right balance will either leave the race or will need to buy in skills to support their organizations.

Digital has enabled marketing, like human resources, to personalize and as a result, starts to go into the area of ethics. For example, you can personalize an advert based on what an individual looks at. You could then profile that individual based on their behaviours and insights from multiple data sources and tailor the advert accordingly. You can then look at the psychological triggers of that individual and start to manipulate their behaviour to your advantage. Called Neuromarketing, this is part of a new portfolio of behavioural science approaches to marketing that have allowed rapid innovation and new streams of marketing to evolve. Neuromarketing is the application of neuropsychology, which is about how the brain and nervous systems impact behaviours, to look at the effect of marketing stimuli. Marketing has always been about influencing people, the ethical question is, when does influencing become manipulative? The line appears to sit somewhere between conscious and unconscious awareness, people are okay with the attempts to influence or watch them if they are aware of it. But the line is grey, a line many psychologists would argue does not exist, and is a line many marketers will need to tread carefully. As Netflix's 2020 docudrama *The Social Dilemma* explains, stacking super computers and world-class psychologist up against consumers with 10,000-year-old brains seems like an unfair battle. No doubt marketing regulation will follow to protect consumers.

Digital has also enabled consumer feedback to become interactive and instantaneous and consumer behaviour to be monitored live. Organizations can now monitor social media and what customers are talking to each other about and how their brand and products are perceived. A very sensible consumer insight approach to identifying what your customers really think and want. Nestlé S.A. suffered online attacks in 2010[64] and built an internal centre to monitor online conversations to both respond to hostile comments and to develop their organization. The food and beverage company was looking to identify through social media what people were saying to each other, in order to make improvements through their entire value chain.

L'Oréal became a world leader based on its ability to identify the preferences of women, innovate and make beauty products more accessible worldwide. However, the hair colour market, particularly the home-colouring segment, was lacking sparkle,

[64] http://www.babymilkaction.org/nestlefree

with very few innovations and a particularly saturated market. In 2012, there were two emerging hairstyles, 'ombre' and 'tie-dye', and L'Oréal needed to decide whether they were fads and whether to invest. The press was claiming that the ombre trend was dead and was being substituted by tie-dye amongst the coolest people. Meanwhile, every day there were more and more Facebook posts and YouTube 'how-to' videos on both styles, however YouTube's most-watched videos were on 'DIY Ombre Hair'. Movie stars and models were holding strong to ombre, while younger pop idols preferred tie-dye. L'Oréal's analysis was that tie-dye was more of a fad, uses non-permanent colouring methods and is a look that consumers will tire of, whereas ombre was a longer-lasting trend so they invested accordingly and they were right.

CMOs to maintain competitive advantage for their organizations will need to master neuromarketing and gain unique insights into what their current and potential customers are thinking. They need to spot market opportunities and trends earlier, behave more like entrepreneurs and founders and try and get ahead of their customer's needs. Customers can also be used as sources of innovation, be engaged in the development process and then potentially turned into an extension of your own sales team. Organizations used to talk about converting customers into ambassadors. Now imagine you have one salesperson for every 100 customers. If you can convert those customers into salespeople, you have effectively increased the size of your sales team by 10,000 per cent. Support this with viral marketing and you may well achieve exponential growth.

Behind the scenes this is supported by a well-thought-out marketing tech stack, with real-time dashboards, real-time feedback and the ability to respond and address customer needs in real time. The CMO of the future needs the ability to orchestrate this new marketing technology, with neuromarketing, unique market insights, viral marketing campaigns, engaged customer groups and to respond creatively and convincingly. CEOs for some time have spoken about the importance of being customer-centric: this is about understanding and responding to customer needs.

The CMO's role has been one step ahead of this and has been genuinely real-time customer led. The evolution is to accurately predict customer behaviours and needs and this can now be done with increasing accuracy.

Chief Information, Digital & Data Officer (CIO & CDO)
Technology is changing sector dynamics, the competitor landscape and ultimately, the way business models create value. IT departments have picked up the digital responsibility and increasingly, the data responsibility from marketing. To do this, IT functions have reskilled their own people, raised their digital and data literacy and recruited and replaced people appropriately just to keep up.

Simultaneously, employees now demand to be able to use their own devices (Bring Your Own Device or BYOD), each of which comes with their own sensors. Combine this with the new Software as a Service (SaaS) applications and the many new application programming interfaces (APIs) these create and you have a system with many entry points and many sleeping sentries. The FBI estimates only a fraction of cyber attacks are ever detected, which makes the role of cyber and big-data security a perennial task for the CIO and a material ongoing risk for the organization. Boards and senior management are seen as a weak point, with the saying 'to senior for security' or TSFS, a problem arises when passwords are not kept secure and changed often enough. IBM Research[65] found that quantum computers may be able to instantly break the encryption of today's strongest security.

Customers will ultimately own their own data, the data lake organizations hold will be cleaned through cleaning the rivers into it and people will eventually be savvy to the tricks of cyber criminals, making the organization increasingly immune to their attacks.

---

[65] https://www.zdnet.com/article/ibm-warns-of-instant-breaking-of-encryption-by-quantum-computers-move-your-data-today

The CIO role is one of the most rapidly evolving in the C-Suite. The need to continue to keep the lights on and systems running, while trying to replace legacy systems with agile and scalable cloud-based systems on a single platform stack. They need to defend the organization against an ever-evolving and entrepreneurial cyber threat, where the results can be crippling and your greatest weakness is the organization's own people. They also need to understand and be able to leverage the data, interoperability and digital opportunities available ahead of the competition, in real time and lead on innovation. And all that needs to be orchestrated into a coherent map and hardwired into the organization.

New approaches like design thinking, crowd sourcing solutions, innovation labs and community hubs all continue to help CIOs, who can help create a digital culture through:

- Lunch & Learn – Using junior team members who have a deep understanding of the digital channels to deliver ten- to fifteen-minute training sessions on digital.
- Champions Programme – Getting the leadership to build a 'senior-level digital champions programme'.
- Advocates Programme – Create advocates below the senior leadership team to build engagement with the leaders of the future.
- Innovation Workshops – Organize gatherings where teams identify the biggest opportunities and flesh out what they could look like.
- Celebrate Digital – Celebrate and share successes.
- 30-Day Challenge – It takes 30 days to drive an incremental change in behaviour according to neurological science. Have a different (competitive) digital challenge every day for 30 days (i.e. best use of Yammer, LinkedIn, Twitter, Facebook, Snapchat, digital ideas, etc.).

In truth, others in the C-Suite may propose the business model but it is the CIO who is its architect, they are the engineers of its creation and the people who make it work. So, the CIO has moved into strategic business model design, has the deepest knowledge of the business model and they touch every part of the business and may understand some areas better than the people who actually run them. As a result, it is not surprising that computer science is now the most common first degree for a CEO.

Chief Innovation Officer (CINO)

The Chief Innovation Officer (called CINO to avoid confusion with CIOs) is also sometimes known as a Chief Technology Innovation Officer or CTIO. They are responsible for stimulating and managing the process of innovation, creative development and change in an organization and are sometimes involved directly in the process and even generate ideas. The role is to also capture innovations, sometimes in patent or legal form, and support the commercialization of them. They may also collaborate with other organizations and groups or invest in or buy start-ups and early-stage entrepreneurial ventures. This innovation often includes initiatives that have a positive societal impact, which for many is a source of genuine interest and personal satisfaction. Whether it is a bank running schools in Peru, ASOS's 'Bring Your Parents To Work' days or a swimwear company collecting plastics from the oceans, organizations are getting more involved and becoming increasingly prepared to take a stance.

In 2000, the CINO role was virtually unheard of, but today, almost a third of Fortune 500 companies have a CINO. It is considered by some to be a key new C-Suite role and by others to be something everyone else does. The argument is the same for risk: by creating a role and department, do you unwittingly allow everyone else to dodge the responsibility? The reality is that for many organizations and sectors, the process of innovation is still relatively immature and therefore to have an individual who knows how to stimulate, manage, capture and commercialize ideas and innovation is an important investment. So, it is not about the size of the team and instead the focus should be about having a big output. For example, at Telefónica, the Spanish telecoms giant, they have a number of innovation practices including:

- Academia – Who they create challenges for, fund research groups, share knowledge and work in collaboration with;
- New Ventures – Who they encourage, identify, invest in and sometimes acquire;
- Idea Scaling – Scaling and embedding early-stage ideas into general corporate practice;
- Inspiring – Creating a culture that inspires their own people to innovate continuously.

To lead on innovation, you need to have a clear map of the competitor environment, value chain and all relevant influencers. Historically, the Harvard Business School Professor Michael E. Porter taught us about the five competitive forces, which looked at direct competitors, new market entrants, substitutes and the power of buyers and suppliers. He also created a value chain model about how organizations supply to each other, where you sit in the chain and this can be linked back to his competitor model and the power of supplies and buyers. Now we need to add the all-pervasive digital giants to the ecosystem and all the soft power influencers, including indirect stakeholders. Combined, we call this the organization's ecosystem and the Chief Innovation Officer has a key role in deciding which set of ecosystems the organization sits in, what the organization's role should be in each system and how the dynamics of the ecosystem will affect the organization and can be effected by the organization. For example, Fidelity Investments Inc., one of the largest asset managers in the world with $3.3 trillion under management, not surprisingly tracks the Fintech market in detail. In their innovation centre in California, they have mapped the entire financial services market, have looked at where Fintech start-ups are making headway and decided what role they should play in this Fintech ecosystem. They have positioned themselves and connected with multiple groups to reap the maximum benefits from this rapidly evolving ecosystem.

CINOs need to be tapped into innovative ecosystems and to be able to utilize crowd access. The era of 'move fast and break things' as famously coined by Facebook founder Mark Zuckerberg is over. The Creative Strategy team at Snap Inc., who own Snapchat, Spectacles and Bitmoji, explain that Snaps innovation strategy is not 'move fast and break things' but rather to 'build by design' and 'don't be afraid' and to always be consistent with your values, which for them are Kind, Smart, Creative. Some parts of innovation development can be automated and funnelled through the company process, others can just be great ideas from employees and customers. One night, an employee at Metro Bank left his card behind a bar and on his train home, suddenly remembered. He worried about what would happen and had a light-bulb moment: wouldn't it be great if I could freeze my card in the banking app? Within a month, the app functionality was up and running and has off-the-charts customer satisfaction scores.

Chief HR Officer (CHRO)

Society, and as a result HR, is going through substantial upheavals in terms of expectations and behaviours and they don't look to end soon. Bundle this with the technology revolution and new working practices, including the huge amount of work being done in the area of diversity and inclusion, and employee psychological contracts and you have very busy CHROs. CHROs are combining and aligning purpose, values, agile, flexible working and new contracts.

Like CMOs, CHROs are looking to personalize HR activities and empower all staff at the same time. The personalization element looks at what is important to staff through a combination of surveys, face-to-face (F2F) interviews, focus groups and digital tracking. These insights are used to focus on 'moments that matter' in the employee's lifecycle and to develop agile and flexible benefits that adapt through their career journey. The empowerment comes through direct communications, flexible working and reward and recognition, and providing the best learning and tools for the individual and role. The benefits should be better motivation, recruitment, retention, performance and cost reduction, leading to improved return on investment (ROI).

Technology will enable increasingly frequent and detailed communication, monitoring and measurement of staff attitudes and behaviours. This can be analysed to identify individual drivers and motivations, as well as gain insights across departments, functions and geographic locations. The recruitment and on-boarding processes have been transformed by technology, resulting in a 30–40 per cent reduction of costs, and this is key to capability planning. With a smaller core team and higher use of external people, effective hiring and onboarding will be essential, for example:

- Candidates can be found through social media platforms such as LinkedIn, Facebook and Twitter.
- Artificial Intelligence (AI) is being used to match candidates to roles with ever-increasing accuracy. AI is also being used to profile people and help form the high-performance teams they will be joining.
- The front end of mass recruitment is being accelerated through CV-matching technologies.
- Speeding up on-boarding process for new hires through the digital delivery of learning and development tools.
- Five-minute vetting calls over Zoom and MS Teams are being used for graduates and experienced hires. Vodafone, the UK telecoms giant, ask potential hires to send in a short video: why them.
- AI-backed robotics can interview candidates and exit leavers PepsiCo, Inc. have used Vera, a robot in Russia, to conduct interviews with job hunters at a rate of 160 candidates an hour.[66]

[66] https://www.computerweekly.com/news/252438788/PepsiCo-hires-robots-to-interview-job-candidates

The surge in remote home working during the Covid-19 pandemic accelerated the adoption of mindfulness, meditation, well-being and mentor apps. Tech can also ensure compliance and Virtual Reality (VR) and Augmented Reality (AR) can be used to train and direct staff and is increasingly also helping employees to live healthier and happier lives. This will mean that aptitude and potential will become more important than experience. Happiness is also high on the agenda, sentiment tracking important and organizations like HSBC can spot employees about to resign through behavioural pattern recognition. As a result HSBC know the interventions most likely to retain staff and can deploy these or not depending on how valued the member of staff is.

Much of this can now be managed through 'one-stop shop' HR software that can personalize benefit bundles and run engagement practices. This data also leads to greater equity as performance is evidenced in an increasingly transparent manner. A challenge on the near horizon for CHROs is the end-of-time based contracts and their replacement 'outcome' based contracts. As data improves, outcomes will become easier to measure and people more easily compared and managed.

As in marketing, CHROs who can get the right balance between the data approach and the engaging solutions will not be common. CHROs who have strategic HR mindsets and perform well in the digital arena while staying on purpose will be in high demand. They will need to have built and have access to talent ecosystems that can be drawn on as needs arise.

Chief Legal Officer (CLO)
Legal functions have never been busier dealing with regional legislation such as General Data Protection Regulation (GDPR) and what can appear to be an endless list of sector-specific regulation. As a result, CLOs have been spread-sheeting incoming legislation, looking at the impact of non-compliance in terms of fines and reputation risk and making decisions on what to prioritize. Simultaneously, they have created triage systems,

increasingly automated, to assess work prioritization based on risk and value.

Legal departments are at the forefront of capital protection. They provide the legal protection behind nearly all assets and the enforcement ability behind contracts and resulting cash flow. Their ability to recognize, capture and monetize digital assets and intellectual property is an important skill.

As with CFOs, digital has presented substantial opportunities for automation such as litigation, case preparation and due diligence (e-disclosure). Contracts have been standardized, processes unbundled and templates created. These standard contracts and templates are now available to business units through legal self-service portals that will increasingly merge into broader shared service portals.

CLOs need to be good internal consultants, understanding the business, implementing risk mitigation initiatives and mapping risk as they become more embedded in the business. Large-project contracts will become smart, reminding parties of their obligations in a timely fashion and when necessary, highlighting non-compliance.

As we have seen, commercial lawyers can be redeployed onto more complex work thanks to the rise of automation. And this has led to a temporary increase in legal work as uncovered issues end up surfacing thanks to the transparency of technology. However, budgets remain tight and false economies of under-investment have held back many legal functions.

The work of legal departments is polarizing into volume and automated work, such as insurance claims, and to highly complex specialist work, such as international regulation frameworks. This volume work in larger functions is increasingly spun off as a separate entity that can do work for other organizations, as CLOs try and turn their legal functions into profit centres. In time, it is likely that these legal processing houses merge with each other to create substantial new legal tech companies that could eventually be bigger than the organizations that founded them.

CLOs, alongside their CIO peers, are looking at data capture, their interest triggered by legislation like GDPR (the EU General Data Protection Regulation), bringing them to the forefront of conversations about data and digital ethics with the CMO peers. More importantly, they are recognizing, registering and protecting their new Digital Assets.

Chief Multi-Disciplinary Officers (CMDO)
Under the role of COO, we introduced the idea of unbundling processes. In psychology, they call this 'chunking', where a pattern of activities can be grouped together and quickly recognized. If you reflect for a moment, each C-Suite role is really a collection of activities or disciplines and it is expected that in the future these are likely to be unbundled, chunked and their movement between roles will be more fluid. When I started writing this book, Katja Tautscher was the Chief Legal and Procurement Officer of Borealiz AG, a billion-dollar Austrian chemicals company. By the time of editing, she had dropped procurement and picked up on human resources to become the Chief Legal & HR Officer, all the while staying a member of the executive committee. Like the modern organization model in the previous chapter (*see also* pp. 202–206), the C-Suite is expected to become more fluid, calling on deep knowledge experts for periods to help an organization on its path.

As C-Suite departments become more tech-orientated, their departments more automated and diamond-shaped, the role of their C-Suite executive will become easier. This will enable C-Suite executives to move their gaze to be more client-, innovation- and forward-looking, while covering more disciplines. So, in the end, a CXO becomes a CXXXXXXXXO, with around eight areas of expertise in their multi-disciplinary function or MDF – maybe we should call them CMDO, a chief multi-disciplinary officer. This in turn should accelerate the whole organization's evolution so we should expect an acceleration of innovation in every aspect of business.

The New C-Suite

There is no clean answer to what the future C-Suite will look like as it will vary as it does today from organization to organization and will be impacted by many factors. In Chapter 1 (*see also* pp. 34–38), we looked at nine strong C-Suite executives led by the CEO, with five staff C-Suite roles and three line C-Suite roles. In the digital giants, all the line roles were product focused and it is expected that in time, most organizations will follow the lead of the digital giants. So, based on what we know today and what we expect to happen in the future, we can take an intelligent view of what a future C-Suite may look like. This is captured in the image below and explained afterwards.

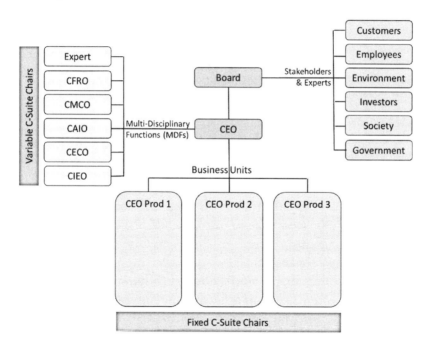

In the modern C-Suite, the number of people is expected to stabilize at around nine, the Group CEO and three fixed seats for the three divisional product CEOs. Then there will be five variable seats for the advisory and multi-disciplinary functional leads. These will usually be allocated to the five CMDOs, but the Group CEO may also choose to bring on an expert for a period of time to help with an initiative, such as helping to take the organization through a development stage or expand into a new market. That may mean that there will be a CMDO that needs to stand down, or their disciplinary areas are reallocated to a smaller number of CMDOs. Regardless, it once again illustrates the importance of the line roles in the C-Suite as it is the staff roles that will be playing musical chairs while the line roles stay seated as the music changes.

THE MODERN C-SUITE

1.	Group Chief Executive Officer	6.	Chief Marketing & Customer Officer (CMCO)
2.	CEO Product 1	7.	Chief Architect & Technology Officer (CATO)
3.	CEO Product 2	8.	Chief Ethics & Capabilities Officer (CECO)
4.	CEO Product 3	9.	Chief Innovation & Ecosystem Officer (CIEO)
5.	Chief Financial & Reporting Officer (CFRO)	10.	Initiative Expert (CEO-appointed adviser)

In the C-Suite, the constituents all have additional roles, are all leaders of MDFs (Multi-Disciplinary Functions), some have been merged and renamed, there is a healthy balance of internal- and external-facing people.

The CEO role remains entirely linked to value creation for the stakeholders, is transfixed on achieving the purpose and is there to create, propose and implement the strategy.

> **CFRO** – The CFO role is replaced by a chief financial & reporting officer (CFRO), who is a finance and data wizard. They are the central point for all finance, a collator and analyser of all data, the producer of the key performance indicators (KPIs) and the company dashboard.

CMCO – The CMO remains externally-facing and gains the customer title to ensure they are outward-facing and always representing the customer and the customer experience. So, they are renamed the Chief Marketing & Customer Officer (CMCO). This CMCO role should also include investor relations to ensure the stakeholder connectivity.

The COO role has been chunked up and given to other roles and no longer has a seat in the C-Suite. However, they may survive as a deputy CEO if the organization's CEO has a particularly arduous external-facing role or existential challenges to deal with.

CATO – The CIO, CTO and CDO roles all get absorbed into a chief architect & technology officer role (CATO), who is the key architect and engineer behind the design, building and delivery of the business model and its operational effectiveness. This includes the data flows that support decision making and enable digital services.

CECO – The Chief Legal Officer and Chief HR Officer roles are merged into a chief ethics & capabilities officer (CECO) with responsibility for the performance and capabilities of the organization, sitting within an ethical framework that directs its legal, risk and property protection work. Interestingly, Aviva, the global insurance company, legal department appear from their vision to be reflective of this journey already, as they state, 'We are passionate, collaborative and innovative. We protect Aviva by doing the right thing and delivering the best possible outcomes for customers.' Rob Chesnut became the Chief Ethics Officer of Airbnb from the General Counsel role, and is adamant that someone in the C-Suite needs to have strategic ownership of integrity. 'In the 21st century, integrity has to be intertwined with the business – having a greater purpose that truly drives decision-making motivates employees and turns customers into ambassadors. Silence is the enemy of integrity. It cannot be assumed, it must be pursued with intentionality.'

CIEO – The last of the CMDOs, but definitely not the least, is the Chief Innovation & Ecosystem Officer (CIEO). This individual will be extraordinarily well connected and has a deep understanding of the innovation process and the ecosystem in which they operate. Most importantly, they will be able to influence both to the benefit of the organization.

It is expected that the three product CEOs will have fixed seats in the team as they represent the more mature 'cash cows' of the organization and the high growth more early-stage businesses. Processes will be put in place to ensure the effective transition of the new innovative products from the CIEO to the product CEOs to scale them.

Finally, there will be an expert seat on the C-Suite, the King's advisor, the person who has a unique skill or knowledge that can take the organization to the next level on its journey to its massive transformative purpose. This person may be appointed or come from the stakeholder group.

As mentioned, the CMDO roles are expected to be more fluid, with roles merging and unmerging and different Xs being managed by different CXOs. A good example of this is that at Santander UK, a Top 20 global bank, they have the role of chief customer & innovation officer, which takes two of the above double titles and merges them.

Key Learnings from Chapter 5

Team & Values

- Decide on who you want to be and live by those values. This will make your personal decision making easier and less stressful. Always be honest with your staff, then they are more likely to be honest with you and may well work with you again.

- Your role within the C-Suite and when leading the C-Suite and other teams is to make that team the best team you have ever been in and you already know what that looks and feels like. When building a team, look for the underpinning values that produce the best attributes.

Follow a CEO

- C-Suites have been steadily growing with the same proportion of staff and line executives. New CEOs tend to have larger C-Suites and then reduce them over time so following the next potential CEO may be a good career move. Decentralized organizations may also have smaller C-Suites as they act more like investors than managers.
- CEOs know that who sits in the C-Suite also reflects the organization's strategic priorities. They also know that changing responsibilities keep them fresh and valuable. Therefore, C-Suite executives should either keep evolving their responsibilities or expect to have them changed for them.

Chief Multi-Disciplinary Officers

- The modern C-Suite is likely to consist of nine seats, the Group and three product CEOs, who have fixed seats and five other variable seats for staff CMDOs and experts, creating a fluid and dynamic environment.
- The C-Suite roles and their departments are being transformed by technology, ethics, innovation and their broader ecosystems. HR and Marketing are personalizing and empowering staff and customers alike, COOs and CIOs are building new agile, scalable and defendable business models, while CFOs and CLOs are capturing, valuing and protecting capital.
- C-Suite Executives run Multi-Disciplinary Functions (MDFs). The disciplines in their MDF are likely to be fluid, which makes the role more interesting and refreshing.

They could also be referred to as CMDO, Chief Multi-Disciplinary Officers, and their tiara of knowledge turns their CXO role into a CXXXXXXXXXO.

- To stay in the C-Suite, it is important to oversee an area of strategic importance. These can be acquired through volunteering and internal landgrabs and the more areas you cover, the more secure your role may be. A balance between breadth and ability to add value needs to be struck.
- The C-Suite team is becoming more fluid, with new and temporary experts and new and merged C-Suite roles like the Chief Financial & Reporting Officer (CFRO), Chief Marketing & Customer Officer (CMCO), Chief Architect & Technology Officer (CATO), Chief Ethics & Capabilities Officer (CECO) and Chief Innovation & Ecosystem Officer (CIEO).

Connecting People & Knowledge

- Good leaders are collegiate, build bridges, think central and act local. A great career starting point is a degree in computer science, followed by a role in business development or consultancy and then bolstered with a management degree like an MBA.
- Siloes are created by the person who leads them and their formal education or lack of management education is likely to make them narrower in their thinking and therefore more prone to siloes. Business partnering breaks down silos and can be partly automated and partly achieved through allocated account specialist bolstered by niche internal consultancies or centres of excellence.
- Executives and organizations need to create strategic contacts in key organizations including clients. Everyone in the C-Suite is in the sales team and each key account needs to have a member of the C-Suite allocated to them, someone they can call when things go wrong or float ideas past.

Stakeholders & Governance

- C-Suite executives should be meeting a client and a stakeholder once a month. On top of this once a month, they should be meeting a relevant expert or joining an innovative forum. This is key to maintaining and building their commercial antennae. These antennae must be alert to innovation, competition and material sector movements.
- Governance, boards and C-Suite teams all need to flex with the environment but this is a brief summary of good governance in numbers:

    1. Away day a year and a detailed one-year plan.
    2. Each board paper needs a one- or two-page summary and non-executive directors should meet on their own twice a year.
    3. All organizations should have a three- or five-year plan.
    4. Board meetings should be around four hours long.
    5. *See* 3.
    6. The CEO report should start the board meeting and should be around six pages long.
    7. Is about the limit for number of material issues on a board agenda.
    8. Average number of board meetings a year.

6

C-Suite Musical Chairs

'Stay in the room and don't get left standing.'
John Jeffcock

We have called this chapter after the children's game, Musical Chairs, as once you are in the C-Suite, you need to know how to keep your chair and then when things start moving around, how to find a new chair and ultimately, what do you do when you are left standing. Similarly to the game, you will experience bigger children who push you out of the way or pull the chair closer to them. We also now know from the previous chapter that the staff CMDO roles are likely to move around more often than the product CEO roles, so a product CEO role should be a safer seat in the C-Suite. However, this is not necessarily the case as someone may stay in a CMDO role for longer, say nine years, compared to a product CEO, whose average tenure may be closer to five years. So, for a product CEO to stay in the C-Suite, they need to be seen as Group CEO succession and to ultimately get the top job. They will also need to have had staff or central business experience, like a chief strategy officer, to be in best place for a promotion. Whereas a CMDO may stay in the C-Suite for longer than a product CEO by playing Musical Chairs and like the product CEO, they will need to have a breadth of experience.

How to Get the Chair Closer

If you are rightly concerned about Musical Chairs in the C-Suite, how do you ensure you are closer to a chair when the music stops, or when the change around happens? There are three fundamental ways of ensuring the chair is closer to you:

- **Extra X** – As mentioned in the previous chapter, an extra X in your CMDO role should give you greater longevity. This is sometimes referred to as a landgrab, but you need to make sure that the X you are grabbing is on the ascent not descent in terms of strategic importance. If the latter is the case, the land grab may do the reverse and illustrate a lack of strategic insight or your importance.
- **O & Succession** – If you are identified as a material candidate for succession for the Group CEO role, your chair in the C-Suite is almost guaranteed. To do this, the right people need to know that you are interested and you should be seen as someone developing lots of 'O'. As discussed in previous chapters, there are many ways of doing this, including adding a useful non-executive board role to what you do.
- **Stakeholders** – This is where the politics comes in. If certain stakeholders or stakeholder groups particularly like you, it makes it more difficult to move you – in effect, stakeholders make your seat in the C-Suite stickier. In the previous chapter, we talked about the importance and frequency of meetings with stakeholders and clients (*see also* pp. 235–238). Every relationship you make in this space shifts the chair another centimetre towards you.

How to Disarm the Chair Hoggers

Many C-Suites will suffer from a bully or internal power blocks, and a seasoned executive who says they have never experienced dysfunctional behaviour in a top team is inexperienced. Within every team, there are groups of people who are closer than others and these may form separate power groups. This is why people rightly campaign for more than one woman or minority group on a board as a single voice may have limited influence. Similarly, you will have some people with stronger characters, louder voices and more experience than others and these people and groups can hog chairs and ultimately make your chair the variable one.

- **Build Allies** – We will recommend a non-executive director (NED) as an ally later in this chapter, the key is to have one or two people who have your back. In the best team list of attributes, everyone respected each other equally and you will need to demonstrate that you are worthy of that respect as fast as possible. Like networking to create an ally, the best approach is to offer to support them in their work and to create that social debt. Then, over time, to convert that social relationship into one of professional friendship. A C-Suite friend of mine has lunch with the Chief Financial Officer once a week to talk about what is going on and as a result, their thinking is more often aligned and they do not need to ask for each other's support as it becomes assumed.
- **Break Power Blocks** – Power blocks in the C-Suite are bad news and you should do what you can to break them up and to ensure the C-Suite is the team. Some people may advise you to join the power group and you can find situations where there is, for example, a younger power group waiting to replace an old guard. The advice would be along the lines of 'If you can't beat 'em, join 'em.' A problem that may arise from this approach is that the others, who may feel threatened, may pick on weaker team members to depower the group. The better advice is to stick to your values and when they align with

a group vote with them and when they don't, do the right thing. Keeping your integrity is a more powerful weapon, it is better to position yourself as a potential partner than to join them. This approach helps balance the power, as from time to time they will need you onside. The rational heads usually win and even when a power block successfully organizes a coup d'état, they will want the rational executives on side as it legitimizes their behaviours.

- **Master Conflict Management** – In Patrick Dunne's book, *Boards: A Practical Perspective*,[67] he explains how conflict often seen as a negative can be a force for good, as it can create a more rigorous decision process and better outcomes. All members of the C-Suite need to be practiced and skilful at managing conflict and the best starting point is to understand the facts and motivations and to act in alignment with the organization's purpose. If you combine McKinsey's 'Leave your ego at the door' and Canon's 'Have we made the best decision for the organization?' rules, you should get good results.

    During the meeting, you need to choose your conflict position and how assertive or co-operative you should be and is appropriate. Dunne highlights the Thomas and Kilmann[68] conflict model, which offers five alternative stances: avoiding, accommodating, compromising, competing and collaborating. To take on the bullies, you will need to choose your times to conflict with them wisely and to call out their poor behaviours, without making it personal. You need to get them to let go of your chair and to do this, you need to look them in the eye from a level playing field.

---

[67] Dunne, Patrick, *Boards: A Practical Perspective*. Governance Publishing and Information Services, 2019

[68] https://en.wikipedia.org/wiki/Thomas%E2%80%93Kilmann_Conflict_Mode_Instrument

BOARD ADVICE TO NEW CXOS

So, as the song goes in *The Sound of Music*, when you read you begin with A-B-C ... And when you join the C-Suite, you need to begin by learning what the Board advice is to new C-Suite executives. New CXOs will have a lot of new expectations on them and they will need to:

1. **Understand their Role** – Need to understand the business and their role in the current environment and what they are expected to deliver, which in smaller companies can include a wide variety of functions reporting in. CXOs need to remember that they are a board director in the boardroom and a member of the C-Suite executive team in the executive committee.

2. **Whole Business** – Understand that they are no longer reporting to a functional lead, that their role now encompasses the whole business, ensuring everything important is being looked at, that there are no blind spots and that the things that the organization needs to be concerned about are known.

3. **Internal Network** – Need networks of information that tell them what is going on. This is obviously harder for people coming from an external organization as they can take some time to develop.

4. **Internal Relationships** – Should expect to have resource conflict with other departments, such as marketing, legal, finance, technology and HR, and should become an adept negotiator with good conflict resolution skills.

5. **Answers & Questions** – Need to realize that the KPI or metric is not the answer. To understand where your strategic focus should be and to move from having the right answers to asking the right questions.

6. **Board Friend** – Need to find an ally on the Board. This is typically an appropriate committee chair and is particularly important when you have a strong CEO.

7. **Be Brave** – Need to stand up to the CEO and Board, be brave but not foolish, understand their issues and have your 'brave pants' on when you talk with the Board.

8. **People Skills** – Need to check their ego, develop strong people skills and be a change driver in the business.

9. **Get the Basics Right** – Ensure the department or business unit is the appropriate size for the organization, that risks are estimated and mitigated well, controls are strong, that there is enough resource in place and that there is a keen eye on money and where it comes from.

10. **Early Wins & Advertising** – Secure early wins to earn confidence and influence with stakeholders. Do not be shy about telling people how you helped win and improve the outcomes of business activities and deals.

First 100 Days, for New C-Suite Executives

Although research conducted by Michael Watkins at Harvard Business School estimated that it took, on average, 6.2 months to reach the 'breakeven point', the point at which new leaders have contributed as much value to their organization as they have consumed from it, most stakeholders, peers and team members will expect to see the impact of a new CXO within the first three months.

In effect, you have a window of opportunity of around 100 days to make your mark and to begin to define your place within the organization. However, it is a mistake, and potentially dangerous, to focus on the first 100 days as an entirely make-or-break opportunity, as there are a variety of factors that make it a false timeline.

You should approach the first 100 days like the beginning of a marathon, set a pace and adjust it, as required. Although you need to make an impact, you should remember that a short burst may negatively impact your medium and long-term performance, making it difficult to complete the marathon. You also need to be conscious that it is highly likely that within your first 100 days, something will happen that will need your attention, so you need to build in time for the unexpected.

It is useful to start by creating your own hypothesis of where the organization is, a top-level view of the organization, its environment, its workings and how you fit into it. Take notes and draw a picture; this will help you set your direction and priorities, understand the complexities and operate effectively. First, you need to start with and understand the purpose and strategy of the organization, its objectives and what needs to be done to achieve these. You need to get the view of the CEO, at least one stakeholder and at least one NED and while doing this, learn about the internal dynamics. You need to identify what they expect and want from you, what good looks like to them, how they would prefer to work with you and what support they could give you. Look to also create your personal stakeholder map while doing this.

You also need to understand the organization's external environment, understand its market places, competition, the cultural differences, how the organization is perceived on social media, what former and current employees are saying on social media platforms, such as Glassdoor. Finally, look at external advisors, organizations and people with power, like rating agencies, and see what they say.

A common regret cited is becoming too tied to head office or the leadership at the centre. It is therefore better to meet with as many operational and regional site managers as possible. It is important to be visible to the whole organization and particularly if you are business partnering. The advantage of being new in role is that people are more likely to be honest with you, so you have a window of opportunity to truly understand what they think.

It can be useful to work with a questionnaire in your head, with key questions you may want to ask. For example:

- Where does authority in the business really lie, both officially and unofficially?
- Where and how does decision-making take place?

- Who are the established key personnel: who is respected, who is feared, who do you go to get things done?
- What motivates people to want to come into work? Why do people leave?
- What's their view of your area, what it gets right and wrong, and should be doing more of?

The key activities to do well on in the first 100 days are getting your relationship with the CEO off to a healthy start and learning the regulatory governance and governance structure, so you can be an effective member of the C-Suite. Your team and reports will also be keen to meet you and develop their own relationships with you. Remember, there may be someone who also applied for your role and they would be a good place to start. You will need to be involved in internal politics and it is important to remember you are in the role to make the organization successful and not to make friends, so stay on purpose. Do a deep dive into the three Ps: People, Processes and Purpose, identify and review your centres of excellence and how you interface with other parts of the organization. Take the opportunity to set up regular feedback sessions within your team and with your business partners, then adapt these as necessary.

At Winmark, we created different first 100 days best practice guides for each of the C-Suite roles, but there was much commonality between them. Below is the first 100 days checklist from the Winmark CHRO network:

- Discuss goals with CEO, agree them and be flexible;
- Arrange meetings with key individuals;
- Work out a few quick wins as soon as possible;
- Understand the organization's context, operating model and culture;
- Understand and learn the general and specific governance requirements as a board member;
- Understand the complexity and ambiguity and embrace it;
- Outline vision and objectives for HR;

- Conduct skills audit of HR team;
- Do the basics really well;
- Conduct health check of HR core processes, policies and systems;
- Establish HR operating rhythm: regular 1:1s and tracking measures of success;
- Applying an 80:20 approach – 80 per cent of the time to get the most impact.

What Board Directors Want from C-Suite Executives

Once established in the role, the expectations of the Board evolve and C-Suite Executives will need to demonstrate:

1. **Clarity of Vision** – Boards admire executives who have absolute clarity of vision for the business and their business area. With this vision should come clear thinking, an independent mind and a clarity of personal purpose. Leading C-Suite executives take the organization's purpose and translate it into a vision for their area and do not wait to be allocated objectives.
2. **Great Antennae** – That is supported by a strong internal network mitigating any potential blind spots and entrepreneurial external antennae that pick up on trends, opportunities and threats earlier than others.
3. **Integrity & Courage** – Tell the Board the whole story and how it is, make it real, making sure there are no information reality gaps. The best executives do not always come to the Board with the answers. C-Suite executives need to be credible and able to look themselves in the mirror and say, 'I have done the right thing.'

    'I always tell new team members that I will never fire them for getting something wrong, but I will fire them for not telling me about it' – CEOs should expect the same honesty from their reports.

4. **CEO** – Build a healthy relationship with the CEO, become the CEO's partner, flagging issues as they arise, and also act as the CEO's check and balance. Be a trusted, balanced and realistic advisor to the CEO, using your influential position to balance the CEO's natural optimism with a realistic approach from a cool head.

5. **Board & Stakeholders** – Earn the respect of the Board, be strong strategically and stand up as an independent board director. Spend more time researching stakeholders, understanding their motivations and then communicating with them appropriately in their language.

6. **Department Strength & Levers** – Be functionally strong, ensure you have built your own department or business unit so it is now self-running. Your functions should also be real in their reporting, not afraid to report bad news. Ensure that their assumptions are realistic and that you understand the levers you can pull to increase performance, including profitability and reduce risks.

7. **Strategic Insight, Data & Complexity** – Be able to explain where the organization is today, where it is going and what the headwinds are. Become better at recording, managing and utilizing data and data analytics to support and justify decision making. Be well connected, so you can influence and manage sensitive and complex discussions, and stay abreast of what is happening in the marketplace so you can see the headwinds early.

8. **Strategic Action:** Think more long-term like the Board while ensuring the competition does not get ahead and that decisions are not put off. The Board recognizes the short-term pressures it places on the C-Suite but still needs the CXO to be able to step back and think broader and more long-term.

9. **Communication, Focus & Responsibility** – Treat Board Directors with respect, be humble and do not go on transmit and do not talk when you don't know what you are talking about. Ensure that what you do makes

common sense and do not get lost in an idea, creative concept or the detail. Choose your words wisely and show clear responsibility of decisions made and do not hide behind people, governance or the environment.

10. **ROI & Problems** – Ensure you understand the business model and know where and how the organization makes money, stay focused on this and don't be distracted by governance. Do not return with the same problem to the Board too often as it suggests non-performance, that you are unable to manage it and the Board may lose confidence. Be a rational problem solver in the executive team and on the Board, flexing between your own area and commercial, as appropriate to the context.

11. **Risk Priority** – Prioritize and anticipate external risks, as the Board perception is that operational risks are decreasing while external risks, such as cyber and competition, are underestimated and continue to increase.

12. **Board Reporting** – Plan ahead of meetings and ...

- be timely, submit reports a week ahead of meetings;
- understand what the reader needs to know to make the best decision;
- show the full picture with its context, more than the historical information and ensure forecasts are accurate;
- access broader information and illustrate the more important connections;
- share and motivate the resulting priorities;
- be articulate and accurate, ensuring fair representation and
- avoid making late changes.

13. **Governance** – Understand how the governance works, who is involved and their roles. This includes knowing relevant regulations and what the committees do. Ensure rigour and governance checks and balances behind activities, always ensuring that there are alternative views.

14. **Good Behaviours** – Should exhibit good behaviours coming from sound values, are considerate and do not jump to conclusions. Your behaviours should not be defensive and should motivate staff and carry people when they need it. You need to be able to take feedback without feeling personally criticized.

If you get all the above areas right, you will probably make a great success of your C-Suite role for you personally and for your organization. May I wish you every luck on this journey. There will come a point when there is no longer a chair for you, that may be your choice or it could come earlier than you may have hoped or expected. The big question is, what next? You could also join another C-Suite at some point, you could work for a smaller organization, such as the banker who became CEO of London Zoo, but there will eventually come a time when you decide to no longer go for a chair in the C-Suite and instead, you stand back honourably and let someone else take your place.

WHAT NEXT? WHAT HAPPENS POST C-SUITE

If we are now all retiring when we are 80 years old, it is likely that you have another 20 years of good work left in you before you hang up your boots. As Martin Luther King, Jr once said, 'The time is always right to do what is right.'

Those who enter this last chapter of their careers, if they choose not to take up another executive role, have four routes they can take: the board and plural non-executive route, the educator and university lecturer route, the consultancy route or the service to humanity route. None of these routes are exclusive – in fact, they are all complementary – and most people after a while find a hybrid situation that suits them and their lifestyle well. They are also not fixed options – for example, your mix of NED roles, consultancy and academia can evolve over time. Those that have done particularly well financially sometimes go down the investor route and combine this with a board role, as illustrated in the model below.

Post C-Suite Career Options

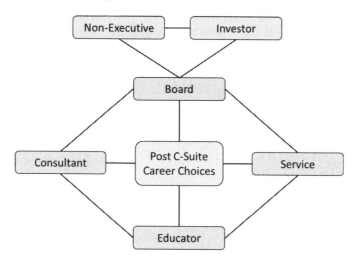

Because of what I do many people who plan to step down from their executive roles come knocking on my door to ask for my advice. Normally, when I get asked for career advice by people planning to leave their executive role, I start by asking them how rich they are. They are initially taken aback but then they quickly understand that the need to have a regular substantive income has a significant impact on their choices and the number of six-figure NED roles is very limited. The majority have now paid for their house, educated their children and are looking for something that they want to do. Some have weddings on the horizon to pay for and others still need to earn significant salaries, which means their choices are limited to the consultancy and plural NED routes.

I then share with them the fact that the big four accountancy firm exiting partner programmes tend to be devised around five years and that's because it takes that long to build up your new career. Armed with this knowledge, if they need the money, my advice is usually to reduce their executive role to two to three days a week if possible for at least a year. This income should ideally cover their base costs and give them time to build up their supplementing income through their consultancy work or NED portfolio.

Many former C-Suite executives assume that they can transition straight into setting up their own consultancy and immediately win business. Some do and are successful, but for the majority it takes several years to build up a client base. They had forgotten their early years and how tough winning new business was and are usually unconscious of the already vibrant consulting market. People often say to me, 'I wish someone had told me that three years ago.' Even the most senior business leaders find it difficult building their consultancy or portfolio of NED roles. Rather than go down the pure consultancy route, some go down an educator route and more commonly, a hybrid consultancy educator route. The academic body, a book and sometimes their research gives them more authority in the marketplace.

However, if you get the consultancy offer right, for some your C-Suite role may not be the pinnacle of your career or the pinnacle of your financial earnings. The first company chair I reported to was a New Zealander and a rugby coach, particularly skilful in people-related areas. The pinnacle of his career in terms of earnings was not when he was managing partner of a top consultancy or chairman of a public company but rather when he was part of a four-strong team who knew how to do one thing particularly well. He did this for five years of his life, worked incredibly hard, but it was those five years that set him up financially for life.

Some people will develop plural careers, becoming a non-executive director on multiple boards, and will have a lot of wisdom to share and considerable value they can bring to the table, if they choose their boards well. Focusing on NED portfolios, there is then the choices of sector, type of organization, where it is on its lifecycle and what the organization needs from its board. The trick is not to pigeonhole yourself into one area and to look for areas where you can add genuine value beyond governance. When looking for a new NED role, there are several things you should keep in mind:

- **Open Mind** – Do look at all the options and keep an open mind as you may find something you had not previously come across, which may be the perfect fit.

- **Honest Reflection** – Not all executives make good NEDs, so be sure it is the right route for you. CEOs can find the transition particularly hard and some people have short-lived NED careers as it does not suit them.
- **Best Fit** – Consider the type of organization most suited to your personality and skill set, such as entrepreneurial or a large public company.
- **Aligned Passion** – Demonstrate real passion and genuine interest in the role you want to undertake, otherwise it will be difficult to land a position and you may not give it the focus it needs.
- **Add Value** – Think critically about your own skill set and connections, think about where you can add material value and what you can offer as a board member.
- **Knowledge & Challenge** – Remember, your role is non-executive and you should only consider taking on the role if you understand the governance issues for that organization and are prepared and ready to become a 'critical friend' to the executive.
- **Your Time** – If a chair role is two or three days a week and a NED role three to four days a month, that tells you that your portfolio of roles is limited to two to three chair roles or four to seven NED roles and no more. Be real about your time and conscious of the extra time a NED role may take.

I always remember the plural NED, who took up the role of chair of the British Schools Exploring Society (BSES). He thought this not-for-profit role would take up a small amount of his time, would be a fun role and his opportunity to give back to younger people. Soon after being appointed chair in August 2011, a polar bear in the Arctic Circle attacked one of his expeditions and killed a 17-year-old schoolboy called Horatio Chapple. BSES became front-page news and the Chair rightly spent the majority of his time as chair working on the case and ensuring it could never happen again.

For those people who are in the lucky position of already having built their tangible assets and who want to do something that interests them, the world can be a very exciting place. They have a broad range of unique skills, a wealth of knowledge, huge social capital in the form of their connections and reputation, a high level of professionalism and behavioural skills that can make them very valuable to a whole range of organizations, people and initiatives. The difficult question is, what to do next? Life has presented them with an opportunity to spend 20 years or less of their life doing something that interests them. They have the opportunity to make the world a better place than it was when they joined it, to make sure that their dent in the universe is a good one. But still, what is that going to be? They need to find their passion and purpose.

I know executives who have left powerful roles and dedicated themselves to raising money for a charity for a year, entrepreneurs who have sold their businesses and become charity CEOs and drawn no pay, but not all of them have found what they were looking for. In Anita Hoffman's 2018 book, *Purpose & Impact: How Executives are Creating Meaningful Second Careers*,[69] she advises people to start by searching for their passion: who are they? What are they passionate about? She suggests you should do this through talking to lots of people, interesting people on the fringes of who you know to discover what they do. Then to talk to people who know you well and ask them what they appreciate about you. Through a process of discovery and reflection your passion may quickly or slowly emerge. As reputation is connected to brand, passion is connected to purpose, so the next phase is to identify your purpose: what will your dent in the universe be? What question are you going to help answer or problem help solve? She suggests for inspiration you start with the 17 Sustainable Development Goals (SDGs) set in 2015 by the United Nations General Assembly, which range from poverty to equality to education. But your impact may be far more local and greater for it.

[69] Hoffman, Anita, *Purpose & Impact: How Executives are Creating Meaningful Second Careers*. Routledge, 2018

On inspiration leadership courses, they often ask you to draw a graph of the happiest and saddest times of your life. The horizontal axis is time and the vertical axis is the height or depth of your emotional state. You then label the peaks and troughs with what was going on and like most people, you will have an image of mountains and valleys. Then think back to when you were happiest and try and find a purpose that links with or helps create that environment. As Apple founder Steve Jobs puts it, 'Your time is limited, so don't waste it living someone else's life. Don't be trapped by dogma – which is living with the results of other people's thinking. Don't let the noise of others' opinions drown out your own inner voice. And most important, have the courage to follow your heart and intuition.'

Key Learnings from Chapter 6

Keeping your Seat and Integrity

- There are three ways of minimizing your chances of being rotated out of the C-Suite and these are acquiring an extra area, preferably an area of increasing importance, being a material candidate for CEO succession and being popular with stakeholders.
- In the C-Suite do not build power blocks, instead break them up and act with integrity, have allies on the Board and in the C-Suite and master conflict management.

Being Successful in the Role

- The key to starting in a new CXO role is to understand the organization's environment, internally and externally, and to create a hypothesis. This enables you to set your priorities and where you spend your time. Then it is about building internal networks and relationships, particularly with the board, the CEO and your own top team.

- Once the CXO has set a clear vision for their area, they need to be brave, to get the basics and team fit right and address issues early on.
- They need great antennae, strategic and competitive insight and a firm handle on their area and company data. Be regularly in touch with stakeholders and other parts of the business supporting them, mitigating their risks and asking for their feedback and advice.
- Remember, the boardroom is a shop window for you and your area's performance, so prepare well, be organized and engage.

Your Next 20 Years

- When stepping down from the C-Suite, there are four complementary routes to take: the plural or investor non-executive route, the educator route, the consultancy route or the service to humanity route.
- Money has a significant impact on your post C-Suite choices, which you need to start preparing for five years ahead and it can be necessary to secure a part-time executive role to help with the transition.
- To find a NED role, reflect on what value you can bring, where you are personally best suited, what you are passionate about and where your governance understanding is high enough. Be careful not to underestimate the time involved.
- Those that are in the privileged position of being able to pursue a passion and have a positive impact on the world should spend some time working out where and how. So, start with a period of discovery and reflection and decide to spend your precious time wisely, aligning your happiness, passion and purpose to ensure a legacy you can be proud of.

A Final Word

Hopefully, you now have a clearer view of what the C-Suite looks like today, could look like in the future and where you could fit into it. You should have a better picture of how to plan your career, what path you will take and be more able to overcome the challenges and spot the opportunities life presents en route to the 'The Suite Spot'. You will have learnt many strategies and tactics that will hopefully make your journey easier and less daunting and your time at work more successful and fulfilling. Most importantly, I hope that this book will inspire you to be better at what you do for the betterment of everyone.

To ensure you make it through the whole journey, please do look after yourself. Learn how to breathe deep, how to sleep well and turn off from technology and your work. People are who they are, not what they do, and the purpose of life is to be the best of who we can be. You are not framed by your role or what you have done at work, being a C-Suite executive, a PhD from Harvard or the author of a book. No one will write any of these on your gravestone. What they may write is that you were a loving parent, a good person and a generous friend.

On that note, may I wish you luck, a life full of love and a moment in 'The Suite Spot', whatever yours may be.

Index

Note: page numbers in **bold** refer to diagrams, page numbers in *italics* refer to information contained in tables.